Business Opportunities in the Yangtze River Delta, China

THIS BOOK CONTAINS an exceptionally useful compendium of articles both for the generalist interested in China and foreign investors who are targeting the Yangtze River Delta, which generates about 70% of China's GDP and is destined to be the hub of China's industrial activity well into the next century.

Roger S. Leeds (Managing Director, Patricof & Co. Capital Corp., New York, U.S.A.)

Titles in the Nanyang Business Report Series

Business Opportunities in Penang, Malaysia

Business Opportunities in Sichuan Province, China

Business Opportunities in India

Business Opportunities in the Philippines

Business Opportunities in Myanmar

Business Opportunities in the Yangtze River Delta, China

For further enquiries, information or feedback on the series, please write to the Editor at e-mail: prenhall@singnet.com.sg or Simon & Schuster (Asia) Pte Ltd, 317 Alexandra Road, #04-01 IKEA Building, Singapore 159965.

NANYANG BUSINESS REPORT SERIES

Business Opportunities in The Yangtze River Delta, China

Edited by

Tan Teck Meng (Dean)
Low Aik Meng (Vice Dean and Director of MBA Programme)
John J. Williams (Chief Coordinator, Business Study Mission)
Cao Yong (Coordinator, Business Study Mission)
Shi Yuwei (Coordinator, Business Study Mission)

Nanyang Technological University
Singapore

Prentice Hall
Singapore New York London Toronto Sydney Tokyo

First published 1996 by
Prentice Hall
Simon & Schuster (Asia) Pte Ltd
317 Alexandra Road
#04-01 IKEA Building
Singapore 159965

Printed in Singapore

1 2 3 4 5 00 99 98 97 96

ISBN 0-13-713083-X
ISBN 0-13-713059-7 (pbk)

Prentice Hall International (UK) Limited, *London*
Prentice Hall of Australia Pty. Limited, *Sydney*
Prentice Hall Canada Inc., *Toronto*
Prentice Hall Hispanoamericana, *S.A., Mexico*
Prentice Hall of India Private Limited, *New Delhi*
Prentice Hall of Japan, Inc., *Tokyo*
Editora Prentice Hall do Brasil, Ltda., *Rio de Janeiro*
Prentice Hall, Inc., *Upper Saddle River, New Jersey*

CONTENTS

ABOUT THE EDITORS

TAN TECK MENG is Professor and Dean at the Nanyang Business School. Since joining academia in the early 1970s, Professor Tan has combined his university responsibilities with extensive consultancy work, largely in the field of accountancy. He holds senior positions on a number of institutional boards and committees in Singapore including the Accounting and Auditing Services Working Group of the Economic Committee, the Public Accountants Board, the Board of Directors of Singapore Reinsurance Corporation Limited, the Institute of Certified Public Accountants of Singapore (ICPAS) Annual Report Award Competition Committee and the Income Tax Board of Review. Professor Tan is founding Director of the Entrepreneurship Development Centre (ENDEC) and in 1992 was elected to the Board of Governors of the MIT Sloan School of Management Society for Senior Executives. He is a council member of the ICPAS.

LOW AIK MENG is Associate Professor and Director of the MBA programme at the Nanyang Business School. He worked for five years as an accountant and an internal auditor before joining academia in 1975. He was Vice-Dean of the Faculty of Accountancy and Business Administration at the National University of Singapore until he joined the Nanyang Technological University in 1987. He is currently Vice-Dean at the Nanyang Business School and has been the Director of its very successful MBA Programme since its inception in 1991. Under his leadership, the MBA Programme has been building a network of contacts with businesses and government bodies in Singapore and overseas. He spearheads the thrice-yearly Business Study Missions which are an integral part of the MBA Programme. Associate Professor Low continues to be active in the accountancy profession and serves on several committees in the Institute of Certified Public Accountants of Singapore.

JOHN J. WILLIAMS is Associate Professor at the Nanyang Business School and Chief Coordinator of the MBA Business Study Mission programme. He has taught and carried out research projects in several countries including Canada, the U.S., Kenya and Singapore. Throughout the latter part of the 1980s, Dr. Williams served as Vice-Chairman and Chairman of the Final Accreditation Exam Board for the Society of Management Accountants of Canada, which admitted him as a Fellow in the Society in 1992. Although active in consulting for government agencies in the U.S. and Canada during this period, he has published extensively in leading academic and professional journals and he continues to pursue the study of emerging regional economies in the Asean region.

CAO YONG is Lecturer at the Nanyang Business School and Head of the Chinese Economic Study Unit (ACES). Dr. Cao Yong received his PhD degree from the Australian National University. He was a research economist for the Institute of Economics of the Chinese Academy of Social Sciences and the Australian National University. He started his study of the Chinese economy in 1982 when he joined the Chinese Academy of Social Sciences in Beijing. Since then, he has participated in many study missions in China and has had intensive contacts with Chinese enterprises and economic organisations. His research focus is on the reforms of Chinese industrial enterprise and Chinese business practice. He has published papers in the *Journal of Applied Economics, Asian Economic Journal, Economic Systems, Journal of Far Eastern Business, Accounting and Business Review, Jingji Yangjiu* (Economic Research) and other international journals and books.

SHI YUWEI is Lecturer and Deputy Director of the MBA (Management of Technology) Programme at the Nanyang Business School. He holds a PhD degree from University of Texas, U.S.A. in organisation, strategy and international management, a Master of Comparative Laws degree in international business laws from Southern Methodist University, U.S.A., and a Bachelor of Engineering degree in mechanical engineering from Shanghai Jiao Tong University in Shanghai, China. Dr. Shi specialises his teaching, research and consulting in the areas of MNC management, corporate strategy, strategic alliance, organisational development, technology and innovation management, and management of SOEs and their reform. Dr. Shi has an enriched industry experience through actively involving himself in numerous consulting and training projects for distinguished business organisations, such as AsiaInfo Services, Bank of China, BOC Gases North Pacific, the China Aerospace Academy and DuPont Asia-Pacific.

PREFACE

The Master of Business Administration (MBA) programme of the Nanyang Business School at Nanyang Technological University requires participants to complete a Business Study Mission (BSM) before graduation. The purpose of these visits to other countries is to expose MBA participants to business opportunities and the realities of doing business in cultural environments that are different from Singapore.

This book presents the business reports emanating from the MBA Business Study Mission to China in December 1995. The cities of Shanghai, Suzhou and Nanjing were the focus of the BSM which covered a period of 13 days. The reports are the outcome of a much longer effort involving six months of pre-trip preparation and post-trip debriefing. These cities were chosen because they represent the economic pillars of the Yangtze river delta which is emerging as the single most powerful economic zone in China as it marches towards the 21st century. In fact, Shanghai is now portrayed as the "Dragon Head" swinging the body and tail of a powerful economic "Dragon" which encompasses the Yangtze river valley hinterland including the provinces of Jiangsu (where Suzhou and Nanjing are located), Zhejiang, Hubei, Sichuan, Anhui, Jiangxi and Hunan.

The analogy could not be more fitting; the economic might of this region is simply awesome. For example, just under 40% of China's total gross domestic product, or approximately US$120 billion in 1995 merchandising trade alone, is generated within this geographical area. Moreover, the Yangtze river delta is home to almost 80% of the behemoth state-owned enterprises which employ more than 125 million workers. And, equally important, is the significant presence of the town and village enterprises which have been the financial saviour of China's unwavering commitment to the economic growth and development of what was, as recently as a decade ago, one of the poorest nations on earth. Understanding the nature and structure of these state and non-state-owned entities is tantamount to knowing the ingredients for successfully doing business in China. Insights into these institutions, combined with the attractions of special economic zones in the region, the unbelievable rise of Pudong New Area as the "new" Shanghai, and the burgeoning real estate and tourism industries constitute the motivation for this BSM to China. Lastly, this visit complements an earlier volume in this series on part of the "Dragon" entitled *Doing Business in Sichuan Province, China.*

In Shanghai, the Pudong Jinqiao Hotel was the venue for the opening ceremony of the BSM led by the Secretary General and Deputy Chief Administrator, Mr. Hua Guowan, of the Shanghai Pudong New Area Administration and Associate Professor Low Aik Meng, Vice-Dean of the Nanyang Business School. This was followed by site visits to the Pudong New Area including Waigaoqiao Free Trade Zone, Shanghai Harbour and Lujiazui Financial District.

After subsequent site visits to the state-owned Shanghai Guo Mai Communication Company, the Shanghai Stock Exchange Centre and the Multinational Security Company, the delegation travelled to Suzhou by coach. The Suzhou Bamboo Grove Hotel was the venue for a series of seminars led by Mr. Zhang Xinsheng, Mayor of Suzhou Municipal Government. Following a site visit to the China-Singapore Suzhou Industrial Park, our delegation visited Suzhou Old and New Town before proceeding to Shengze Town near Suzhou. Shengze is famous for the development of its Chinese-style architecture and was popularised by the study of Professor Fei Xiaotong, the Vice-President of the Chinese People's Congress in the early 1930s. It is presently renowned for its township and village enterprises and commodity markets.

An afternoon of travel by coach from Suzhou brought our delegation to Nanjing where we were hosted by a number of representatives from the Jiangsu Provincial Government and the Nanjing Municipal Government. In Nanjing, site visits included Huafei Co. Ltd (a joint venture with Philips from the Netherlands), Nanjing Automobile Co. Ltd (a joint venture with Italy's Iveco), Panda Electronics Co. Ltd (a joint venture with Japan's Matsushita), Yangzijiang Petroleum Company.

A four-hour train ride brought our delegation from Nanjing back to Shanghai for site visits to the giant state-owned Baosteel Company, Shanghai Jiaotong University, Shanghai Textile Machinery Group Company and Shanghai Family Chemical Product Company. Although the presentations and seminars at these locations, as well as those at other site visits, were all conducted in Chinese, they were simultaneously translated into English by various bilingual members of our delegation. It was frequently necessary to change interpreters because of the subtle differences in dialect and common word usage. However, every attempt has been made to authenticate and substantiate the final translation of material that is incorporated throughout various chapters of this book.

The information in this book is unique for two reasons. First, the authenticity of the information is less in doubt because our delegation was not there in the capacity of investors but, rather, as academics. Thus, we obtained first-hand information from top business and government officials in the region who did not perceive that they were negotiating with us and, therefore, tended to be more straightforward. But at the same time, we are business people ourselves and, consequently, our insights might be different from those of journalists or economic analysts. Hence, on matters of practical judgement, our views may be closer to the ones that you, the reader, would have in these situations.

The knowledge amassed through the experience of this mission to China defies a simple calculation. The spirit of business as most of us know it in more advanced and developed countries is prevalent everywhere. There are enormous opportunities waiting in China for international investors. It is our hope that sharing the contents of this book will contribute to a knowledgeable understanding of the environment and specific contexts which now exist in the Yangtze river delta for a variety of business opportunities. The appeal of the book, therefore, is global as well as regional: to firms or entrepreneurs eager to provide capital, training or technology; to government agencies contemplating trade or infrastructure development; to organisations servicing expatriate subsidiary operations in China; to executives and managers of professional services; and to educational institutions for pedagogical and research purposes.

Editors:
TAN Teck Meng
LOW Aik Meng
John J. WILLIAMS
CAO Yong
SHI Yuwei

ACKNOWLEDGEMENTS

The success of the Business Study Mission to China is attributable to considerable effort undertaken by many individuals and organisations. In Shanghai Pudong New Area, we extend our appreciation to the Shanghai Pudong New Area Administration for their hospitality and untiring efforts to make our visit to Shanghai thoroughly rewarding. Thanks go particularly to Deputy Chief Administrator and Secretary General, Mr. Hua Guowan, who arranged for an excellent series of seminars and spent hours happily informing our MBA participants of economic developments in the area, including Shanghai and Pudong New Area. Thanks also to the Director of Comprehensive Planning and Land Bureau, Mr. Liu Zi Qiang; the Director of the Economic and Trade Bureau, Mr. Wang Xin Ling; and the Director of the International Exchange Centre, Mr. Dai Hui Xing. All of them graciously provided detailed information on various economic policies implemented in the Shanghai Pudong New Area and their presence throughout our site visits was invaluable. We also thank the Director of the Human Resource Management Institute at Shanghai Jiaotong University, Professor Xu Jiliang, for arranging our visits to Baosteel and the Shanghai Family Chemical Product Company. Of course, our deep appreciation is extended to the many individuals at the various companies who gave so willingly of their time and knowledge to the MBA participants. At the Shanghai Guo Mai Communication Company, thanks goes to Vice-General Manager, Mr. Ji Ti, who hosted informative seminars on state-owned enterprises and the operations and role of Guo Mai in the Chinese economy. Thanks also to Mr. Li Peizhong, Guo Mai's Director of Office, who led us through their entire operating facilities.

In Suzhou, we extend our gratitude to Mr. Zhang Xinsheng, Mayor of Suzhou Municipal Government, who led the seminars on economic development and presented an exciting overview of the China-Singapore Suzhou Industrial Park. For hosting our BSM and delivering the keynote address in Nanjing, thanks to Mr. Chen Deming, Deputy Chief Secretary General of the Jiangsu Provincial Government. Thanks also to Professor Hong Yinxing, Dean of the International Business School at Nanjing University, for sharing his valuable insights on economic reforms with us, and to Mr. Xie Yongmin, Deputy Chief Secretary General of Nanjing Municipal Government, for sharing with us his incredible knowledge on state-owned enterprises, town and village enterprises and joint ventures within the Yangtze river basin.

Many cultural and historical institutions received our delegation throughout our visit to the three cities. Their hospitality was simply overwhelming and they added that special cultural dimension to our economic knowledge which is indispensable to understanding how China's society functions, and how they are assimilating foreign investment into their new found prosperity.

We are grateful to the many pre-trip seminar speakers in Singapore who helped us prepare for the BSM to China. Without question, we are proud of the MBA participants who prepared well for the mission and conducted themselves professionally on a difficult information-gathering, and exhausting, trip. A special thanks is extended to project supervisors, Associate Professor Chew Seng Beng, Dr. Choo Teck Min, Dr. Patrick Gibbons, Dr. Low Kee Yang and Dr. Shi Yuwei for their diligent efforts in guiding the MBA participants; and to Mr. Ivan Polunin, Miss Valerie Low, Mr. Jack Teo, Mr. Victor Yeo and Dr. Austin Pulle for commenting on earlier drafts of the various chapters.

Thanks also to the MBA office, to Grace Cheng and Adelene Ang for attending to incredible administrative details; without their efforts, the trip would not have worked. Finally, our thanks to our Publisher, Prentice Hall, for their guidance, and to Alison Soo for her unfailing patience in bringing this book to completion.

INTRODUCTION

Chapter 1

China and the Yangtze River Delta

BY
TAN Teck Meng
LOW Aik Meng
John J. WILLIAMS
CAO Yong
SHI Yuwei

INTRODUCTION

AGAINST A BACKGROUND of pockets of recession and low growth scenarios worldwide over the past several years, China's economy has been growing rapidly and consistently. In terms of purchasing power parity, China is now ranked as having the world's second largest economy after that of the U.S.A. (International Monetary Fund, 1993; Randall and Telesio, 1995). Moreover, the dynamic Chinese economy is attracting the interest of investors from all over the world who are eager to participate in this giant emerging market. However, this economy is still in the throes of transforming from a centrally planned economy to that of a market-oriented system. This mixture of central planning plus a market mechanism overarching China's economy is puzzling to many foreign investors, and it creates some degree of uncertainty and risk for foreign investment projects.

The Critical Choice

On the eve of economic reforms in 1978, China was one of the poorest economies in the world and she was clearly an insignificant participant in international markets for goods and capital. At the time, the opinion of world gurus leaned towards political reform as the strategic choice necessary to salvage an impoverished China. Ironically, the developed nations of the world had no proven economic formula for rescuing a nation with one billion two hundred million people from the depths of poverty. But Deng Xiaoping and other top Chinese leaders created a vision which placed economic reform ahead of political reform. Beijing harnessed its central control with one objective in mind — economic development aimed at world supremacy in the 21st century.

Initially, China was faced with decentralising the fiscal system in both the rural and urban areas. The former was accomplished by returning the land to the farmers while the latter required working around the formidable burden of the state-owned enterprises (SOEs). Dismantling these giants would have meant utter chaos and the potential ruin of the entire country.

Instead, Beijing concentrated on developing private and non-state-owned enterprise on a small-to-medium-sized scale. These entities were flexible, transparent and manageable. They required relatively small amounts of capital and could be initiated in the most favourable locations for trade such as along vital waterways and adjacent to coastal cities. Significantly, their turnover was rapid which led to increased cash flows, larger savings and more intensified new capital investments. With these decentralisation measures in place, the miracle started to happen.

Economic Progress

The Chinese economy has grown rapidly since economic reforms were started in the late 1970s. With an annual average gross domestic product (GDP) growth rate at double digit levels over the past 18 years (see Table 1–1), China has not only been one of the fastest growing economies in Asia but also in the world. The high growth rate has been mainly due to the rapid expansion of the non-state sectors of the economy which consist of township and village enterprises, private and joint venture enterprises. Since these enter-prises have had to compete with each other in many areas, ranging from the supply of industrial materials to the sale of final products, their growth has perpetuated the phenomenal expansion of China's market economy.

Since the late 1980s, China has advocated an "open door" policy or, in other words, an outward looking set of trade and industrial strategies.

TABLE 1–1
The Key Economic Indicators of the Chinese Economy: 1978 to 1995

Year	Per Capita GNP	GDP Growth Rate	Merchandise Trade	Foreign Direct Investment (Actually Utilized)	Fixed Capital Investment	Domestic Savings	Inflation (Overall Retail Price Index)	Exchange Rate (1 US$:RMB Yuan)[a]
	RMB	%	billion US$	billion US$	billion RMB	billion RMB	%	RMB
1978	379	11.7	20.64	N/A	66.87	113.45	0.7	N/A
1980	460	7.8	38.14	0.36[b]	91.10	166.11	6.0	N/A
1985	856	13.5	69.60	1.66	254.32	427.30	8.8	N/A
1990	1634	3.8	115.44	3.49	444.93	1164.48	2.1	5.60
1991	1883	9.3	135.63	4.37	550.88	1665.79	2.9	5.85
1992	2288	14.2	165.53	11.01	785.50	1889.11	5.4	7.20
1993	2926	13.5	195.70	27.52	1245.79	2323.03	13.2	8.50
1994	3679	11.8	236.73	33.77	1637.03	2932.78	21.7	8.44
1995	N/A	10.2	280.80	37.70	2000.00[c]	N/A	14.8	8.25

a. Figures from 1990 to 1993 are rates in the swap market. Figures from 1994 to 1995 are rates published by the People's Bank of China.

b. Average value between 1979 and 1983.

c. Estimate from *Zhongguo Zhenquan Bao* (*China Security Daily*), 4 February 1996.

Sources: (1) State Statistical Bureau, People's Republic of China, *Statistical Yearbook of China*, various years, China Statistical Publishing House; Beijing.

(2) The 1995 figures are quoted from various reports released by China Xinhua News.

This political stance has effected a rapidly changing industrial structure and has sustained growth in industrial output and international trade (see Table 1–1). To compete internationally, Chinese enterprises have had to continually improve their existing products, develop new products in the same industry, and adopt new and more sophisticated levels of technology. China has also tried to obtain advanced technology through foreign direct investments. The adoption of more sophisticated and better quality products, together with well-managed foreign enterprises, has dramatically improved the quality of human capital. Product quality through increased levels of technology in the work place and human capital, hence, are mutually reinforcing. Moreover, exports have shifted noticeably, from primary products to manufactured goods, and from simple labour intensive production techniques which require unskilled labour (e.g., handicrafts, textiles, apparel, footwear, leather products and simple electronic goods assembly) to more capital and skill intensive products (e.g., shipbuilding, automobiles, consumer durables, chemical production and computer software).

The Flow of Foreign Investment

The rapid economic development and export growth in the Chinese economy has attracted considerable foreign investment into China. Initially, investment flows from Hong Kong to the special economic zones in Guangdong province sparked the reallocation of industries between these two regions. Next, investors from Taiwan, Singapore, South Korea and Thailand followed Hong Kong's initiative but they located mainly in other regions such as Fujian, Guangdong and Jiangsu provinces. Some scholars have described these investment flows from Asian countries into China as the "big Chinese economic area" (Jones *et al.*, 1993).

This perspective, however, is superficial because it presupposes that the "Chinese" factor alone was responsible for attracting early foreign investment into China and it ignores more fundamental economic and business factors. On the one hand, the newly industrialised Asian economies, such as Taiwan, Hong Kong, South Korea and Singapore, had already achieved a high degree of industrialisation and cost factors mandated a reallocation of their labour intensive industries to China where labour was abundant and cheap. But on the other hand, the opening up of the Chinese economy and its rapid growth simultaneously presented opportunities for capital flows from these sources. In fact, these investment patterns were only part of a larger picture of growing trade and investment patterns among countries in the Asian region (Dowling, 1994). Thus, the so called "big Chinese economic area" is simply part of an emerging regional integration and expansion of trade and investment between Asian nations.

Inflation

Over the past 18 years, the Chinese economy has experienced two periods of high inflation: the year 1988 when the inflation rate was 23%, and the year 1994 when the inflation rate reached 21.7%. In 1988, many people seriously thought that inflation would destroy the foundations of economic order in China, and perhaps even shake the dominance of the Chinese communist regime. But high inflation was effectively brought under control in 1990 by the central government's austerity programme.

Then in 1994, high inflation again led many outsiders to harbour suspicions about the overheated Chinese economy and its ability to sustain long-term growth. However, the Chinese people were generally very calm in response to the price index published by the Chinese Statistics Bureau. This was because consumer goods were abundant while wage levels were keeping pace with, or even exceeding, the rising cost of living.

With an increased savings rate and another round of austerity programmes from Beijing aimed at tight control over the money supply, and targeting foreign investment at large-scale infrastructure projects and certain heavy industries (which absorbed excess labour from bankrupt state-owned enterprises), inflation was capped at an annual rate of 14.8% for 1995.

Beijing is determined to lower the inflation rate to below 10%. This is a realistic objective if one understands that the pricing mechanism in the Chinese economy is still in a process of transition. Therefore, some of the factors responsible for the spiralling inflation are a consequence of the move to a market economy. For example, price reforms were targeted at previously planned products which were fixed at very low levels. Naturally, the sudden exposure of these products to the forces of supply and demand in a free market created strong upward pressure on prices. Also, upgrading the industrial structure has produced higher quality industrial products. In this case, calculating a price index does not differentiate the quality difference in products but, instead, treats old and new products equally.

Inflation which is attributable to price reforms is temporary; it will disappear as soon as the equilibrium price level is reached. Thus, it is a necessary part of China's market oriented economic reform. Of course, inflation arising from product quality differentials is not at all harmful. But inflation caused by an overheated economy is harmful. This condition is usually accompanied by high levels of capital investment in combination with increasing levels of disposable income. Therefore, fiscal policy must match the intended outcome of price reforms.

Government Initiatives

Each wave of high inflation in China has precipitated a more market oriented system. In the early 1980s, reforms in the state-owned enterprises through the profit sharing system degenerated into a wage maximisation scheme. Retained earnings and reinvestment declined while wage bills soared. The government implemented a bonus and wage tax ranging from 20 to 200%, depending on the growth of each enterprise's total compensation bill. This tax effectively dampened wage growth and consequently inflation. In addition, the inflationary pressure of wage maximisation was reduced by the diminished importance of the shrinking state-owned economy.

Inflation in the 1993–94 period was largely caused by distortions in the financial system, particularly with substantial bank credits pouring into the new real estate market and causing prices to rise at triple digit inflation rates. The Chinese government then adopted a conservative macroeconomic policy stance, including the control of monetary aggregates and fiscal deficits, as well as transforming government banks into commercial banks. As a result, more funds were directed to priority sectors, particularly to large-scale infrastructure projects. At the same time, implementation of a value added tax provided more funds to the central government while the partially liberalised foreign exchange system generated considerable government reserves.

Critical Success Factors

The ability to maintain high domestic savings and increasing foreign reserves are the two crucial factors underlying the success of the Chinese economy. The average saving rate over the past 18 years has been well above 35% of GDP and it has been increasing dramatically (see Table 1–1). Due to a healthy international trade surplus and foreign direct investment in recent years, the Chinese economy has accumulated more than US$60 billion in foreign reserves. The increasing level of foreign reserves enabled the central government to liberalise the foreign exchange system under the current account in early 1994. Since then, the RMB has appreciated slightly against the U.S. dollar. The government is planning to liberalise the foreign exchange system further and make the RMB fully convertible in the near future.

The Chinese economy is expected to move increasingly towards a well-functioning market economy given the substantial reforms in finance, taxation, banking, investment and trade. The Chinese economy will continue to grow rapidly in the next five years or so, although the growth rate may be lower than in 1994 and 1995 mainly due to stricter macroeconomic controls. But moderate inflation is expected as a result of the rapid structural changes in the economy. The trade balance is also expected to improve further due to the increased export of non-traditional products such as electronic items and transportation equipment.

THE RISE OF SHANGHAI AND THE YANGTZE RIVER DELTA

Shanghai is destined to spearhead China's economic development into the 21st century. Shanghai is a municipality and, together with Jiangsu province, it represents one of the most powerful economic centres in all of China. In a comprehensive study involving 29 provinces and municipalities in China, Yang *et al.* (1995) reported that Jiangsu ranked number one in total industrial output, using 1992 data, while Shanghai ranked fourth. Interestingly, on a per capita industrial output basis, these rankings were reversed. In terms of total exports and net exports, Shanghai ranked third which suggests that it has a large capability for generating foreign exchange.

However, these economic indicators do not reveal the real status of Shanghai *vis-à-vis* the role that it played in China's new economic reforms nor its potential for the 21st century as seen by Beijing. To begin with, Shanghai's contribution to China has been achieved at the expense of a large investment base and the lack of foreign capital relative to other prosperous regions in China. Furthermore, Shanghai has been the most heavily taxed economic unit in China. Thus, Beijing explicitly used Shanghai to finance the economic miracle of the coastal regions and it ensured that foreign investments were diverted from Shanghai so as to fuel the economy and welfare of other regions (Yang *et al.*, 1995).

The Yangtze River Valley

There are four natural geographical regions in China and they include the Yangtze river valley, the Yellow river valley, the Zhujiang (Pearl) river valley and the north-east area. Table 1–2 is adapted from Yang *et al.* (1995) and it shows that the Yangtze river valley and the Pearl river valley are nearly equivalent on a weighted ranking of the following five economic indicators: production capacity; foreign exchange generation capability; size and structure of capital investments; structure and importance of foreign capital; and the financial strength and resources of the provincial/municipal government.

Using an even broader measure, GDP in 1993 for the Yangtze river valley was RMB 922.1 billion as compared to RMB 425.3 billion for the Pearl river basin. This spread is increased in favour of the former if the GDPs of potential provinces are considered. In fact, the GDP for the Yangtze river valley is nearly two and one-half times larger in percentage terms. It is little wonder that Shanghai is now referred to as the "Dragon Head" and the other regions of the Yangtze river valley as the "Dragon" in China's economic march towards the 21st century. Moreover, it now becomes evident after examining the GDP data why Beijing is resurrecting Shanghai to become a world-class economic power.

Other Economic Factors

To restructure the economic base of Shanghai, the central government has embarked on a bold new plan. Part of this new directive is the development and construction of a "new" Shanghai called the Pudong New Area. The enormity of the project is staggering. It covers 350 square kilometres and, in terms of the 14 economic development zones in the coastal provinces, it is 12-fold larger. This strategic decision was necessary given the decadent state of the old city of Shanghai. It would have been impossible to rejuvenate Shanghai and simultaneously

TABLE 1–2
Comparative Profile of the Four Most Rapidly Growing Regions in China

Region	Key Provinces (Municipalities)	Average Weighted Average Rank	Average Overall Rank	GDP in 1993[a] (RMB billions)	Percentage of Total GDP	Potential Provinces	GDP in 1993[b] (RMB billions)	Percentage of Total of GDP
Yangtze River Valley	Shanghai, Jiangsu, Zhejiang, Hubei, Sichuan	6.67	6.80	922.1	29.4	Anhui, Jiangxi, Hunan	1,209.5	38.5
Yellow River Valley	Beijing, Tianjin, Shandong, Hebei, Henan	7.87	8.60	725.2	23.1	Shanxi, Shaanxi, Gansu, Ningxia Inner Mongolia	946.4	30.2
North-east Areas	Heilongjiang, Jilin, Liaoning	8.47	10.70	725.2	23.1		355.7	11.3
Zhujian (Pearl) River Valley	Guangdong, (Fujian)	6.43	5.50	425.3	13.6	Guangxi, Hainan	526.7	16.8

[a] GDP is deflated by price deflator (1980 = 100).

[b] The sum of GDP from key provinces and GDP from potential provinces.

Source: State Statistical Bureau, People's Republic of China, *Statistical Yearbook of China,* 1993, 1994. China Statistical Publishing House, Beijing.

develop a new industrial base on the same site.

To accommodate the commercial and financial expansion envisioned for Shanghai, the government is shifting some of the manufacturing base up the Yangtze river to neighbouring provinces. Moreover, the focus is on new technology and modernised plant facilities. At the same time, the government is intent on re-establishing Shanghai's service sector which fell from 52% of GDP in the 1950s to a mere 18% by 1978. As of 1994, the service sector contributed 40% to Shanghai's GDP and 52% is the target for the year 2000 (*Asiamoney*, 1994; Xu, 1994).

Social Factors

China's economic reforms created several serious problems which were not entirely unexpected. In the first place, the new prosperity of the coastal regions has outpaced the economic levels in the hinterland. This outcome has prompted a large migration to the already overcrowded large cities and, therefore, employment is problematic. But more serious is the agency problem associated with the labour tied up in the SOEs. Failure in these entities means massive unemployment, something that Beijing will not tolerate.

To combat the problem Beijing has begun to spin-off profitable SOE segments while syphoning off the employees from the bankrupt shells into new foreign entities. This reduces the need for social security payments and solves the unemployment problem simultaneously. Foreign firms pay higher wages and these, in turn, are subsidising part of the social cost (Yang *et al.*, 1995).

Political Factors

The economic and social factors constituting China's strategies for change cannot be separated from political factors. It is clear that social and economic stability are paramount goals for Beijing and, despite the phenomenal economic success story, incrementalism is fundamental to Beijing's strategy for growth. This explains the government's neglect of Shanghai in the beginning, but its full support at the present time. The philosophy here is embedded in the idea of triggering reforms from the countryside to the city. Hence, emphasis was on shifting from the small cities and the countryside to the big cities; from small enterprises to big enterprises and from the private economy to the state-owned economy.

It is patently clear that Shanghai was not a candidate for early reform. It is China's largest city with a massive industrial base and home to a disproportionate share of China's SOEs. In fact, the whole plan was to make sure that Shanghai's cash contribution to Beijing was not disturbed by any elements of reform. Shanghai was the bank and, some would argue, this enhanced its decline after reforms were instigated in 1978 (Lehner, 1994).

There was only one city in China that could have withstood the bold initiative from Beijing for China's future prosperity and that was Shanghai. However, not overtly planned by the central government was the surge in voluntary trade between Shanghai and the coastal cities with their new found wealth. In reality, this phenomenon was mutually beneficial for both regions. Shanghai desperately needed the increased trade and had the market potential to absorb the new inflow. In turn, trade with Shanghai generated even more prosperity in the coastal cities. It was a turn of good fortune both ways, especially for the central government, and demonstrates the unleashed power of market forces within China's internal economy.

Towards the 21st Century

The present irony is that Beijing has now chosen Shanghai over Hong Kong as the centre for China's future economy because the former is a socialist city. In some sense, the entrepreneurial spirit fell by default to Hong Kong over the last several decades because Shanghai's commerce and financial activities were decimated by the communist reform in 1949. Shanghai's large Chinese banks were moved to Beijing and trading operations were virtually halted. All that remained was a "factory" under Beijing's tight control (Yang *et al.*, 1995).

Arguably, some analysts view the success of the southern coastal cities as emanating from foreign investment from Hong Kong, Taiwan, South Korea, Singapore and even Japan. If this view is accepted, then the success here is one of capitalism and not socialism. But Beijing is sending signals to the world that socialist reforms are the most important factor behind China's future progress. Thus, Shanghai will now enjoy the free market spirit of business and trade, much like Hong Kong in the past, but combined with the full financial and economic might of Beijing. Beijing does not want to fail in this experiment at any cost (Rohwer, 1995) and the Pudong New Area is testimony to what can transpire economically when the central government focuses its power and resources. Perhaps Beijing believes it would be easier to successfully control the socialist substance of Shanghai over the capitalist substance of Hong Kong after 1997 (Bluestein, 1994).

With this terse overview of the Chinese economy since 1978 and the resurrection of Shanghai currently taking place, there is unprecedented opportunity for business and trade in the Shanghai region. As noted above though, there are economic entities operating in Shanghai and Jiangsu province which are unfamiliar to many foreigners. However, to seriously consider doing business in the region, some basic understanding of the economic progress, location of special economic zones (including the Pudong New Area) and the nature of the mammoth SOE structures are prerequisite to survival. The contents of the following chapters are specifically directed towards a deeper understanding of these elements in Shanghai and the Yangtze river delta.

OVERVIEW OF CHAPTER CONTENTS

The remainder of this book comprised 13 chapters which are grouped into four major sections. These sections have been arranged to feature the broad attributes of Shanghai's location, special economic zones in the Shanghai area, an economic sector analyses of major business opportunities and, finally, a set of case analyses focusing on large state-owned enterprises.

Location

This section has two chapters which deal with the geographical and infrastructural facilities of Shanghai and the neighbouring cities of Suzhou and Nanjing, located in Jiangsu province. In Chapter 2, Lien *et al.* take on the task of evaluating Shanghai as an international hub for northern Asia. They use a model which features the financial, commercial, market access and industrial output capabilities of an international hub and contrast these attributes for Shanghai with those of world centres such as New York, London, Singapore and Tokyo. The latter part of the chapter examines the potential for Shanghai's industrial base to service the domestic market. Finally, the authors present arguments supporting Shanghai as China's major international hub of the future rather than Hong Kong.

Phua *et al.*, in Chapter 3, continue with the theme of locational attributes but extend this to a comparative analysis of Shanghai, Suzhou and Nanjing. The main thrust of the chapter is on identifying the competitive advantage of each location as well as the synergistic features of locating in any one of the three. More specifically, a number of factors are contrasted which include natural resources, land use, access to capital, infrastructure, building and rental costs, government problems, legal framework and tax incentives. In the second half of the chapter, the authors discuss local market demand, analyse labour conditions, examine regional clusters and compare each city to other major global cities. They conclude by asserting that all these centres are poised for growth into the 21st century.

Special Economic Zones

This section has three chapters which cover the important concept of special economic zones within the Yangtze delta region. In Chapter 4, Tan *et al.* examine the options which are available to potential investors who are interested in any of Pudong's four special economic zones. Attention is then directed to three special zones located in the Puxi area (i.e., the old city area of Shanghai) and several of Shanghai's lesser economic zones. The authors then develop a comparative ranking across ten SEZs on a number of infrastructure characteristics, status of development and competitive advantage factors. The chapter concludes with some very useful suggestions for investors on matching industry types and size with the different zones.

Abdual Halim *et al.* pursue the focus on trade zones by specifically examining developments and opportunities in Pudong New Area. As the authors clearly point out, Pudong is not a special economic zone but, rather, it is an extension of Shanghai across the Huangpu river. The chapter discusses foreign investment trends over the last five years as well as infrastructure development. Of particular interest to investors, the authors analyse a number of preferential investment policies specific to Pudong. The chapter concludes with a discussion of forms of business ventures, major issues impeding foreign investment, opportunities for small-and-medium-sized enterprises and, finally, opportunities for multinational corporations.

The China-Singapore Suzhou Industrial Park is the focus of Chapter 6. Ng and Tan describe the nature of the development and the benefits that it can offer potential investors. The Appendix is particularly useful because it summarises a number of geographical characteristics, infrastructure facilities, investment criteria and tax incentives associated with the park.

Economic Sector Analyses

Four chapters are included in this section and they deal with major sectors that are particularly prominent and appear to dominate the economic expansion under way in the Shanghai region. Chapter 7 presents a comprehensive overview of China's banking system and the manner in which it operates in Shanghai. Next, the authors discuss the financial services offered by both Chinese and foreign banks as well as the extremely important aspect of doing business in Shanghai.

Chapter 8 covers the dynamic, but critically important, real estate market in Shanghai. Lim *et al.* begin by posing some sobering problems faced by real estate investors and follow this with an assessment of related legal issues. Next, the authors highlight important problems faced by foreign investors during a project's development and construction stage. This is followed by an overview of the office property market, the retail property market, the hotel property market, the residential property market and property for industrial use. This discussion, and related tax implications, are supplemented by a comprehensive set of Appendices with much detailed comparative data.

In Chapter 9, Choy *et al.* analyse the tourism industry, its potential among the three cities of Shanghai, Suzhou and Nanjing, and the comparative advantages among the three locations. The early part of the chapter focuses on macro issues covering administration, travel agencies, travel restrictions, major markets and China's tourism development plans to the year 2000. The remainder of the chapter isolates specific areas and highlights major tourist, recreational and hotel facilities within each area. Once again, a substantial set of Appendices accompanies the main chapter with details of tourism data contrasted with other major tourist destinations across China.

The last chapter in this section, Chapter 10, is somewhat unique relative to the other chapters in this section. Chian *et al.* present a thorough documentation on the nature and functioning of town and village enterprises (TVEs) in Jiangsu province. This chapter is included here because TVEs are considered to be a major industry sector in

China's economy. The authors begin by contrasting TVEs with SOEs and private enterprises. Next, four different types of TVEs are contrasted in terms of their economic significance to China's economy for revenue generation and employment. The latter part of the chapter then discusses the structure and administrative operations of TVEs followed by an analysis of relevant success factors. Chian *et al.* conclude the chapter with a look at specific business opportunities (through joint ventures) in the silk, textiles and food processing industries.

Firm Analyses

The final section of the book contains four chapters which build on the theme presented in Chapter 10. China's giant SOEs are the focus of each chapter and, collectively, they cover industries ranging from steel production and electronics to cosmetics. It is appropriate to suggest that no one can successfully do business in Shanghai without having an understanding of the nature of these economic monsters.

Chapter 11 is the first in the series and it examines Shanghai's Baosteel project. Ang *et al.* initially characterise the nature of SOEs in China prior to reform in 1979 and then describe operating conditions under the new economic reforms. Before examining Baosteel, the authors discuss a number of current challenges that face SOEs. With this background, Ang *et al.* use McKinsey's 7-S framework to analyse the structure and performance of Baosteel before presenting several future challenges faced by Baosteel.

In Chapter 12, Tan *et al.* employ the same grounding as in the previous chapter to analyse the critical success factors of Huafei which is the largest joint venture in Jiangsu province to date. There are two Chinese partners while the third partner is Philips Electronics N. V. from the Netherlands. The authors next analyse Shanghai BOC Gases with the British multinational BOC Group which is a joint venture. In summarising the chapter, the authors identify five common factors attributable to the overwhelming success of each joint venture.

In Chapter 13, Ng *et al.* analyse the Panda Electronics Group which is one of the largest SOEs in China. Of interest here, are the shifts in strategy and structure that Panda has had to endure to maintain its leadership status in the consumer electronics industry. The authors employ D'Aveni's (1994) four arena analysis and within each factor they evaluate Panda's opportunities for searching out foreign joint venture partnerships.

The final chapter of this section focuses on Shanghai Jahwa Corporation. Here the authors are primarily concerned with the firm's marketing strategies associated with its skincare and cosmetic products. In addition, Lim *et al.* use the classic four Ps framework from marketing theory to contrast Jahwa with the marketing strategies of Proctor & Gamble and Unilever, its two major competitors. For potential investors, this chapter is a good lesson on pricing strategies for urban and rural areas in China.

REFERENCES

Asiamoney, "Cover Story", *Asiamoney*, September 1994, pp. 45–9.

Bluestein Paul, "Shanghai Seeking a Renaissance: China Looking to City as Model of Economic Reform", *International Herald Tribune*, 1 June 1994.

Chyau Tuan and Linda Fung-Yee Ng, "Hong Kong's Outward Investment and Regional Economic Integration with Guangdong: Process and Implications", *Journal of Asian Economics,* 6(3), 1995.

D'Aveni R. A., *Hypercompetition: Managing the Dynamics of Strategic Manoeuvring*, Maxwell Macmillan Inc., New York, 1994.

Dowling J. M., "Outlook and Prospects for Developing Asia", *The Australian Economic Review*, 4th Quarter 1994.

International Monetary Fund, *World Economic Outlook*, Washington, D.C., 1993.

Lardy N. R., "Participation in International Capital Markets", *China in the World Economy*, Institute for International Economics, Washington, D.C., 1994.

Lehner U. C., "As Goes Shanghai, So Goes China", *The Asian Wall Street Journal*, 22 November 1994, S9.

Jones R. S., R. E. King, and M. Klien, "Economic Integration between Hong Kong, Taiwan and the Coastal Provinces of China", OECD Economic Studies, No. 20, Spring 1993.

Randall D. and P. Telesio, "Managing Risk in China", *World Executive's Digest*, June 1995.

Rowher Jim, *Asia Rising*, KHL Printing Co. Pte. Ltd., Singapore, 1995.

State Statistical Bureau of People's Republic of China, *Waishang Zai*

Zhongguo Dalu Touzhi Jingyan Bijaio Diaocai (Comparative survey on the investment experience of foreign enterprises in the mainland of China), memo, Beijing, 1995.

Xu Kuang Di, *Shanghai, a City Marching Toward the 21st Century*, Seminar Presentation, Nanyang Technological University, August 1994.

Yang Mu, John J. Williams, and Cao Yong, "Resurrecting Shanghai for the 21st Century: the Shift in China's Regional Economic Strategies", *China Business Review*, Dccember 1995.

World Bank, *World Debt Tables: External Finance for Developing Countries*, World Bank, Washington, 1993.

LOCATION

Chapter 2

Shanghai: An International Hub for Northern Asia

BY
LIEN Ber Luen
LEE Kin Seng
Robert CHOO
NG Joo Hee

INTRODUCTION

GIVEN THE TREMENDOUS economic growth of China in the 1980s and 1990s, as well as the grandiose plans for Shanghai and the Yangtze river region, it would seem that investors who ignore Shanghai do so at their peril. Companies seeking a place for siting their China operations should look at Shanghai. Together with the nearby Yangtze river region, Shanghai has advantages both as a business hub for company headquarters as well as a base for industrial operations.

Shanghai's unique geographic endowments, favourable political environment, comprehensive infrastructure development plan, and attractive set of economic initiatives and investment incentives are conspiring to appoint it as the engine driving China's economic modernisation into the new millennium. Shanghai is evaluated favourably *vis-à-vis* other international cities for its suitability as a business hub. The conclusion for domestic production is less clear as some companies may find the inland regions more attractive due to Shanghai's rising costs.

This chapter is divided into two main sections. First, it evaluates Shanghai's claim to be a successful regional hub for companies wishing to site their Chinese, and even Asia-Pacific headquarters, in the Yangtze river delta. This evaluation is carried out through the qualitative description and rating of several renowned hub cities relative to Shanghai. Secondly, attention is focused on Shanghai's attractiveness for firms seeking an industrial base for their Chinese operations. By examining the benefits and cost pressures in Shanghai and the surrounding regions, potential business strategies can be assessed. Figure 2–1 serves as the model to address these issues.

FIGURE 2–1
Shanghai as an International Hub

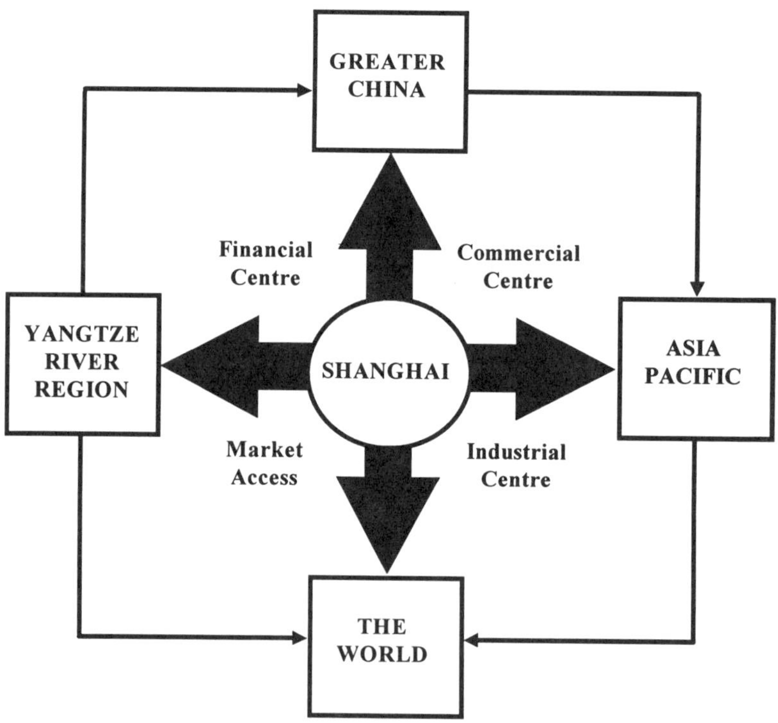

INTERNATIONAL HUBS

The Concept of a Regional Business Hub

Although there is no ideal location for firms to site their headquarters, it is evident that many do so in cities widely perceived to be "business hubs". These hubs are important far beyond their boundaries and they are an obvious anchor for firms seeking a foothold in a particular geographic region. It is generally accepted that any business hub should have several essential activities. These can be divided into primary economic activities for the generation of income, support activities to facilitate the primary activities, and activities to improve the population's quality of life.

The primary economic activities are trade centre activities and financial centre activities while support activities consist of physical transportation and distribution activities, information and communication related activities and business service activities. Activities relating to quality of life would vary from leisure, entertainment and the arts, to educational activities. For a regional hub to successfully engage in these activities, it can be argued that a good alignment of several factors are essential. Based on Kass' framework (1992), nine critical success factors have been identified. These are good geographic location, stable government, good transportation and logistic facilities, good telecommunications, good investment incentives and business environment, good work ethic/human resources, good banking facilities, support from the hinterland and a good quality of life.

Some of these factors are the *sine qua non* of activities. For example, to successfully engage in physical transport activities, it is obvious that good transportation and logistic facilities be a prerequisite. Others, however, are more subtle such as a stable government. The support from the hinterland is important since it provides support for the growth of hub cities. In particular, there is a market support region which has buyers and sellers in large quantities, and a ready pool of talent and other resources which can be drawn into the hub city.

In general, for a successful hub, the critical aspect is the linkage between the different sectors of the economy: "A modern international financial centre must be supported by a modern industry and commerce" (Chen and Shi, 1994). Some examples of successful hubs in the world today are New York in North America, London and Randstad in Europe, and Tokyo and Singapore in Asia.

(i) ***New York:*** The city became established at a remarkable confluence of water in upper New York Bay. It is situated on the shortest and easiest route into the American continent from the east and it is the gateway for nearly one-half of the total import and export trade of the U.S. Having leveraged on this unique geographical location, it has become the epicentre of an industrial region containing three-fifths of America's industrial and commercial power. Besides these international routes, the transportation links to the rest of the U.S. are excellent, with fast access to an interstate highway system, express rail services and domestic and international air links to many other U.S. cities via Kennedy, Newark and LaGuardia airports. New York sits in the heart of the American manufacturing belt consisting of the Atlantic coast plain, the Appalachians, the Canadian Shield, the Adirondacks and interior lowlands.

One of the early industrial growth areas was the Boston–Baltimore belt and it was financed through New York which lies right in the centre of this belt. Markets and other infrastructure facilities rapidly sprung up to facilitate this industrial activity. The diversity of thc many businesses located there lends economies of scale which outweigh the higher cost of locating in New York. There are more than 500 prominent commodity broking houses based in New York. As the focal point of American finance, New York organises financial assistance and investment in virtually all parts of the globe through more than 8,000 financial and insurance institutions.

(ii) ***London:*** With the most diversified economy among British cities, London is the single most important banking, insurance and trading centre in Western Europe. As the conduit for much of Britain's annual trade, its geographic position on the Thames and its nearness to the sea have played a major role in its success. As a centre of commerce, five international commodity agreements, namely cocoa, coffee, sugar, tin and wheat are based in London, along with the International Lead and Zinc Study Group and the International Rubber Study Group. Due to Britain's worldwide trading patterns and commercial experience extending through a long history, London has well-developed international markets in money and financial services. It has more than 180 international banks.

London's communications and transportation infrastructure is excellent, with the twin airports of Gatwick and Heathrow serving as gateways into Britain. The Port of London is, at present, the leading port for container traffic in Britain, boasting modern facilities and high levels of productivity. Numerous trunk roads, railways and waterways link London to all parts of England and Europe, especially with the completed Channel Tunnel. The south-east region of the U.K. surrounding London provides a supporting hinterland for trade, financial and business services. With all these benefits, it is not surprising to note that many multinational companies have placed their European headquarters in London, in spite of generous tax incentives from neighbouring countries.

(iii) ***Randstad:*** Rotterdam and Amsterdam, as part of Randstad Holland (*Corporate Location*, 1994a), has an entrenched position as Europe's business gateway due to its sophisticated transport, logistics and distribution infrastructure. It comprises multiple city regions serving as an integrated growth engine. The mutual reinforcement of the Rotterdam port and Amsterdam's Schiphol Airport (mainports) serves as a vital nexus between international connections and the Ruhr industrial belt in Germany, supported by the Netherlands's excellent road network, efficient customs and educated workforce. Another strong transportation link is the network of rivers and canals linking Rotterdam to Frankfurt and beyond (*Corporate Location*, 1994b). Randstad is the vital distribution headquarters for numerous companies.

(iv) ***Tokyo:*** As one of the world's largest banking centres, Tokyo is the focal point of finance and insurance in East Asia, with more than 9,000 financial and insurance institutions. It is therefore no surprise that Tokyo is the headquarters city of Japan, with many domestic and international firms opening offices there. With the many business services units in Tokyo, the headquarters officials are well supported. The transportation links of Tokyo are good with the two major airports, Narita (international) and Haneda (domestic). Narita in particular serves as a major trans-Pacific stop while the Port of Tokyo and Yokohama rank among the busiest in the world. Regional and inner-city transport is supplied by publicly and privately operated railways, subways, buses and electric railway systems, together with major highways for automobiles. Railroad links to other major Japanese cities like Nagoya, Osaka, and Sapporo are efficient.

(v) ***Singapore:*** The city-state is an established regional hub for commerce and trade in South-east Asia and it is fast becoming an important international centre for finance. Although it has limited resources, Singapore has exploited its unique geographical location at the southern end of the Strait of Malacca to the maximum to become a centre of trade for the South-east Asian region. Riding on the back of the growth in trade is that of the banking sector, facilitated by the Singapore government's strong push for a technologically literate and oriented society (Kass, 1992). Physical infrastructure, such as air and sea port facilities, are excellent, and the level of automation is high, partly to compensate for the small pool of human resources. Partly as a result of physical constraints and the effects of rapid growth, Singapore has had to concentrate on providing regional hub services, in particular for financial services, communications and technological research and development.

SHANGHAI'S POSITION

Macroeconomic Indicators

The pace of development in Shanghai is impressive. Foreign trade continues to boom, its import-export turnover was valued at RMB 41.05 billion as of November 1995, with processing trade growing at RMB 16.1 billion. The value of foreign investments in Shanghai during 1995 rose 5.1% to US$10.54 billion. As of mid-December 1995, Shanghai had 13,584 foreign projects with a contracted investment value of US$34.27 billion. Further growth of the six pillar industries is expected in 1996, with total sales reaching RMB 220 billion (US$26.5 billion) led by automobiles and telecommunications, followed by power equipment, petroleum refining, steel and household appliances (Chen, 1995a).

The traditional heavy industries of Shanghai, such as steel and warehousing, contribute greatly to Shanghai's economy. This is particularly so in the Baoshan district where 158 state-owned large and medium-sized enterprises producing 90% of Shanghai's steel and 58% of its electricity are based (*Shanghai Star*, 8 December 1995).

Pudong's recent designation as China's latest special economic zone

(SEZ) will spur its already impressive development. Trade volume reached RMB 6.27 billion in 1995, up 62.5% over 1994. As of October 1995, there were 5,000 on-going projects in Pudong,[1] with a total investment of US$10.4 billion. The investors include multinationals such as DuPont, Ford, Siemens and Sharp. Growth is expected to remain at 20% over the next five years (Lu, 1995a).

The Near Future

Between 1996 and 2000, the gross domestic product (GDP) of Shanghai is expected to increase by 10 to 12% annually and to reach RMB 650 billion (US$78.3 billion). Imports and exports are expected to reach RMB 38 billion and contractual foreign capital income to come to RMB 37.5 billion. The breakdown of activities as a percentage of GDP in Shanghai is shown in Table 2–1.

TABLE 2–1
Breakdown of Activities by Sector

	1990	**2000 (est.)**
Agriculture	2.0%	4.4%
Industry	53.0%	64.6%
Services	45.0%	31.0%

Source: Hua Guowan, Vice-Administrator of Pudong Local Government.

Finance and insurance, and domestic trade, are expected to account for 20 and 16% of GDP, respectively, while industrial and high technology industries are expected to take over 60% of the city's industrial output value. Shanghai has the ambition to become a regional and even an international service centre. From 1993 onwards, more than 50% of new asset investments have gone to the service sector. It is estimated that China will have the world's largest economy by the year 2010.[2]

1 Presentation at Pudong on 6 December 1995 by Hua Guowan, Vice-Administrator of Pudong Local Government.

2 The World Bank projects that China's GDP, calculated on a purchasing power parity basis, will reach US$9.8 trillion in the year 2002 as compared to US$9.7 trillion for the United States. If these forecasts hold, China will become the world's biggest economic pole.

Finance

One keystone of Shanghai's blueprint is its maturation as a financial centre. The central government is determined to open its finance and insurance market, as highlighted by Vice-Premier Zhu Rongji (*China Daily*, 11 December 1995). According to Mao Yingliang, Governor of the People's Bank of China Shanghai branch (Xiao, 1995), Shanghai has successfully completed the first phase of a three-phase plan to develop Shanghai into a financial centre by 2010. In phase one, Shanghai laid the foundations for a supervisory framework. Further growth is expected during the second phase which should be completed by 2000. During this second phase, Shanghai will optimise its market set up, improve personnel training and establish electronic banking services. In the final phase, Shanghai's international profile will be raised as it attempts to overtake London and New York. It is projected that more than 300 foreign financial institutions and 500 headquarters of multinational companies will be established in Shanghai by 2010 (Chen, 1995a).

The convertibility of the RMB remains a pressing concern for potential investors. Steps are currently underway for the RMB to be freely convertible, at least for the current accounts, which should facilitate trade and lead to a truly open financial system. Vice-Premier Zhu Rongji announced that China would be able to do so "well ahead of a 2000 deadline", and this would lead to the renminbi becoming an internationally tradeable "hard" currency. Besides banking activities, Shanghai has started many specialised financial markets. Shanghai's Oil Futures Exchange, which has been in existence for many years, is ranked fourth after New York (NYMEX), London (IPE) and Singapore (SIMEX). The Shanghai Foreign Exchange Transaction Centre that was set up in 1988, introduced forward currency contracts in June 1992. These contracts allow the trading of U.S. dollars exclusively at an agreed rate against the renminbi on a specified date in the future. In 1992, the Metals Exchange and the National Coal Exchange were started while the Grain and Cooking Oil Exchange opened in 1993.

The Shanghai Stock Exchange (SSE) share trading floor was opened in December 1990 and it presently has 218 class A and B stocks listed. However, the current financial market accounts for only 10% of the total funds used in the country. The development of a capital market is still in the primary stages and it is difficult at the moment to use market mechanisms to distribute resources in an optimal and rational manner. In response to criticisms that the SSE was unregulated and subject to obvious manipulation (Kahn, 1994), the SSE has been tightening its regulatory environment through the introduction of new rules in December 1995. Already, the demand for financing has reached insatiable proportions. Investments in projects as diverse as infrastructure, heavy industry, textiles, chemicals, electronics, real estate, food and animal husbandry are actively courted (SITC, 1995). Also, colossal projects such as the Lou Jing Coal Terminal (US$350 million) and the Light Rail Transit Line to Pudong (US$704 million) have enormous price tags.

Transportation

Shanghai's key geographic position makes it a natural choice for a hub both for East Asia and the Asia-Pacific. Its location at the mouth of the Yangtze river on the Pacific Ocean's western rim is ideal. One can visualise Shanghai at the centre of a vast web, with multiple links radiating in all directions regardless of the mode of transportation.

(i) ***Shipping:*** Shanghai's facilities for water-based transportation are well established. They support shipping, both domestically along the Yangtze river and Grand Canals, as well as internationally via the Pacific Ocean. The harbour is China's biggest port and one of the ten largest in the world with more than 70 10,000-tonne berths and with a handling capacity of 200 million tonnes per year. Plans are underway to build another 20 10,000-tonne wharves at Pudong's Waigaoqiao harbour which will add 20 million tonnes per year in handling capacity. The presence of nearby ports, such as the deep water 300,000 dead-weight tonne Beilun port in nearby Ningbo (Wu, 1995), and others in Nantong, Zhangjiagang and Zhousan, will facilitate an integrated shipping centre for the whole region.

(ii) ***Aviation:*** Air transportation is equally important especially in view of Shanghai's close proximity to many other growth areas in North Asia. Although Shanghai's Hongqiao International Airport is overcrowded, the construction of the new four-runway Pudong International Airport, with a capacity of 80 to 100 million passengers per year, will alleviate the problem.

(iii) ***Rail and Roads:*** Although Shanghai's traffic congestion has been chronical, new road and railway networks are being planned to link the airport, seaport and the financial, trading and industrial zones.

Ten billion renminbi will be spent to build seven highways over the next five years, including the local sections of Shanghai–Nanjing and Shanghai–Hangzhou expressways. The urban and suburban light railway, metro and highway networks will transform the landscape of rail and road links from Shanghai to other cities.

Telecommunications

Although not widely publicised, telecommunication links are well established. For example, market quotations on the Shanghai Stock Exchange can be transmitted by satellite to 3,000 locations across China while information on "B" shares are readily provided on Telerate to international investors.[3]

Warehousing

Warehousing facilities, such as those provided by the Waigaoqiao Free Trade Zone in Pudong, will encourage the rapid turnaround and light assembly of transported products. When completed, it will have 37.8 hectares of bonded storage area to the southeast of the Waigaiqiao Port. At present, 1.1 square kilometres are already operational with more than 100 construction sites and over 200 buildings under construction.[4] More than 70 office buildings, workshops and warehouses have already been built with commercial, processing, transportation and storage functions.

Construction

With the massive number of projects underway in Shanghai, the construction industry has developed rapidly. However, the industry is forecasted to slow down in 1996 to 10% from the heated 30 to 40% growth rates of the early 1990s. The slowdown is due to falling investment, a credit squeeze and a general shortage of funds (*Business Times*, 1 December 1995). At present, bank loans are only providing 22.4% of the capital needed by property developers (Tang, 1995).

Education and Human Resources

Shanghai has a solid institutional foundation in education, culture, sci-

---

[3] Presentation on 8 December 1995 at the Shanghai Stock Exchange.

[4] Presentation by Hong Renrong, Vice-President of Shanghai Waigaoqiao Free Trade Zone No. 3, United Development Co. Ltd., on 6 December 1995.

ence and technology. At present, Shanghai has 50 colleges and universities with a total enrolment of over 120,000 undergraduate and graduate students. At the end of 1994, Shanghai had more than 1,600 research and development institutes with over 901,000 professionals in the science and technology fields. Recently, the demand for human resources, especially in finance, insurance and trade, has been high (*Shanghai Star*, 8 December 1995b), although plans to open training centres may alleviate the problem. A comparison of wages among several coastal provinces is shown in Table 2–2 and Shanghai's wages are clearly the highest.

TABLE 2–2
Annual Per Capita RMB Wages in Selected Coastal Provinces: 1994

Shanghai	Jiangsu	Zhejiang	Anhui	Fujian	Jiangxi	Shandong
7,401	4,974	5,594	3,793	4,890	3,450	4,338

Source: *Coastal Region Statistical Handbook*, China Unified Statistical Publishing Board, Shanghai, 1995.

Housing and Property

Housing remains a large concern of the Shanghai populace because the local government is gradually easing the subsidies on housing. It is expected that as house prices continue to rise, ordinary middle class Shanghai residents will have increasing difficulty in funding their housing purchases unless there is some form of mortgage available (Tang, 1995). One key barometer of the inflationary pressures in Pudong are its property prices, which have risen five-fold in five years to US$120 per square metre in contrast to only US$40 to US$50 per square metre in the Singapore-Suzhou Industrial Park (Lu, 1995a).

The Hinterland

Beyond Shanghai, the surrounding provinces also have a high potential for growth, in particular the region from the Yangtze delta right up to Wuhan. Surrounding provinces, and even remote areas of China, are ready to use the city of Shanghai as their service base. A number of the provinces have already made investments in this respect in the Pudong New Area. The Yangtze river industrial belt will become the largest in the world in two or three decades. It is predicted that the region along the river, including the seven provinces and a municipality directly under one central government, will contribute about 45% of the country's GDP by the year 2010, an increase of 6% from the 39% in 1994. It will become the most dynamic part of the Asian and Pacific Rim early in the next century (Shanghai Municipality, 1995).

Years of construction have turned the region into a major area for the developed raw materials, extracting and processing, iron and steel, petrochemicals, machinery, electronics and automotive industries. The key iron and steel works in the region produce 45% of the country's steel and steel products. Exports totalled RMB 55.15 billion worth of products in 1994, up 46.2% over the previous year and they accounted for 20% of China's total exports. The nine economic spheres within the region and a chain of cities, including the three major cities of Nanjing, Wuhan and Chongqing, will further strengthen the overall advantages of the region as an industrial belt and its ability to absorb investment into the region.

INVESTORS' PERSPECTIVES

The above factors illustrate the strength of Shanghai as a business centre. Moreover, the rapid growth of Pudong has bolstered Shanghai's ability to lead the Yangtze delta region towards greater economic development. This, in turn, will serve Shanghai as a springboard for inland economic expansion. For Asian economies, this means a bigger market for exports, as well as a shorter supply line for components or manufactured goods.

According to a report by the Academy of Pudong (1991 to 1994) which was cited by Hua Guowan, Vice-Administrator of Pudong Local Government, the success of the Shanghai developmental zones can be attributed to several events. First, the integration of the Shanghai, Jiangsu and Zhejiang economies provided an economic synergy that attracts one-third of China's foreign investment. The foreign investors were mainly MNCs, with 120 companies located in Shanghai and 100 companies located in the other two provinces. Secondly, these foreign investments were sizeable and normally in the high-tech industries. Thirdly, most of the joint ventures were with large to medium-sized SOEs.

However, despite all of these favourable conditions, it is worthwhile to study the merits of Shanghai as a hub for the North Asian region. One way to assess this is to evaluate Shanghai relative to other major hub cities on the basis of the critical success factors highlighted previously. This is pursued in the following section.

Shanghai as a Hub for Northern Asia

Table 2–3 shows that Shanghai ranks below other international hubs. However, Table 2–3 also shows that many weaknesses are structural in nature and they will improve as Shanghai develops. The advantages provided by its natural endowments, location and supporting hinterland, give Shanghai a potential that is waiting to be fulfilled. Improvements in finance, education, and infrastructure will make Shanghai one of the most attractive regional hubs in the near future.

Shanghai's claim to be a hub for northern Asia will also strengthen in the near future given its proximity to many important cities. Tokyo, Seoul, Beijing, Nanjing and Hong Kong, to name a few, are a three-hour flight away. With improvements to telecommunication facilities, Shanghai's sphere of influence will consolidate. Furthermore, Tokyo as a main rival in northern Asia, has structural problems of its own, such as a rigid Japanese economic framework, political turbulence and a sluggish, expensive economy.

There are already signs that Shanghai will be used mainly as a site for company headquarters. American firm J. D. Edwards and Company, a software and consulting firm, announced plans in December 1995 to set up offices in the Waigaoqiao Free Trade Zone, partly to support the high growth energy, chemical, construction and manufacturing industries (Xiao, 1995). Shanghai's mayor, Xu Kuangdi, is optimistic that growth in the Singapore-Suzhou Industrial Park will also boost Shanghai's prospects as companies make use of Shanghai's airports and seaports. Clearly, there is a reciprocal benefit to both locations from any increase in trade, investment or commerce. Shanghai is well poised to serve all of its neighbouring high-tech industrialised areas, "just like Singapore is the hub of the whole of South-east Asia" (Teh, 1995). In Deng Xiaoping's own words, "I think in 20 to 30 years, Shanghai will become a comprehensive international centre for industry, finance and high technology. It will leave Hong Kong and Singapore in its wake" (Lam, 1995).

TABLE 2–3
Comparison of International Hubs

Hub Cities	New York	London	Ranstadt	Singapore	Tokyo	Shanghai
Location	*** Increasing competition from other U.S. cities.	** Pressures from other European cities.	**** Good location as gateway to Europe.	**** At crossroads of Straits of Malacca.	** Good hub for Japan but internationally distant.	**** Head of Yangtze and Chinese coast, near to many parts of Asia.
Government	*** Some possibility of political opportunists.	** Present government lacks confidence.	*** Stable, unassuming government.	**** One party has held power since independence.	** Government suspect to tinges of scandal.	** Favoured by central government but China situation volatile.
Transport	** Good, although subject to congestion.	*** Improving with opening of Channel Tunnel.	**** Good rail and road links to Europe.	**** Great air and water links. Renowned seaport and airport.	**** Good international shipping and air links.	** Large plans but present situation still frustrating.
Telecoms	***** Exceptional, high technology links.	**** Good national and international links.	*** Good links to Europe.	*** Good links to rest of the world.	**** Good.	* Good for China but not international standard yet.
Business Environment	**** High tax though large market.	** Economy still in doldrums.	*** Good, pro-business climate.	*** Low taxes and good incentives.	** Heavy regulation for foreign firms.	*** SEZ status and willing government.

TABLE 2–3 (cont'd)

Hub Cities	New York	London	Ranstadt	Singapore	Tokyo	Shanghai
Human Resources	**** Good entrepreneurial spirit.	*** Well-trained.	**** Multilingual population with good English.	*** Knowledge of English, high productivity.	*** Good, literate, hard-working population.	** Well-educated but shortage of English speaking people.
Finance	***** Home of Wall Street.	**** City has good financial base.	*** Good.	**** Stringent regulatory climate, sound.	**** Good financial infrastructure.	*** Improving especially with development of Pudong.
Hinterland	**** Good support from surrounding region.	*** Smaller English home base.	**** Good support from the Ruhr.	* No natural hinterland, reliance on neighbours.	*** Tokyo-Yokohama conurbation well built up.	***** Tremendous potential of Yangtze region.
Total	**30**	**24**	**27**	**26**	**24**	**22**

* Moderate
** Good
*** Very Good
**** Excellent
***** Exceptional

SHANGHAI AS AN INDUSTRIAL BASE OF THE DOMESTIC MARKET

China is a huge country which many investors want to exploit in terms of a production base as well as a market. Strategically, Shanghai offers a good manufacturing centre for export-oriented products. However, if production is targeted for the local market, does Shanghai offer similar advantages? Assuming an affirmative answer, are certain types of enterprises favoured over the others?

Factors of Production

Domestic production requires low cost, good infrastructure, available labour and proximity to markets. High business costs in Shanghai will affect its competitive edge over other inland production sites. However, this is somewhat counterbalanced because of Pudong's SEZ status. Also, Shanghai is in the process of developing excellent infrastructure facilities. Correspondingly, Shanghai has a solid supply of skilled labour and a densely populated local market. As Table 2–4 shows, Shanghai is slightly favoured over other inland cities in the region in terms of factors of production.

The Push Inland

As cost pressures rise in Shanghai, it is evident that some investors will find the lower cost inland areas more advantageous. "Wages are increasing and the standard of living is increasing, so costs are increasing," says a manager of a Taiwanese electrical appliance company in Shanghai. The trend inland is already starting and China reported that the number of contracts signed for foreign investments in SEZs dropped 42% in the first half of 1995 as compared with a year earlier. Profit margins for many firms have been squeezed due to rising wage and land costs.

The desire by the central government to develop the inland region is attracting investment. To reflect the theme of China's Ninth Five-Year-Plan for raising incomes, inland regions are receiving priority in infrastructure projects and there is a shift of primary and labour intensive industries from coastal to inland areas (Yang *et al.*, 1995). In addition, Beijing will authorise the opening of more inland cities. Currently, only 359 Chinese cities are open to foreign investment (*Business Times*, 16 October 1995).

TABLE 2–4
Comparison of Attributes Between Shanghai and Inland Cities

Attributes for Domestic Production	Shanghai Pudong and Other ETDZs (Puxi, Hong Qiao)	Other Inland Yangtze Cities (Nanjing, Suzhou and Hangzhou)	Remarks
Low Business Cost	** SEZ treatment on taxes, but with increasing business costs.	* No SEZ treatment.	SEZs preference will be shifted inland to balance investment and check inflation.
Good Labour	**	**	Major inland cities such as Nanjing have good labour resources comparable to Shanghai.
Good Infrastructure	***	*	Inland cities lag behind Shanghai in communication networks. Nanjing offers a good alternative as an expressway is currently under construction and will be ready by the end of 1996. An international airport is also under construction.
Proximity to Huge Market	**	**	Same for major cities.
Total	**9**	**6**	Shanghai appears to be more attractive.

* Good
** Very Good
*** Excellent

There is also the possibility that China will redraw its taxation laws which will drastically change, or even abolish, the SEZs. With special privileges being given to many other development zones and the SEZs' economic advantages diluted by cost pressures, it is difficult to present a case to maintain the SEZ's special tax position. Furthermore, with China's entry into the World Trade Organisation (WTO) it is expected that a unified taxation approach will have to be adopted. (Kao, 1995).

These tax changes will drive firms away from the SEZs and into other regions. Furthermore, "while multinationals can afford to wait, many small export oriented foreign funded enterprises with thin profit margins may be wiped out in the meantime" (Lu, 1995b). However, the net effect is that firms have to become more competitive in the long run, especially in Shanghai where cost pressures are high. Table 2–5 shows the comparative investments in Shanghai, Jiangsu and Zhejiang by industry class.

TABLE 2–5
Comparative Investments in Shanghai, Jiangsu and Zhejiang by Industry Class (in RMB 100 Million, 1994)

Industry Types	Shanghai	Jiangsu	Zhejiang
Primary	16.6	86.3	53.6
Secondary	454.5	1,073.7	531.6
Tertiary	680.5	858.9	600.8
TOTAL	1,151.6	2,018.9	1,186.0

Source: *Coastal Region Statistical Handbook*, China Unified Statistical Publishing Board, Shanghai, 1995.

From the above analysis, cost and infrastructure are two competitive factors for domestic trade. In this respect, Shanghai ranks higher than other inland cities. While SEZ treatment is currently given to investment in Pudong, other economic and technological development zones (ETDZ) are not. In the long term, SEZ preference will be shifted inland to balance investment and check inflation. Thus, investors may have to weigh the advantages and disadvantages of investing in Pudong *vis-à-vis* industrial bases such as Nanjing and Hangzhou. Shanghai ETDZs are not recommended for domestic production since their business costs are likely to rise with Pudong in the long term.

As China enters the WTO, it will also lower import tariffs to keep in line with the international regulations. While domestically manufactured products may not be internationally competitive in several ways, such as packaging and quality, local companies will have to maintain their strategy on cost and value for money. In fact, the inflation rate across China differs between coastal cities and inland cities. Shanghai's inflation rate ranks one of the highest due to its international trade and influence. Inflation caused by high import prices and escalated economic development will drive up business costs, particularly land prices and wages. With increasing wages, consumers' purchasing power will also increase. Thus, foreign manufacturing companies can invest in Shanghai profitably provided their product quality and price are competitive with the imports.

On infrastructure, there is a concerted effort to build up the transportation network linkages in the Yangtze river basin. The construction of the Nanjing bridge is important since it opens up the city as the strategic gateway for domestic trade and distribution. Furthermore, by the end of 1996 an expressway linking Shanghai and Nanjing will be completed, contributing to Nanjing's importance as a complementary distribution centre to Shanghai.

HONG KONG'S ROLE RELATIVE TO SHANGHAI

As Shanghai develops its infrastructure, the city has a vision to compete with Hong Kong not only to be the national business centre for China but also to be the business hub for North Asia. However, according to an *Economist Intelligence Unit* report (Davis, 1996), it is unlikely that Shanghai will overtake the position of Hong Kong as the regional business centre in the near future. Currently, Hong Kong plays an important role in boosting the development of south China. In addition, it has already taken the pseudo role of a "national business centre" for China well before 1997. Notwithstanding competition, Hong Kong will continue to be a major contributor to China's economic development. Table 2–6 in particular, lists four business sectors of Shanghai's development linked to Hong Kong's contribution.

TABLE 2–6
Hong Kong's Contribution to Shanghai's Development

Business Sectors	Areas of Contribution
Investments	Source of capital for the development of industrial base and services sector.
Infrastructure Development Expertise	Source of technology transfer.
International Trade and Financial Services	Source of revenue and trade. Provides excellent financing facilities and instruments to support China's economic activities.
Global Market Network	Source of market contacts and distribution to expand China's network of markets in the world.

Hong Kong's initial investments in Shanghai were in the labour intensive, light manufacturing industries and the outputs were export oriented. Subsequent investments expanded into medium and high value added industries that are targeted for both export and domestic markets. Hong Kong overtook Japan to become Shanghai's biggest investor in 1995. Besides capital investment, Hong Kong has been involved in Shanghai's rapid infrastructural development through the transfer of technological expertise.

Hong Kong will remain as a centre for international finance and trade in the near to medium term. China's central government is not prepared now to liberalise its financial market. It is unlikely that the government will give up the control necessary for Shanghai to become a true regional financial centre (*The Straits Times*, 29 August 1995). Hong Kong is also an important trading partner of China, accounting for 35% of China's total foreign trade, both as a final market and an entrepot. With an established marketing and distribution network worldwide, Hong Kong has become a channel for China to open new markets for Chinese products and expand trade relations with Hong Kong's traditional partners.

Shanghai is unlikely to pose any threat to Hong Kong as a business centre for China in the near future. This view is shared by Mr. Hua Guowan, the Vice-Administrator of Pudong New Area, who was quoted as saying "China is like a big hall, and Shanghai and Hong Kong are the lamps. We need more than one lamp to illuminate the whole hall." Both cities will play a pivotal role in China's economic development.

In the long term, Shanghai is more likely than Hong Kong to emerge as the international hub. The Yangtze river industrial belt is expected to grow and surpass the industrial belts along the Rhine river and Tokyo Bay to become the largest in the world in two or three decades according to the results of a report entitled *Comprehensive Research on the Construction of the Yangtze River Industrial Belt* by the Municipality of Shanghai (1995).

CONCLUSION

The challenges to Shanghai are many, both internationally and domestically. In international business, Shanghai has the potential to be the business hub for North Asia with the advantages of excellent trade and finance infrastructure. However, it will face intense competition from other regional hubs such as Tokyo and Singapore. For Shanghai to succeed by the year 2010, Shanghai needs more than just infrastructure development. The government has to liberalise its financial market so as to gain global acceptance. In addition, it needs to develop its human resources to achieve a world-class standard.

On the domestic front, however, Shanghai is less attractive as a long-term manufacturing centre since lower production costs can be found in the inland Yangtze river region. The city has large concentrations of manufacturing industries and, as a result of rising costs, low value added operations are moving inland. In summary, Shanghai has all of the necessary facets to propel it towards becoming an international hub for northern Asia, equivalent in status to any of the extant international hubs in the world today.

REFERENCES

"Beijing to End Tariff Exemptions for Foreign Firms", *Business Times*, 10 November 1995.

Bernard Bruce, "Gateway Europe", *Europe*, March 1995, pp. 10–12.

Bowman Robert J., "Who's on First", *World Trade*, January/February 1992, pp. 102–9.

"Call to Reform Housing System", *Business Times,* 13 November 1995.

Chen Qide, "Planned Development", *Shanghai Star*, 15 December 1995a.

Chen Qide, "Shipping Centre to Rise Up", *Shanghai Star,* 8 December 1995b.

Chen Qingbai and Shi Wei, "Re-establishing Shanghai as an International Financial Centre", *Beijing Review*, 15–21 August 1994.

"China May Allow Currency Convertibility Next Year", *Business Times*, 13 November 1995.

"China to Open Inland Cities to Foreign Investors", *Business Times,* 16 October 1995.

"Coastal Cities Opening to Foreign Investors", *Hong Kong Standard*, 5 December 1995.

Coastal Region Statistical Handbook, China Unified Statistical Publishing Board, Shanghai, 1995.

Comprehensive Research on the Construction of the Yangtze River Industrial Belt, Survey, Shanghai Municipality, 1995.

"Construction Growth Easing Off ?", *Business Times,* 1 December 1995.

Dai Huixing, Director of Pudong's International Exchange Centre, paper presented at NTU's Business Study Mission Seminar, 8 December 1995.

Davis K, *Hong Kong After 1997*, Economist Intelligence Unit, 1996.

"Financial Centre Shapes Up", *Shanghai Star,* 5 December 1995a.

"Golden Megaport Colours Movement", *Corporate Location,* January/February SS4-7, 1994b.

Hong Renhong, Vice-President of Shanghai Waigaoqiao Free Trade Zone No. 3, paper presented at NTU's Business Study Mission Seminar, United Development Company, 8 December 1995.

Hua Guowan, Vice-Administrator Pudong New Area, paper presented at NTU's Business Study Mission Seminar, 8 December 1995.

Kahn Joseph, "Beijing Holds the Cards", *Asian Wall Street Journal,* 22 November 1994.

Kao Chen, "Is It Time to Level the Economic Playing Field for All of China", *The Straits Times*, 31 October 1995.

Kass Rochelle, "A Light In the Asia Pacific", *International Banking*, March 1992, pp. 36–44.

Keith Richburg, "Can Shanghai Overtake Hong Kong in Business", *The Straits Times,* 29 August 1995.

"Key Industries Excel", *Shanghai Star,* 8 December 1995.

Lam Willy, *China After Deng Xiaoping,* John Wiley, London, 1995.

Lehner U. C., "As Goes Shanghai, So Goes China", *The Asian Wall Street Journal*, 22 November 1994.

Lu Ning, "Pudong to be China's Sixth Special Economic Zone", *Business Times,* 8 September 1995a.

Lu Ning, "How Tax Changes Will Affect Foreign Firms in China", *Business Times,* 6 November 1995b.

Masuda Tatuhiro, "Pointers on Investment in the Chinese Market", *Jetro China Newsletter*, July/August 1994.

Quak H. W., "HK to Remain Global Hub for Trading China Stocks: HKSE", *Business Times,* 24 October 1995.

"Randstad Holland – Gateway to Europe", *Corporate Location,* January/February SS2-3,1994a.

Schwieterman Joseph P., "Turbulence Over Hong Kong", *China Business Review,* January/February 1994.

"SEZs Likely to Keep Corporate Tax Rates", *Business Times,* 13 November 1995.

Shanghai Internet Trading and Consultancy (SITC) (shaintnt@ public.sta.net.cn.), 1995.

Shanthi K., "China Investors Head Inland As Cost Loses Its Appeal", *Asian Wall Street Journal*, 21 October 1995.

Tang Ivan, "80pc Mortgage Plan a First", *Hong Kong Standard,* 7 December 1995.

Teh Hooi Ling, "Suzhou Project Will Boost S'pore–Shanghai Ties: Mayor", *Business Times,* 10 October 1995.

"The City of Glitter and Ghosts", *The Economist*, 24 December 1994.

Wu Jingshu, "Landmark for World-Class Port", *China Daily,* 11 December 1995.

Xiao Li, "JD Edwards Enters Free Trade Zone", *Shanghai Star*, 8 December 1995.

Xin Bao, "New Rules", *Shanghai Star*, 8 December 1995.

Yang Mu, John J. Williams and Cao Yong, "Resurrecting Shanghai in the 21st Century: The Shift in China's Regional Economic Strategies", *China Business Review*, December 1995, pp. 11–29.

"Zhu Explains Economic Situation", *China Daily,* 11 December 1995.

Chapter 3

Comparative Study of Shanghai, Suzhou and Nanjing Business Locations

BY
Karen PHUA Oong
LEE Way Tuck
David SOH Buck Leng
WONG Yew Cheong

INTRODUCTION

THE PURPOSE OF this chapter is to present a comparative analysis of the three business locations in China – Shanghai, Suzhou and Nanjing. The focus is on identifying the competitive advantages and complementary features of each location that foreign investors can leverage upon when they invest in the three locations.

To fully appreciate the discussion presented in this chapter, it is important to gain an overall perspective of the unique geographic relationships of these three locations and the economic, social and political developments in a broader regional nature. Therefore, this chapter begins with an introduction which traces the development of the Yangtze river valley region. This region spans the three business locations and extends right into China's hinterland, covering Zhejiang, Hubei and Sichuan provinces.

Following the introduction, discussion turns to the framework used to analyse the comparative advantages in each location. This section identifies the various parameters or elements used to compare the locations. Next follows a detailed discussion and analysis of these elements on both a competitive basis and also on a complementary basis in the form of integrated regional clusters. A brief review of major cities in the world is also included to project the region's continual growth possibilities. The chapter concludes with a matrix outlining the comparative analysis of these three locations.

DEVELOPMENT OF THE YANGTZE RIVER VALLEY REGION

The ten-year Cultural Revolution, which ended in 1976, completely devastated China. To regain its past glory and prominence, China reopened its doors to the world through a series of incremental reforms aimed at economic expansion and social stability, and the upgrading of living standards for the general population.

The first major policy decision was to embark on a "socialist modernisation" of the economic structure in the countryside by returning the farms back to the farmers. Following the success of the rural reform, more complex urban economic reforms were implemented in 1984. These included the decentralisation of the centrally planned economy by focusing on the development of private and other non-state-owned enterprises. These urban reforms started in Shenzhen and soon after, spread to other Special Economic Zones (SEZs) including Zhuhai, Shantou and Xiamen (Yang *et al*., 1995). With the influx of foreign funds, these reforms very quickly extended to the southern coastal areas of Guangdong and Fujian provinces which constitute the Pearl river valley region and represent the first wave of development.

The set of strategies which guided the first wave of development along the Pearl river valley region has certainly contributed immensely to the economic prosperity of the coastal provinces and the SEZs. However, in another way, this has created some serious problems. These problems include a widening of the income gap between coastal regions and the hinterland; social problems associated with migration from the hinterland and the consequent unemployment in these urban centres; and lastly inflation. The main cause of these problems is that the growth of the hinterland has lagged too far behind those of the coastal regions. In addition, the reform strategies have not been able to address the problems associated with the state-owned enterprises (SOEs) including inefficient operations and the high cost of social security. It is thus the priority of the central government to address these issues in the 1990s, (Yang *et al.,* 1995).

The strategy for the 1990s is one of promoting growth for the hinterland so as to achieve a more balanced economic development across the country. It is also time to address the problems of the SOEs, a significant portion of which reside in Shanghai. The second wave of development, therefore, was centred on the Yangtze river valley region which includes Shanghai, Jiangsu, Zhejiang, Hubei and Sichuan provinces.

This wave started in 1992 after the government ended the austerity campaign aimed at cooling off the overheated economy. Many companies are now looking for investment opportunities in this growth region which centres around Shanghai, referred to as the "Dragon Head" and Nanjing which represents the "Dragon Neck". Together, they will enhance the economic growth of the entire hinterland (Yang *et al*., 1995). Suzhou, which is situated between Shanghai and Nanjing, is of strategic importance to Shanghai in its course to spearhead the nationwide economic development into the 21st century.

FRAMEWORK OF ANALYSIS

The framework employed to study the competitive and complementary interactions of the three business locations is derived from an article written by Michael Porter (1995) on "The rise of the Urban Entrepreneur". In this article, he states that there are four attributes which contribute to the potential competitive advantages of cities. These attributes interact individually, and as a system, to define the business climate that each city establishes and operates for its industries. These attributes include the following:

(i) ***Strategic Location:*** With the rapid growth of concepts such as just-in-time delivery, strategic supplier and customer relationship, service quality and so forth, the choice of locating a business is a critical business decision. By virtue of the location, a company can tap on to the available resources and operating conditions necessary to compete in a given industry. The elements selected for comparing the three cities are: geographic location; natural resources and land use; access to capital; infrastructure; building and rental costs; and government policies and incentives.

(ii) ***Local Market Demand:*** This concept refers to the nature of home market demand for the industry's products or services. The element selected for the comparison of the three cities is population and wealth.

(iii) ***Human Resources:*** This concept refers to labour conditions such as cost, quality and availability of the labour force.

(iv) ***Integration with Regional Clusters:*** This concept refers to the relative ease and ability to leverage the financial, technological and other capabilities of the nearby regional business clusters. This creates opportunities for new and growing companies to provide services and production inputs as well as the opportunity to sell downstream products and services. The complementary interactions explored in this chapter are the Shanghai-Suzhou Link and the Nanjing-Shanghai-Suzhou Link.

ANALYSIS OF STRATEGIC LOCATION

Geographic Location

(i) ***Shanghai:*** Located at the mouth of the Yangtze river, Shanghai lies mid-way along China's coastline, covering an area of 6,341 square kilometres. In 1984, the Shanghai municipal government submitted to the state council a "report outlining Shanghai's economic development strategies" and put forward a proposal concerning the development of Pudong, an area on the east bank of the Huangpu river. The Pudong New Area is almost 12 times larger than the total completed area of all the 14 economic development zones in the coastal provinces. It covers 350 square kilometres, of which 177 square kilometres is planned to be an urban area with a population of 1.7 million. Its aim is to develop five districts specialising in different activities, becoming in effect, tomorrow's new Shanghai.

These districts will include a large commercial and financial sector to be located across the Huangpu river from the Bund which is the historical financial area located on the western side of the river. Shanghai's plan is to extend the financial quarter from the Bund across the river into Pudong on the eastern side of the river.

To succeed, the task is to relocate manufacturing facilities to neighbouring provinces where labour costs are lower, but to retain people to work in hotels, shops and other service industries.

Since many industries have moved out of the city to make way for the development of Pudong, the future growth of the western part of Shanghai is likely to be less spectacular, a view shared in an article in *The Economist* (1995, pp. 29–30). Thus, concentration outside of Shanghai will result in attention being focused on the whole region, the Yangtze river delta, of which Shanghai is only a small part.

(ii) ***Suzhou***: The historic and cultural city of Suzhou is situated between Shanghai to the east and Lake Tai to the west. It is a municipality of Jiangsu province on the eastern coast of China. There are already three economic and technological development zones (ETDZs) in the province, namely Lianyungang, Nantong and Kunshan. Suzhou is located 80 kilometres (or two hours) away from Shanghai, and 170 kilometres (or five hours) from Nanjing. Its close location to Shanghai allows easy access to established infrastructure facilities in Shanghai such as an international airport and a port. It can also be used as further access to inland cities.

Also known as the "Venice of the East", Suzhou is connected to the other two cities via the Yangtze river. Suzhou's success has been to market itself as the most convenient alternative in the Yangtze delta to Shanghai, but with lower costs, less job-hopping and bureaucracy, and a clear commitment to the manufacturing industry. Suzhou is located near to key industrial parks in Wuxi and Shanghai which have attracted foreign investments.

Suzhou can serve to support these areas with supplementary factory and residential space which is a cheaper alternative to Shanghai. Suzhou can offer potential advantages to businesses that benefit from the proximity to downtown business districts which are equipped with logistical infrastructure, entertainment and tourist destinations, and concentrations of companies. Its strategic location also creates opportunities for relocating warehousing, data processing, food preparation, and other activities that benefit from a downtown proximity but do not need to be near the more expensive downtown headquarters (or other company locations). The successful companies locating here will leverage access to nearby regional business clusters.

The Singapore-Suzhou Township, planned at national level by the Chinese and Singapore governments[1], aims to grow into a satellite city of 600,000 people over the next 15 years (*The Straits Times,* 10 September 1995). However, according to Suzhou's Mayor Zhang,[2] agriculture still maintains a 3% growth rate despite the growth of the industrial area. The Singapore-Suzhou Township comprises a total area of 70 square kilometres out of the 8,488 square kilometres of Suzhou municipality. Suzhou, well known for its beautiful gardens, is still relatively undeveloped. With the exception of the industrial park, much farmland and few buildings are to be found. However, with the further development of Shanghai, the scenery in Suzhou will change.

(iii) ***Nanjing:*** Jiangsu's capital city of Nanjing has a rich history, having served ten times as the capital of various kingdoms or dynasties over the last 2,500 years. Nanjing's fundamental asset is its importance to the domestic economy and its location. Nanjing lies 300 kilometres west of Shanghai on the south bank of the Yangtze river, right in the middle of the basin supplying the bulk of east China's food produce.

The cities along the Yangtze river have become a priority for the state planners' next great "dragon of development", with Shanghai as the dragon's head, Nanjing the neck and Chongqing the tail. A few Beijing planners even foresee the eventual development of a continuous megalopolis between Shanghai and Nanjing. As such, Nanjing's location is crucial to China's interior markets. The city's Yangtze River Bridge carries all highway and rail traffic between Shanghai on the coast and Wuhan, 1,810 kilometres upriver, and it also connects road traffic with the largest railroad marshalling yard in east China. Nanjing's city area is 6,516 square kilometres including an urban area of 867 square kilometres. By the end of the century, China's former capital plans to double in size and to establish industrial satellites in five nearby counties where numerous high-tech and economic zones have been set up over the past six years.

---

1 Brochure printed by China-Singapore Suzhou Industrial Park Development Co. Ltd., 1995.

2 Official banquet and seminar with the Joint Working Committee of the Singapore-Suzhou Industrial Park, co-chaired by the Mayor of Suzhou, Zhang Xinsheng and representatives from the Suzhou Municipal Government, Suzhou Bamboo Grove Hotel, 9 December 1995.

Natural Resources and Land Use

The availability of natural resources in a city and the optimal usage of land within the city will contribute to its competitiveness.

(i) ***Shanghai:*** In Shanghai, the adopted layout for the Pudong New Area is to form five relatively independent complex sub-areas: Waigaoqiao-Gao Qiao sub-area, Qingningsi-Jinqiao sub-area, Lujiazhui-Huamu sub-area, Zhongjiadu-Liuli sub-area, and Beicai-Shongjiang sub-area. In these five sub-areas, particular emphasis is to be put on the development of free trade zones, export processing zones, services concerning finance, trade, and real estate, non-polluting manufacturing, and education and research. The Pudong project covers an area of 350 square kilometres.

(ii) ***Suzhou:*** The town of Suzhou has always enjoyed the reputation of being a land of plenty, the home of silk and a paradise on earth. The Singapore-Suzhou Township enables manufacturers to set up operations and build their own factories operating within the integrated self-sufficient industrial park with a one-stop approval under the Suzhou Industrial Park Administration Committee (SIPAC) which is a pro-business organisation empowered by the State Council.[3] Lease period is up to 70 years for residential use, 50 years for industrial operations and 40 years for commercial operations. Other information on prepared plots of industrial land of various sizes, fees, deed tax and other duties can be obtained from the China-Singapore Suzhou Industrial Park Development Co. Ltd.

(iii) ***Nanjing:*** Location aside, Nanjing also has a comparatively developed industrial core. The city ranks second in terms of China's electronics and chemical production, and third in the manufacture of trucks and passenger vans. According to a study conducted by the central government in December 1992, Nanjing is China's fifth most powerful industrial centre. Since 1949, Beijing has plowed more than RMB 18.9 billion into 70 key projects in the Nanjing area, accounting for more than 36% of total capital investment. The city itself invested RMB 30.6 billion in light and heavy industries

---

3 Official banquet and seminar with the Joint Working Committee of the Singapore-Suzhou Industrial Park, co-chaired by Mayor of Suzhou, Zhang Xinsheng, and representatives from the Suzhou Municipal Government, Suzhou Bamboo Grove Hotel, 9 December 1995.

during the same time period, helping to build Yizheng Chemical Fibre Co., China's largest synthetic fibre plant and Yangtze Petrochemical, one of the country's largest petrochemical firms (Mr. Xi Yongmin, Deputy Chief General, Nanjing Municipal Government, 12 December 1995).

Access to Capital

Shanghai, Suzhou, Nanjing: In comparing the three locations, Shanghai may have the best access to capital in the long run and it is undoubtedly set to become the financial centre of China. The emphasis given repeatedly by the central government in declaring Shanghai as the "Dragon Head" has put it in centre stage in the recent reform efforts.

At the national level, the National Foreign Exchange Trade System has been set up in Shanghai and is in operation. Currently, Shanghai's financial market is more established as compared with other cities in China such as Suzhou and Nanjing.

There are some favourable conditions for re-establishing Shanghai as an international financial centre. These include its ideal geographical location, a modern and diversified industrial and commercial base, the opening of branches in Shanghai of numerous international financial organisations, the development of the Pudong New Area which needs financial support, access to a legion of financial expertise, and a solid infrastructure with advanced transportation and telecommunication systems. Shanghai has made tremendous progress in preparing for what it considers to be its destiny. However, there are still problems such as the restriction banning foreign banks from doing business in renminbi. The main business of most foreign banks branches in Shanghai is currently servicing joint venture companies. With the recent central government anti-inflation policy, there is tight control over credit (Leung, 1995). Therefore, in order for Shanghai to become a true international financial centre, the government has to change its policies in terms of its restrictions on the development of Shanghai's banking sector.

Infrastructure

(i) ***Shanghai:*** With its historical background as a financial centre of the East combined with its location in the coastal region, Shanghai has relatively good infrastructure as compared to the other two locations. It also has the largest port along the Yangtze river and it is the fourth largest port in the world.

Shanghai intends to expand the existing Hongqiao International Airport to enhance its capacity. On the other side of the Huangpu river, a new Pudong International Airport will be built, with a capacity of 60 million passengers and 2 million tonnes of cargo per annum, to serve mainly the Pudong New Area. In the past five years, Shanghai has invested RMB 25 billion in ten infrastructure projects and it will continue to build infrastructural facilities over the next five years. According to Dai Hui Xing, Director of the Shanghai Pudong New Area International Exchange Centre, with the momentum already built up, the development in the next five years can be faster than that of the last five years and in about 20 years the city will be completely developed (Porter, 1995). Currently, there are about 5,000 projects in progress in Pudong.

Shanghai has around 50,000 IDD lines and the number continues to grow. Shanghai now accounts for one-third of the country's international post and telecommunications volume. The optical cable communication system completed recently will enhance the telecommunication capability in Shanghai.

(ii) ***Suzhou:*** The business location of Suzhou is a two-hour drive from Shanghai's Hongqiao airport and it is three hours from Shanghai's port. In addition to Shanghai's port, Suzhou is also served by Zhangjiagang, about 90 kilometres away which is an established river port with container facilities along the Yangtze river. A Singapore consortium is developing a river port at Changshu, 62 kilometres from the township. Suzhou is located on the main Shanghai–Nanjing railway line which links into the national trunk rail network. Express trains travel south-east to Shanghai in 75 minutes. Travelling time to Shanghai (100 kilometres) is often over two hours despite the upgrading of the main highway. Suzhou's downtown area remains congested. A Nanjing–Suzhou–Shanghai expressway is scheduled to be opened in the latter part of 1996. There are limited domestic services from Suzhou's Gangfu airport but they include Beijing and Guangdong. Travelling time to Shanghai's airport (90 kilometres) where there are many international flights is around two hours.

(iii) ***Nanjing:*** As the former capital of China for ten dynasties, Nanjing has a better developed infrastructure than Suzhou but it is still poor compared to Shanghai. Nanjing's port is the second largest along the Yangtze river after Shanghai and it is the city's main infrastructure advantage. Located up river, and with the narrowing of the river, ships more than 10,000 MT need to unload their goods into smaller vessels before they are transported into the hinterland. This has created an opportunity for Nanjing to become a critical transportation node (MacInnis and Ma, 1995). Similar to Shanghai, Nanjing has an international airport, however, it is far from satisfactory. It is very disorganised and the only international connections are flights to Hong Kong.

The current problems which they are solving are: transportation, telecommunications and power supply, a comment made by one official from the city's Economic Commission.[4] By the end of 1996, highways linking to other cities will be opened and a new international airport will be opened by July 1997. There is also plan to build a second Yangtze river bridge so as to gain access to the north.

In general, the utility facilities for these three locations lag behind demand in the current economic expansion. Shortages in the power supply continue to plague many factories. Water supply shortages are another problem that heavy industrial users need to be aware of. The development of telecommunications has been in progress in Suzhou and Nanjing but improvements have not been as rapid as in Shanghai.

Building and Rental Costs

(i) ***Shanghai, Suzhou, Nanjing:*** The high rent in the Puxi area, which includes the Bund, makes Shanghai the world's fourth most expensive city for office space. People were hoping to move to the Pudong New Area with the expectation that the rents would be about 40% lower. However, this is not the case presently, especially for industrial land. Although Pudong is intended to be a low cost manufacturing haven, the area has high costs for land, which may drive investors away (Sender, 1994). The price for industrial land in Pudong is about five times that of comparable plots to the west of the city. As for office space in Pudong's financial district, rents are equal to the Bund. Supply is no longer a problem as many property developers have rushed in to Pudong area to build commercial of-

[4] Lunch interview with Lui Seow Long, officer from Nanjing Economic Commission, 12 December 1995.

fices and current occupancy is not up to expectation. Overall, Shanghai is an expensive place for business within China.

In the case of Suzhou, industrial land costs about US$50 a square metre for a 50-year lease, undercutting prices in Shanghai's principal investment zones by 100–200%.

Provincial Government Policies

(i) ***Shanghai:*** Shanghai was recently authorised to pioneer an experiment allowing some MNCs to engage in foreign trade as announced by the States Council (*The Straits Times,* 27 November 1995). Prospective partners will be selected from multinational firms to set up joint ventures with Chinese companies. If this experiment proves successful, Shanghai will contribute substantially to the unfolding of a market economy in China. With the backing of Beijing, Shanghai has little chance of failing in this development.

(ii) ***Suzhou:*** Suzhou has the Singapore-Suzhou Industrial Park (SSIP) which promises to provide an interface between investors and the government at all levels, reducing the need for foreign companies to rely on their own connections to get things done. According to the co-chairman of the SSIP, the park is said to be a one-stop administrative and approval centre for investors.[5] The Suzhou Industrial Park Administrative Committee is a pro-business organisation empowered by Beijing to approve projects valued at US$30 million and up. This is one of the key advantages of Suzhou. In China, networking or *guanxi* is an important factor for doing business. The park was set up at the state level between Singapore and China and, therefore, it has a direct link to the central government of China. Mayor Zhang is also very supportive of the SSIP.

(iii) ***Nanjing:*** The administrative procedures for investment in Nanjing are more complex as compared with Suzhou and Shanghai. Investors must deal with both city and provincial level officials. The main complaint foreign investors have about Nanjing is its conservative government (*Business China*, 30 May 1994). The appointment of a new, young governor for Jiangsu, however, could help Nanjing shrug off its conservative reputation. Firms looking to establish

---

5 Seminar on the Singapore-Suzhou Industrial Park hosted by the co-chairman of the Singapore-Suzhou Industrial Park and the chairman of Singapore Jurong Town Corporation, Suzhou Bamboo Grove Hotel, 9 December 1995.

themselves as players in the regional market will have to contend with a municipal government mired in red tape and slower to move on market and enterprise reforms than many of its counterparts. In Wuxi and Suzhou, for example, only firms with investments of over US$10 million are required to go through the provincial government.

Legal Framework

Dispute settlement is of great concern to foreign investors. Efforts are being made to create a more conducive business climate as evident in SSIP. Any major disputes in SSIP are settled by the Joint Working Committee co-chaired by the Mayor of Suzhou and the chairman of Jurong Town Corporation[6] and the channel for settling more serious disputes between the higher government authorities is the Joint Steering Council, co-chaired by Singapore's Deputy Prime Minister, Lee Hsien Loong and the Chinese Vice-Premier, Li Lanqing.[7]

Tax Policies and Incentives

The three locations basically offer comparable preferential tax rates for foreign investors. For example, the term "Income tax exemption for two years after profitable operations and 50% reduction for the next three years" is granted to manufacturing enterprises which have been in operation for a period exceeding ten years, is common for all three locations.

Preferential tax rates can be offered at two levels of authority, either the provincial government or state government. This is also comparable to China's five existing SEZs. These five are Shenzhen, Zhuhai and Shantou in Guangdong province, Xiamen in Fujian province and the whole island of Hainan. These zones offer preferential terms to investors and so far, they have succeeded in attracting large amounts of foreign and domestic investment. The Chinese government recently made it

---

6 Seminar on the Singapore-Suzhou Industrial Park hosted by the co-chairman of the Singapore-Suzhou Industrial Park and the chairman of Singapore Jurong Town Corporation, Suzhou Bamboo Grove Hotel, 9 December 1995.

7 Official banquet and seminar with the Joint Working Committee of Singapore-Suzhou Industrial Park, co-chaired by Mayor of Suzhou, Zhang Xinsheng, and representatives from Suzhou Municipal Government, Suzhou Bamboo Grove Hotel, 9 December 1995.

clear that there is no intention to set up any more new special economic zones (*The Straits Times*, 22 July 1995). This was announced when there was speculation that such zones would be set up in China's western and central regions due to the rising resentment in the poorer regions, which have demanded investment and policies to enable them to narrow the widening gap with the south and east.

On the contrary, the preferential policies enjoyed by foreign investors in these existing zones would be "adjusted gradually" in view of the need to establish a socialist market economy and in preparation for China's bid to join the World Trade Organisation (WTO). It should also be noted that more than 30 ETDZs in the coastal areas also offer tax breaks to foreign investors. The Waigaoqiao Free Trade Zone is the first of its kind on the mainland of China. This has given Shanghai the advantage over the other two locations.

ANALYSIS OF LOCAL MARKET DEMAND

The second potential competitive advantage of the cities lies in the unmet demands of their own populations. Even though average incomes are relatively low in these cities, high population density creates substantial purchasing power and a large market. As incomes are unequally distributed, both among regions and among households, a small increase in average per capita income can lead to much larger increases in the number of households, in particular places, with incomes that are above the threshold for buying goods (*The Economist*, 30 October 1993).

Population and Wealth

(i) ***Shanghai:*** At the end of 1994, the city of Shanghai had a permanent population of 13.5 million, with a birth rate of 5.8%, a death rate of 7.0% and a natural growth rate of -1.2%.[8] The savings rate is over 30% (total volume of savings deposits of the city's residents reached RMB 57.8 billion (US$ 6.96 billion) in 1993). Total retail sales were RMB 65.4 billion (US$7.88 billion) in 1993 of which RMB 7.6 billion (US$0.92 billion) was from the private retail sector. In 1994, Shanghai's GDP was RMB 197 billion (US$23.7 billion) versus RMB 151 billion (US$18.19 billion) in 1993. In 1993,

---

8 *China Statistical Yearbook*, 1995.

total imports and exports through the city reached RMB 256.47 billion (US$30.9 billion); out of this total, RMB 1,162 billion (US$14.0 billion) and RMB 1,411 billion (US$17.0 billion)[9] were for U.S. exports and imports, respectively.

Shanghai's per capita consumption is one of the highest in China. It was RMB 4,162 (US$501.45) in 1993 as compared to RMB 1,415 (US$170.48) for Jiangsu province as a whole. Yong Ser Joo, the Consul from the Consulate of the Republic of Singapore in Shanghai, and Yeo Aik Koon, General Manager of Nippon Paint (China) Co. Ltd., have both indicated that although salaries in Shanghai are higher than the surrounding cities (e.g., Suzhou and Nanjing), they are not high enough to buy houses and cars, and since the Shanghainese do not believe in keeping money, salaries are spent which results in the strong purchasing power. Based on recent estimates of consumer buying power, Shanghai leads the way. It has the highest parity-based spending power and the average consumer spent approximately RMB 20,999 (US$2,530) in 1993 as compared to RMB 9,503 (US$1,145) in Jiangsu while the national average was RMB 8,840 (US$1,065) for the whole of China (Perkins, 1995).

(ii) ***Suzhou:*** Officially, Suzhou's urban population is 860,000; taking account of migrant workers, the total figure is probably near one million. The city has a jurisdiction over six surrounding counties/cities with a population over 5.6 million. The population in the Suzhou municipality is about 6 million and with a per capita GDP of RMB 8,315 (US$970), the city ranks second among major Chinese coastal open cities. It had a GDP of RMB 52.6 billion (US$6.2 billion) in 1993. Suzhou has a high population of well-to-do residents. According to Mayor Zhang, Suzhou takes 52% of the total foreign investment of Jiangsu Province and accounts for 1.7% of the GDP of China.

(iii) ***Nanjing:*** The Nanjing population of 5.2 million enjoys a high standard of living and the political prestige of being the capital of China's third wealthiest province, Jiangsu, which had a GNP of nearly RMB 300 billion (US$36.14 billion) in 1993. Nanjing's GNP for that year was RMB 32.6 billion (US$3.93 billion), a 17% increase over 1992. In 1994, Nanjing's GNP was RMB 47.2 billion

---

[9] Shanghai Municipal Government, *Shanghai Today,* Shanghai, 1994.

(US$5.69 billion), 5.7% higher than the level of average increase for the whole economy. The city generates roughly 15–20% of all provincial revenue, and its employees earn 20% of total wages in Jiangsu. Retail sales were RMB 14.2 billion (US$1.71 billion) in 1993 and RMB 18.8 billion (US$2.27 billion) in 1994. Exports amount to RMB 3,030 million (US$365 million) and import RMB 2,158 million (US$260 million), as of the end of 1993 (Perkins, 1995).

ANALYSIS OF HUMAN RESOURCES

A city with a supply of educated and skilled labour will encourage investors to invest there, resulting in lower unemployment. Thus the availability, the quality and the cost of labour are important factors to companies who intend to invest in any one of the three locations.

Labour Conditions

(i) ***Shanghai:*** The unemployment rate for Shanghai and Jiangsu province are relatively low at 2.8 and 2.1% respectively in 1994. The official national average annual per capita wage of workers and staff was RMB 4,538 in 1994, recording a growth rate of 34.6% in wage levels compared with 1993. The figures for Shanghai and Jiangsu province were RMB 7,405 and RMB 4,974 respectively, both above the national average. Shanghai's figure, in particular, is much higher than the average in Jiangsu province.

The State Labour Bureau monitors foreign joint venture wages closely, restricting them to about twice the level of state-owned enterprises and allowing wage increases only when the joint ventures are profitable.

Shanghai draws quality labour from the surrounding areas due to its economic development and this has resulted in the higher relative wage rates. In 1992, there were 13.6 college graduates per thousand population in Shanghai. At the end of 1993, the city had 49 institutions of higher learning, 1,163 secondary schools including 729 middle schools and 101 vocational schools, and 2,122 primary schools.[10]

---

[10] Shanghai Municipal Government, *Shanghai Today,* Shanghai, 1994.

(ii) ***Suzhou:*** Labour costs are 30 to 50% lower in Suzhou than those in Shanghai and employee poaching and job-hopping in Suzhou are not yet serious problems. Workers imported from outside Suzhou must be housed at employers' expense, but investors report that demand for private housing among the local workforce so far has been muted.

Suzhou's somewhat parochial status within China makes recruitment of skilled local senior managers difficult. Such personnel can be bought from other cities but they require housing and often pressure employers to obtain a right of permanent residence for them. This involves the payment of a "population control" fee of RMB 10,000–20,000 (US$1,175–2,350) per person to the Suzhou government (*Business China,* 23 January 1995). The purpose of this fee is to control the cross migration of population between cities.

At the moment, there are nine universities and 40 vocational institutes and 321 high schools in Suzhou. Suzhou has a higher concentration of graduates than Shanghai but a lower concentration than Guangzhou. Based on 1992 data, there were 16.5 graduates per thousand population in Suzhou compared to 13.6 in Shanghai, whereas Guangzhou recorded 17.8.

(iii) ***Nanjing:*** There is an abundant supply of well-educated labour in Nanjing. There are 16 universities in Nanjing, and a high concentration of skilled labour compared to Shanghai and Suzhou. There are approximately 300,000 engineers in Nanjing's workforce.

In addition, wages are lower than Shanghai. It has been reported that the transportation company, American President Lines, regularly receives 1,000 to 2,000 job applications from graduates for every advertisement placed. The salary package is about 20% lower than in Shanghai e.g. a highly skilled worker would receive RMB 4,000 per month in Nanjing, but closer to RMB 5,200 in Shanghai.

INTEGRATION WITH REGIONAL CLUSTERS

Shanghai, Suzhou and Nanjing, each has its own unique characteristics. There are areas where these locations complement each other in their economic development.

Shanghai–Suzhou

The rapid growth of Shanghai has brought many changes to the local economy, with a huge influx of foreign and domestic investment. The cost of operating a business has thus risen due to the scarcity of most input factors.

Suzhou's proximity to Shanghai and its abundant supply of unskilled labour is readily absorbing spill-over investment, specifically in manufacturing activities. The Singapore-Suzhou industrial township development will further strengthen Suzhou's long-term position as a manufacturing centre for light industries. Shanghai, with its rapid development of financial services, offers a critical capability for Suzhou to leverage upon.

The rapid growth and combined demands of the two locations have created opportunities for infrastructure developments that have benefited both cities economically. This complementary feature enables the Chinese policy makers and both local and foreign investors to make firm-level decisions in allocating resources to this region.

Nanjing and Shanghai-Suzhou

Nanjing's historical position as the capital of China and its skilled labour resources specifically in scientific and technological fields, have attracted many foreign investments. The rapid economic growth has created a huge demand for the services industry in the areas of transportation, insurance, banking and finance.

Shanghai, being the major water transportation link with foreign countries, plays the intermediary role in providing Nanjing's unprocessed and processed input factors and capital needs. Its development in the services sector will certainly be favourably boosted by Nanjing's rapid growth.

Nanjing, being strategically located at the "bottle neck" of the Yangtze river will continue to play an important role for hinterland water access. Manufactured goods from downstream will be loaded into smaller vessels before continuing their journey deep into inland China. Industrialisation in downstream locations like Shanghai and Suzhou will therefore have a positive interconnection with infrastructural expansion in Nanjing.

In addition, rapid parallel developments in Nanjing and Shanghai-Suzhou have created significant economic development in towns and cities that lie between them. Particularly, access to these remote places will be much better with the completion of Nanjing-Suzhou highway by 1997. The improved mobility of input factors and technology will certainly promote economic and technological growth in these towns and cities.

A COMPARISON WITH MAJOR GLOBAL CITIES

Comparative studies on Shanghai, Suzhou and Nanjing as business locations will not be complete without similar reviews of major cities in other parts of the world. Will developments in the three cities eventually complement each other and spur greater growth as seen in the San Francisco Bay area? (Barlyn, 1995).

Views from many researchers describe the importance of inner cities, particularly Porter (1995). In a recent article, Brigadier General George Yeo, Singapore Minister of Information, made an interesting prediction that in the next century, cities will be the most relevant unit of economic production, social organisation and knowledge generation (*The Straits Times,* 10 September 1995).

Half of the world's population are city dwellers and most live in major cities. By the year 2000, 17 of the 21 mega-cities in the world will accommodate more than 10 million people. Shanghai is expected to support over 20 million people by the year 2025.

Generally, in major cities, the high concentration of producers and suppliers bring along many advantages, as Porter (1995) argues. The dense local population provides streams of local demand and makes up the workforce. The interaction of diverse firms participating in active competition for input factors drives towards higher efficiency.

A well-known example is the San Francisco Bay area which consists of numerous cities and towns with a high concentration of well-known tertiary institutions and leading technological firms. These factors combined with the high population (5.6 million) and the availability of a skilled workforce are the main reasons for the success of the many cities in the region.

The stretch along the Yangtze river from Shanghai to Nanjing may provide some similarity to the San Francisco Bay area in terms of potential market, population and industrial diversity. The apparent difference today between the two locations is the lack of sophisticated technology and manufacturing base in the Yangtze river area.

A recent study by *Fortune* magazine on the best cities for business rated Singapore first among major global cities and the San Francisco Bay area as the best location in the U.S.A. Broadly, they look at favourable conditions needed for the workplace today which have equal emphasis on both working and living conditions. Essentially, there are five criteria ranging from market potential to workforce recruitment and retainment (Barlyn, 1995).

An extract of this study is detailed below and the ratings of Shanghai are highlighted in Table 3–1.

TABLE 3–1
Shanghai Relative to Best Locations

Ranking Criteria	Shanghai	Singapore	San Francisco Bay
Market Growth Potential	Excellent	Excellent	Very Good
Business Infrastructure	Fair	Excellent	Excellent
Cultural Acceptance	Fair	Excellent	Very Good
Personal Risk	Good	Excellent	Very Good
Recruitment and Retainment	Fair	Fair	Excellent

Most of the Chinese cities would take a long time to reach to the top rankings of *Fortune* magazine. But the above comparison highlights what it takes to be among the best cities. Broadly, besides the obvious market growth potential, Shanghai is ranked low in other areas and likewise, one can easily relate this to other major cities in China. With Shanghai in position to be China's engine of growth in the 21st century, its ratings will be improved.

SUMMARY AND CONCLUSION

The unique characteristics of the three locations can be conveniently summarised in Table 3–2.

TABLE 3–2
Unique Characteristics of the Three Cities

	Shanghai	Suzhou	Nanjing
Strategic location	Located at Yangtze river mouth, it is the focal point of China economic growth.	Suzhou's proximity to Shanghai renders its strategic complementary role to Shanghai's development.	Being at the front end of the narrowing Yangtze river as it flows towards hinterland, Nanjing is vital to domestic transportation.
Local market demand	High consumption propensity. The locals are relatively more fashion conscious.	Lowest among the three. With the transformation from a largely agriculturally based economy to an industrial one, higher purchasing power is anticipated.	Local market demand is lower than Shanghai but its economical performance and high literacy among its labour force would provide a substantial market demand for goods and services.
Labour cost	As the base for comparison, the labour cost is rated 100%. (A typical production worker earns RMB 5,200 per annum.)	30 to 50% lower than Shanghai.	20% lower than Shanghai.
Population	13.5 million	6 million	5.2 million
New infrastructural development	(a) Pudong's new airport. (b) Two new bridges over Huangpu.	(a) Development of seaport (planned). (b) Suzhou-Shanghai Highway (recently opened).	(a) New international airport (1997). (b) Second bridge over Yangtze river (planned). (c) Suzhou-Nanjing Highway.

We have established four major complementary advantages that contribute to the development of regional clusters in the three locations: a large population which provides the supply of human resource and sustains the market demand; a good geographical location which enables access to regional clusters; a rapid development of financial services to support the industries; and a developed infrastructure to enable the advantages of importing and distribution.

In conclusion, these three locations are poised to grow. They have the ingredients to become successful, complementary mega-cities each with its unique characteristics.

They provide good business opportunities for foreign investors in many aspects of the business spectrum. Early phase development opportunities like power station and industrial plant construction, and low cost manufacturing are emerging. With a large population, telecommunications and consumer goods are in great demand with rising disposable income.

Rapid parallel development in these three areas provide many synergistic advantages. Together, the region that stretches from Shanghai to Nanjing along the Yangtze river, may grow to be like the San Francisco Bay area rated as the best city for business in U.S.A. However this is not an equal comparison as there are structural differences between a socialist and a free market economy.

Given time, if there are no adverse changes on the political and economic scene, Shanghai, Nanjing and the many cities in between will thrive. The disparity between the local standards and practices in technology and management and those of the international community will slowly diminish.

With more liberalisation in the economy, a free market mechanism will take place. An intense concentration of producers and suppliers, skilled workforce and the increasing local demand will create fertile conditions for the growth of Shanghai, Suzhou and Nanjing. To be in the forefront of these activities, it is important that companies locate their businesses there. Its rapid development will certainly result in a cascading effect into the hinterland and, in time, the rest of China.

REFERENCES

"A Challenge from Up-river Nanjing's Make-over", *Business China,* 30 May 1994, pp. 6–9.

"An Upstart Takes Business from Shanghai Forward", *Business China*, 23 January 1995, pp. 8–9.

"Asia-Yangzi Rising", *The Economist*, 9 September 1995, pp. 29–30.

"Buyers and Builders", *The Economist*, 30 October 1993, pp. 15–18.

Barlyn Suzanne, "It's Singapore!", *Fortune,* 13 November 1995, pp. 66–74.

"China to Let Some MNCs Engage in Foreign Trade", *The Straits Times*, 27 November 1995, p. 35.

Editorial, *The Straits Times*, 10 September 1995.

"Jiang: Policy For Economic Zones Will Not Change", *The Straits Times*, 2 January 1996, p. 1.

Leung James, "Beijing Stifles Shanghai Dream", *Asian Business*, October 1995, pp. 24–8.

MacInnis Peter and Ma Ruji, "Nanjing Sets Its Sights on 2000", *The China Business Review*, January–February 1995.

"No New Special Zones in China's Western and Central Areas", *The Straits Times*, 22 July 1995.

Official banquet and seminar with the Joint Working Committee of Singapore-Suzhou Industrial Park, co-chaired by Mayor of Suzhou, Zhang Xin Sheng and representatives from Suzhou Municipal Government, Suzhou Bamboo Grove Hotel, 9 December 1995.

Perkins Peter, "State Figures Belie Spending Reality", *China Business*, 15 June 1995.

Porter Michael, "The Rise of the Urban Entrepreneur", *The State of Small Business,* Vol. 17, No. 7, 1995, pp. 104–18.

Seminar on the Pudong Economic and Development Zone, hosted by Dai Hui Xing, Director of Shanghai Pudong New Area International Exchange Centre, 6 December 1995.

Seminar on the Singapore-Suzhou Industrial Park hosted by the co-chairman of the Singapore-Suzhou Industrial Park, the chairman of Singapore Jurong Town Corporation, Suzhou Bamboo Grove Hotel, 9 December 1995.

Seminar with representatives from Jiangsu Provincial Government and Nanjing Municipal Government at Nanjing Jingling Hotel, 12 December 1995.

Seminar with Yong Ser Joo, Consul from the Consulate of Republic of Singapore and Yeo Aik Koon, General Manager of Nippon Paint (China) Co Ltd., Hilton International Shanghai, 14 December 1995.

Sender H., "Location Isn't Everything", *Far Eastern Economic Review*, 23 June 1994, p. 57.

Shanghai Municipal Government, *Shanghai Today*, Shanghai, 1994.

State Statistical Bureau, People's Republic of China, *Statistical Yearbook of China, 1995*, China Statistical Publishing House, Beijing.

Yang Mu, John J.Williams and Cao Yong, "Resurrecting Shanghai for the 21st Century: The Shift in China's Regional Economic Strategies", *China Business Review*, December, 1995, pp. 11–29.

SPECIAL ECONOMIC ZONES

Chapter 4

Shanghai's Economic and Trade Zones*

BY
TAN Chin Meng
CHONG Chin Hui
TAN Kok Fei

INTRODUCTION

TO FULFIL ITS role as the Dragon Head in the development of the vast Yangtze river basin, Shanghai will have to be transformed into a credible global financial and trade centre. With the establishment of the Pudong area as a Special Economic Zone in 1990 and the subsequent surge in foreign investments in the zone, Shanghai seems to be on a fast track towards achieving its goal. However, the success of Shanghai in attracting foreign investments could be undermined by spiralling land prices and labour cost, especially in the Pudong New Area and the more established trade zones. These trends have already caused a number of large foreign investors to change their choice of location from Pudong to other, more attractive, industrial areas. This chapter examines the options available to potential investors wishing to invest in Shanghai's economic and trade zones.

* The authors are grateful to Dr. Shi Yuwei for his guidance and assistance.

Shanghai as the Dragon Head

China's Yangtze river delta extends from Shanghai Pudong New Area in the east to Chongqing in Sichuan province in the west. This area is widely heralded as the next most vibrant growth area in China. The Yangtze river region is set to become the backbone of China's economic development as it will contribute 45% to the country's gross domestic product (GDP) by the year 2010 from the present 20% (*The Straits Times*, 8 December 1995). More than 180 million people live along or near the Yangtze river, the world's third longest river and one of its oldest commercial waterways. Shanghai, with its strategic location, will play a key role in transforming China's vast hinterland.

Shanghai's roles are clear; the Pudong New Area has been officially referred to as the "Dragon Head" that will spearhead the growth of the largest "market" in Asia. Beijing's strategy is to build up Shanghai as the trade centre by upgrading its manufacturing base and re-establishing its financial services into a world-class trade and business centre. The Pudong New Area, which was first unveiled in April 1990, is an important part of Beijing's attempt to invigorate China's industrial heart land (Brauchli, 1995). The so called "Dragon Economy" of the Yangtze river valley runs through seven provinces, among them China's richest, Jiangsu, and its most populous, Sichuan.

Shanghai's Economy

Shanghai is now the largest industrial and technical base, and trading port in China. Its economic growth is unprecedented in its history. According to China's statistical yearbook of 1995, the GDP of Shanghai reached RMB 197.19 billion in 1994, an increase of 14.3% as compared to the previous year. In 1994, the total volume of foreign trade amounted to US$15.82 billion, an increase of 24%, while exports amounted to US$9.08 billion, an increase of 23% compared to that of 1993. There was a total of 3,802 foreign investment projects in 1994, amounting to almost US$10 billion.

FRAMEWORK FOR COMPARISON

In Shanghai, the economic and trade zones, as in other parts of China, are differentiated based on their status in relation to preferential incentives offered to investors. At the highest level, there are the five official Special Economic Zones (SEZ) in China which include the Pudong New Area. Within the Pudong New Area, there are four separate zones as follows:

(a) Lujiazui Finance and Trade Zone;
(b) Jinqiao Export Processing Zone;
(c) Waigaoqiao Free Trade Zone; and
(d) Zhangjiang Hi-tech Park.

The next group are the so-called national level economic zones which share similar preferential incentives. Currently, there are 32 of these zones in China. In Shanghai, there are three such zones, namely Hongqiao Economic and Technological Development Zone, Minhang Economic and Technological Development Zone, and Caohejing Hi-tech Park.

At the lowest level, there are Shanghai's so-called "lesser zones" which also offer similar preferential incentives as the higher level zones. Specifically, they are Jiading, Xinghou and Songjiang. Figure 4–1 shows the relative location of these zones.

Competitiveness of the Economic and Trade Zones

It used to be that preferential incentives alone would decide the choice of location for a firm contemplating investment in Shanghai. But the recent escalation of land prices and labour costs are affecting competitive advantages. For example, figures from the Bank of Tokyo in Shanghai indicate that factory wages have doubled from 1993 to 1994 (although official statistics show only a 30% rise) to RMB 700 (US$80) a month as compared to US$35 for workers in Vietnam's urban centres. Businesses in Shanghai also are complaining of having to pay unnecessary allowances, such as pension insurance, which make total wages three or four times more than basic wages (Sender, 1994b).

From an investor's perspective, operational needs are becoming top concerns. Increased emphasis is being accorded to the quality of the infrastructure of the zones. Underlying factors, such as road infrastructure, utilities supply, telecommunication networks, port access, availability of trained personnel, are receiving special attention. Thus, infrastructure and its associated business environment are important from an investor's perspective. Some of the most crucial factors that determine the competitiveness of the zones include the elements listed in Table 4–1.

FIGURE 4–1
Location of the Zones

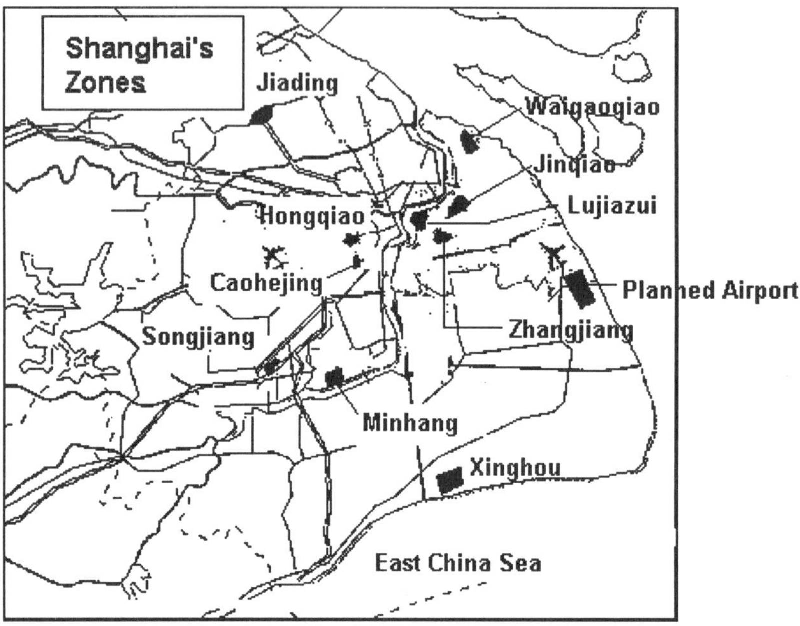

TABLE 4–1
Competitive Factors

Infrastructure	Status of development	Competitive advantage
(i) Land cost. (ii) Labour cost. (iii) Road infrastructure. (iv) Airport accessibility. (v) Port accessibility. Availability of qualified people.	(i) Progress of development. (ii) Successes in attracting MNCs.	(i) Strategic location. (ii) Unique features. (iii) Preferential treatments. (iv) Access to market. (v) Quality of management.

Pudong New Area

Pudong, which is located on the east of the Huangpu river, remained underdeveloped until the establishment of the Pudong New Area economic zone in 1990. Aside from the advantage of its strategic location, Pudong had a fairly established industrial base. At the start of its development, its population was 1.1 million which included 1,930 industrial enterprises employing 380,000 people (Yu, 1993). Pudong's ambitious economic development plan involves transforming 520 square kilometres of land into a full tradc facility and cxport proccssing zonc. Thc attraction of the Pudong New Area zone lies in its preferential incentives and strategic location.

As with the other five special economic zones, Pudong offers preferential treatment for investors but with some added incentives. Among the unique incentives offered to investors are the following. First, foreign investors are allowed to set up banks, financial businesses and insurance companies (only three out of the five special economic zones allow this type of activity). Second, business activities need not be restricted to the zone and may be extended to the whole of the Shanghai Municipality. Third, in the Waigaoqiao Free Trade Zone, there are no duties to be paid and import/export licences are not required so as to promote free trade (*Report On Development of Pudong*, 1995). Although still in its development phase, Pudong (as of May 1994) had already attracted more than 750 leading foreign companies which have invested over US$ 4 billion (*The Banker*, 1994).

Within the Pudong New Area, there are four export-oriented urban zones currently in the final development phase: Lujiazui Finance and Trade Zone, Waigaoqiao Free Trade Zone, Zhangjiang Hi-tech Park, and Jinqiao Export Processing Zone. The following sections briefly summarise the development of these four zones as of December 1995:

(i) ***Lujiazui Finance and Trade Zone:*** This zone is considered to be the catalyst for the development of Pudong as a whole. The 28 square kilometre site is situated just opposite from the Bund and 1.5 square kilometres are already under development. This area has been designated as the new central business district and it will be the financial district of Shanghai. This is also the future site of Shanghai's Stock Exchange building, which is due for completion by the end of 1996. When it is completed, the new stock exchange will be the largest and most modern of its kind in the world, utilising the latest fibre optics based communication links.

Lujiazui is experiencing a phenomenal boom and an enormous number of office buildings, most of very high quality, are now under construction. Among all of the development zones, Lujiazui will have the most advanced facilities and infrastructure. With the anticipated liberalisation of Chinese banking and financial policy, Lujiazui is set to become a premier financial hub in East Asia. However, there are a few major obstacles that need to be remedied, especially runaway land prices and acute traffic congestion.

(ii) ***Jinqiao Export Processing Zone:*** This processing zone is a modernised and comprehensive industrial centre located in the centre of the Pudong New Area. It has a planned area of 19.5 square kilometres, of which 9.5 square kilometres are under development. At the end of 1994, there were 250 committed projects and 80 of these had begun operations, giving an industrial output of RMB 5 billion (US$600 million). Companies that have invested in this area include several large multinationals and Siemens and Shanghai Bell.

Jinqiao is linked and served by Waigaoqiao port and the older Shanghai port, including the new Shanghai Container Terminal. Jinqiao is also experiencing the same problems of high land cost and traffic congestion. For example, *Business China* (2 October 1995b) reported Jinqiao had lost its bid to be the site for the proposed US$2 billion Ford and Shanghai Automobile joint venture factory to a rival zone located in Songjiang. However, Jinqiao still remains attractive to companies that are interested in sourcing goods into Shanghai.

(iii) ***Waigaoqiao Free Trade Zone:*** This is the least successful of the zones. Only a small number of firms have invested in this zone and they are mainly from Japan and Taiwan. Major concerns include the uncertainty over the exact nature of the tax and tariff regime. Inferior port facilities have hampered its effort to attract more investors. The total planned area of 10 square kilometres includes a bonded warehouse area (which occupies 38 hectares), an administration centre, an export processing sub-zone and a residential area (83 hectares).

(iv) ***Zhangjiang Hi-tech Park:*** Located south-east of Lujiazui and Jinqiao this park has a planned area of 17 square kilometres. Its target group of investors are firms engaged in microelectronics, biotechnical engineering, artificial intelligence, laser computer and software, modern telecommunications and information transmission. The first phase of construction, which is nearly complete, consists of a 1.2-square-kilometre industrial area and a 0.8-square-kilometre administration and service centre. Overall, the area will include 20,000 square metres of bonded warehousing and 70,000 square metres of standard factory buildings. Two roads leading to the site have been completed. Zhangjiang faces serious competition from the Caohejing Hi-tech Park in Puxi.

Investment in Pudong

Pudong's economy appeared to be cooling down in 1995. Although actual investment in the first six months of 1995 grew by 11.5% compared with the same period for 1994, the number of pledged investments decreased by 22.2% and their total value fell by 4%. To some extent, this can be attributed to a general reduction of foreign investment in China as the economy cooled somewhat in 1995 (*Business China*, 2 October 1995b).

Lately, concerns are mounting over the effects of soaring land prices in Pudong's development. Pudong is supposed to be Shanghai's answer to the "choking" congestion in the old centre of Puxi but the desire to extract the maximum possible in fees and rental rates has resulted in exorbitant land costs. While many analysts agree that the cost of land should account for the quality of the facilities provided, the wide disparity in prices among neighbouring zones is turning away potential investors. The price for industrial land in Pudong is now five times greater than comparable plots of land to the west of the city (*Business China*, 2 October 1995b).

Sender (1994) offers an explanation by suggesting that the underlying problem lies in the structure of the organisations that have authority over Pudong. The development zone corporations that control these areas are more interested in maximising short-term profits. Gaoqiao and Jinqiao, for example, are listed in Shanghai. But instead of selling land to the most "productive" investors, 80% of it, particularly in Jinqiao, was sold for speculative purposes to local front companies that posed as foreign joint ventures.

SHANGHAI'S OTHER ECONOMIC ZONES

While much of the coverage of Shanghai concentrates on Pudong, the older zones located in Puxi area (the old city area of Shanghai on the west bank of the Huangpu river) are where much of the actual foreign manufacturing has taken place so far (see Table 4–2). Aside from Pudong, there are three main economic and technological development zones in Shanghai which are referred to as the national level zones, namely Hongqiao, Minhang and Caohejing.

TABLE 4–2
Economic and Technological Development Zones 1992

Name	Number of Foreign Investment Enterprises	Foreign Capital Utilisation (US$ Million)	Foreign Exchange Earning (US$ Million)
Minhang	98	331.00	230.17
Caohejing	81	281.06	110.83
Hongqiao	22	490.58	187.99

Source: *Almanac of China's Foreign Economic Relations and Trade.*

The main characteristic of the three zones, Minhang, Hongqiao and Caohejing is that they do not have the same status as the five special economic zones in southern China. Nonetheless, they are "Beijing approved" to operate as economic and development zones and they share similar tax and other incentives usually provided for national-level economic zones (*Business China,* 2 October 1995c). Currently, there are only 32 national level zones in China.

Shanghai Hongqiao Economic and Technological Development Zone

Hongqiao was established in April 1985 as an office and commercial district and remains as the only non-industrial zone in China to enjoy national level status. Hongqiao has been successful in attracting investment. As of April 1995, total investment was US$1.2 billion of which US$888 million was from foreign direct investment (*Business China*, 2 October 1995c). The strength of the Hongqiao lies in its location and overall facilities which are still considered superior to competing zones. Access to the zone has also been enhanced with the completion of Shanghai's inner ring road in December 1995 which connects Hongqiao to the Bund, to Pudong and to the northern parts of Shanghai. The zone has also benefited from its designation as the area for foreign consulates by the municipal government. The American, Japanese, Australian and Czech governments are also planning to move their consulates there.

Shanghai Minhang Economic and Technological Development Zone

Minhang is an industrial zone located 30 kilometres south-west of the centre of Shanghai and it consists of 3.5 square kilometres of development area. Development of the first phase (2.13 square kilometres) is still in progress. Beginning its operations in 1982, Minhang has attracted a number of multinationals including Xerox, Johnson and Johnson and Coca-Cola. As of 1994, there were 122 enterprises representing a total of US$940 million worth of investment. Foreign investment constitutes US$530 million of this total. The breakdown by the type of industries is 20% high technology and 67% export-oriented companies. By 1994, total industrial output reached RMB 20.5 billion, and foreign exchange earnings were US$1.51 billion (*Business China*, 2 October 1995c).

Presently, some major concerns raised by firms include the relatively high land costs and the inadequate transportation facilities. At around US$100 per square metre, industrial land is considered more expensive than the county level zones (see Table 4–3). The route into Shanghai is not convenient; it takes about one hour just to reach the inner ring road near Caohejing. There are, however, on-going plans to extend Shanghai's subway line to Minhang, which was originally scheduled for 1996. The opening of the line has been delayed until 1999 due to the lack of funds.

Shanghai Caohejing Hi-tech Park

Caohejing was first set up in 1984 but it obtained national level zone status only in 1988 and national level hi-tech park status in 1991. The total planned area is about six square kilometres. At the end 1995, 3.5 square kilometres were completed. Caohejing has one of the best locations of all the industrial zones in and around Shanghai. Its aim is to become a centre for advanced technology manufacturing. Compared to the other zones, it is only seven kilometres from Hongqiao airport and even closer to the inner ring road.

TABLE 4–3
Comparison of Land Costs

	Land Cost (US$ per square metre)
Shanghai:	
Caohejing	150
Minhang	100
Songjiang	40
Pudong:	
Jinqiao	110
Waigaoqiao	160
Zhangjiang	80

Source: *Business China*, 2 October 1995c.

As of January 1996, 16 multinationals, including AT&T, 3M, GE, Toshiba, ICI and DuPont have set up operations in the park. American firms are particularly attracted to this zone and they account for 38% of all firms present in the park. These major firms have contributed about one-half of the US$800 million in foreign investment that has flowed into the zone as of the end of the first quarter of 1995. Despite its strategic location, Caohejing is less successful than the other zones. *Business China* attributes this to the land prices. At US$150 a square metre for a 50-year land lease, land prices are higher than anywhere else except Waigaoqiao. The standard factory buildings are on offer for US$300 per square metre. Caohejing is best suited to a company engaged in a specific area of manufacturing. It is also suited to those companies whose processes need highly trained scientific personnel. This follows because there are 70 Chinese companies and development institutes in the park that offer specialised scientific knowledge and expertise (*Business China*, 2 October 1995c).

Future of Shanghai's National Level Zones

The three zones of Hongqiao, Minhang and Caohejing were established about ten years ago and became recognised as national level zones only after proving that they were able to attract a reasonable amount of investments. Most of the development outlined in the first phase are generally complete and work on phase two is underway. It is not certain if authorisation will be given for the third phase of the development (*Business China*, 2 October 1995c).

Shanghai's Lesser Zones

Apart from the larger three zones in Puxi and the four Pudong New Area zones, there are a number of other economic and development zones located in and around Shanghai. Several of these lie within the Shanghai metropolitan borders where an increasing number of counties or districts, usually with the support of the metropolitan government, have established zones to attract foreign investment. The main attractions of these zones are their close proximity to Shanghai, better transportation links and lower land costs. Some of the zones may offer favourable tax regimes comparable to the other established zones. However, few of these zones have been approved by Beijing, which means the tax incentives have little status and could easily be revoked by an order from the central authorities. The following sections summarise the features of these zones based partly on the information provided by *Business China* (2 October 1995c).

(i) **Jiading:** Among the lesser known zones, Jiading is the only zone located within the bounds of the Shanghai urban area. It has a planned area of 24.5 square kilometres and the first phase of a three-phase development, consisting of 8.4 square kilometres, has been constructed. Jiading offers a number of advantages. Although located 25 kilometres from the centre of Shanghai, it is well connected to the Shanghai's inner ring road expressway. It is also about one hour from the container terminals at Wusong and six kilometres from the Nanxiang marshalling yard on the Shanghai-Nanjing railway line.

    There are two universities in the district of Jiading, Shanghai University and Shanghai Science and Administration College. Combined with the fact that they are in an urban area, companies in the zone have an easier time in attracting technical staff.

(ii) **Xinghou:** Xinghou, which is located to the south of Pudong New Area in Hangzhou Bay, consists of a first-phase 7.1-square-kilometre and a second-phase 24-square-kilometre development. As part of the Pudong New Area, the zone enjoys the same status as other Pudong zones. This zone has attracted a number of mainly Chinese ventures in the paper, petrochemical and pharmaceutical industries. At the end of 1995, total investment amounted to over RMB 4 billion.

(iii) **Songjiang:** Songjiang is considered to be the most successful among the lesser zones in Shanghai. Located north of the Minhang zone and 20 kilometres south of the Hongqiao airport, it has convenient access to the Shanghai-Hangzhou railway line, the Hangzhou-Shanghai expressway and the Shanghai-Ningbo expressways. Songjiang is a recent zone which started in July 1992. The total planned area will be 20.56 square kilometres and so far 5.75 square kilometres have been developed as part of the first phase.

Songjiang has surprised analysts by attracting a large number of high-profile companies, particularly Japanese multinationals. Some of the big names include Hitachi Cable, Mitsui Composite Plastics, Minolta Optical Instruments and Kenwood. One of Songjiang's biggest investment opportunities is the proposed US$2 billion automobile plant that Ford Motor plans to build with Shanghai Automotive Industry Corp.

Summary of the Lesser Zones

With regard to the lesser zones, the infrastructure of many of these county level zones are generally not of the same standards as those of the national level zones. The reason for this is that most of the counties have to rely on incoming investment to provide some of the funds for infrastructure development. In general, since cheap land and good transport connections are the main attractions of these zones, they are probably most suitable for companies engaged in large or labour intensive manufacturing businesses that aim at national or regional distribution of their products (*Business China*, 2 October 1995c).

COMPARATIVE PROFILE OF THE ZONES

Based on the data provided by *Business China* (2 October 1995c) and information gathered during site visits to Pudong New Area and Minhang Development Zone, the attributes and strengths of the different zones in Shanghai are scored and tabulated in Table 4–4. This analysis serves to highlight the comparative strength of the lesser known trade zones versus those in the Pudong New Area. The higher scores received by Caohejing, Minhang and Songjiang reflect the overall competitive advantage of these zones in attracting foreign firms. It should be noted that Hongqiao is primarily an office and commercial district whereas Lujiazui is a finance and trade centre.

Analysis and Selection of Zones Based on Industry Types and Size

Although the analysis in Table 4–4 shows that Caohejing, Hongqiao and Songjiang are ranked as the respective top three locations for foreign firms, the ultimate selection of location will have to be made based on the industry type and the importance of location to the firm's strategic plan. For example, consumer electronic manufacturing firms that target Shanghai's huge consumer market will probably favour a zone that has an existing transportation network to facilitate regional distribution.

On the other hand, high technology firms manufacturing semiconductors will perhaps look for a zone that has attracted a substantial number of chemical firms and a reasonable electronic cluster support base, with adequate power and water supply infrastructure in place. For smaller investors, they may find the lesser known zones attractive in terms of close proximity to Shanghai, better transport links and lower land costs.

The suitability of the various zones with respect to manufacturing industry types and firm size are illustrated in the location matrix in Figure 4–2. In this framework, industry types are defined in terms of low or high value added operations. Firm size is partitioned into large and small.

TABLE 4–4
Comparisons of Shanghai's Economic and Trade Zones

	Lujiazui	Jinqiao	Waigaoqiao	Zhangjian	Minhang	Hongqiao	Caohejing	Jiading	Xinghou	Songjiang
Infrastructure Land cost	1	2	1	3	2	1	1	1	4	4
Labour cost	1	2	2	3	3	2	2	2	3	3
Road infrastructure	1	1	2	2	1	4	4	4	2	3
Airport accessibility	1	2	2	2	1	4	4	4	2	3
Port accessibility	4	4	3	2	1	3	3	3	2	3
Availability of employees	3	2	2	2	2	4	4	4	2	3
Status of development Progress of development	4	3	2	2	3	4	4	2	2	4
Successes in attracting MNCs	4	4	1	2	4	3	4	2	1	4
Competitive advantage Strategic location	4	4	2	2	1	4	4	4	2	3
Unique features	4	2	2	2	1	4	4	2	2	1
Preferential treatments	4	4	3	4	3	3	3	2	4	2
Access to market	3	4	3	2	2	4	4	3	3	3
Quality of management	4	4	3	2	4	4	4	2	2	3
Overall Score	38	38	28	30	28	44	45	35	31	39

Legend: 1 – Least desirable (weakness) 4 – Most desirable (strength)

FIGURE 4–2
Location Matric by Industry and Firm Size

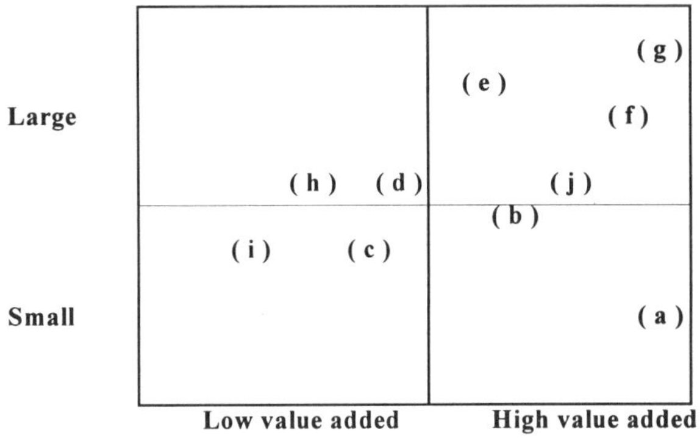

Legend: (a) Lujiazui; (b) Jinqiao; (c) Waigaoqiao; (d) Zhangjian; (e) Minhang; (f) Hongqiao; (g) Caohejing; (h) Jiading; (i) Xinghou; and (j) Songjiang.

From the perspective of industry type, Caohejing Hi-tech Park is an ideal location for high value added manufacturing operations on a large scale. It will not be cost competitive for a labour intensive or low value manufacturing business such as textiles. Manufacturing firms producing electronic parts or components will benefit from the 16 multinationals and over 70 Chinese companies and institutes currently operating in the zone. These firms can serve a sourcing role and a customer base for both components and trained employees.

Firms looking for a quick start-up may view Caohejing as their best choice. Western companies may also tend to favour this zone because 38% of the foreign firms are American and this can provide a familiar environment. In the Minhang Economic and Technological Development Zone, most of the firms are engaged in export markets. However, for firms that have a large employee base and land delivery component to their business, Minhang is less attractive because of its poor location and road infrastructure. The current lack of transportation access also makes the recruitment of employees more difficult.

The Hongqiao Economic and Technological Development Zone, which is the only national level non-industrial zone, is an ideal location for service industries. Jiading, located within the Shanghai urban area, is only 25 kilometres from the city centre and is one hour away by road from the container terminals at Wusong. There are two universities in the area which should facilitate the recruitment of technical staff. Jiading is an ideal location for the light manufacturing of electronic products. Xinghou, located in Pudong, enjoys the same preferential incentives given to the other Pudong New Area zones.

Based on Figure 4–2, petrochemical and pharmaceutical industries may find this location ideal. Located west of Minhang, Songjiang has been highly successful in attracting many high profile companies such as Hitachi Cable, Mitsui Composite Plastics, Minolta Optical Instrument and Kenwood. Newly announced ventures include the Nestle joint venture with Shanghai Sugar, Cigarette and Wine Corp. and the mega US$2 billion automobile plant venture by Ford Motor and Shanghai Automotive Industry Corp., which was originally planned for Pudong. Many analysts attribute Songjiang's success to its responsive management, location and competitive land rates. It is only 20 kilometres south of the Hongqiao airport and offers convenient access to the city centre.

CONCLUSION

Shanghai's growth can best be described as one huge "construction site" working at a "breakneck" pace. The phenomenal pace of development will exact an even greater demand on the already limited land, labour and housing resources. If this growth is not curbed, then Shanghai's progress towards the goal of fulfilling its role as the Dragon Head will be seriously undermined. To provide for more sustainable and smooth development, more has to be done to check the spiralling land and labour costs, and the housing shortages.

Shanghai's long-term strategy is to upgrade its industrial base and revitalise its once dominant services sector, focusing on higher value added industries in the process (Yang *et al.,* 1995). The success of integrating the whole Yangtze region hinges on how well Shanghai succeeds in developing into a world-class trade centre.

In terms of manufacturing, labour intensive industries are best shifted to the neighbouring provinces or counties along the Yangtze to benefit from the cheaper labour and land prices. As the Shanghai economy matures, the focus should be on attracting innovation driven industries as opposed to factor driven. Infrastructure in the economic zones, therefore, needs to be further enhanced. Also, the skills and productivity level of workers have to be constantly upgraded. This is imperative if Shanghai's economic zones are to continue attracting high quality investment under tough competition from nearby industrial zones such as the Singapore-Suzhou Industrial Park.

REFERENCES

Brauchli Marcus W., "River of Dreams: The Mighty Yangtze Seizes a Major Role in China's Economy", *The Wall Street Journal*, 13 December 1995.

Pudong Academy of Development, *Report On Development of Pudong 1991–94,* Shanghai People's Publishing House, 1995.

"Pudong's Day Remains a While Away", *Business China,* 2 October 1995b, pp. 1–4.

"Regional Development: Minhang, Hongqiao and Caohejing – Shanghai Triad", *Business China,* 2 October 1995c, pp. 1–7.

Sender Henry, "Location isn't Everything", *Far Eastern Economic Review,* 23 June 1994a.

Sender Henry, "Passion for Profit", *Far Eastern Economic Review,* 23 June 1994b.

Shanghai Municipal Statistics Bureau, *1995 Statistical Yearbook of Shanghai*, China Statistical Publishing House, 1995.

"Shanghai's Renaissance", *The Banker*, May 1994, pp. 34–8.

State Statistical Bureau, *Statistical Yearbook of China,* People's Republic of China, 1994.

"The Place to Be", *Business China,* 2 October 1995a, pp. 1–5.

"Yangtze Region Set to Spearhead Chinese Economy", *The Straits Times,* 8 December 1995.

Yang Mu, John J. Williams and Cao Yong, "Resurrecting Shanghai in the 21st Century: The Shift in China's Regional Economic Strategy", *China Business Review*, December 1995, pp. 11–29.

Yu George T, *China in Transition – Economic, Political and Social Development*, University Press of America, New York, 1993.

Chapter 5

The Development of Pudong: Implications and Opportunities*

BY
ABDUAL HALIM Bin Selamat
LAM Keng Siak
CHEW Lai Wei
LEE Guan Chong

INTRODUCTION

CHINA STARTED ITS open door policy in 1979. The southern coastal cities were the first to be privileged with the implementation of economic reform. Over a decade of development, the experimental, piece-meal economic reform has proven successful and it has tremendously benefited the economy of China. Shanghai, often dubbed the cash cow that has hitherto financed the economic reform of the targeted special economic zones (SEZs), has been chosen to spearhead economic reform in the north and central regions.

Special emphasis has been given to Pudong because it is the nucleus from which economic wealth will be generated and diffused throughout Shanghai. This will transform Shanghai into one of the best economic, financial and trade centres in the world over the next decade. President Jiang Zemin has guaranteed its "Dragon Head" status in leading the economic development of the Yangtze river

* Thanks to Associate Professor Chew Soon Beng for his guidance and knowledge in developing this chapter.

delta. Pudong has the full assurance of the central government to affirm its catalyst role in revitalisng Shanghai and in opening up the regions in the north. This firm and unwavering support from Beijing is vital to the establishment of Pudong as a new economic frontier for the entire nation. Pudong is thus a political "new born" of Beijing which is to epitomise the success of a socialist market economy.

Pudong is a new district of the Shanghai Municipality. It lies in the estuary of the Yangtze river, just across the Huangpu river that divides Shanghai into two areas, Pudong and Puxi. Pudong is situated on the east bank and faces Shanghai's urban area, the Bund. It covers 518 square kilometres, of which 100 square kilometres will be urbanised by the year 2000. Pudong has a population of 1.38 million. Thus, it houses 10.7% of Shanghai's population and represents 8.2% of the Shanghai Municipality. Pudong is actually much larger if it is compared to urban Shanghai. It is 69.1% of urban Shanghai's size and has 1.84 times the area of Shanghai's central districts. Pudong is about five-sixths of the size of Singapore (Goodman and Segal, 1994).

DEVELOPMENT OBJECTIVE AND VISION

Opening up Pudong is an ambitious move by the central government. The aim is to develop it into a vibrant business centre so as to complement Shanghai in the role of a metropolitan city that is open to the world economy. Pudong, therefore, is bestowed with the mission of leading China into a new era of economic reform. The scope of development is extensive and it is on a world-class scale. The focus is on trade, finance, high technology industries and infrastructure construction.

The far-reaching development plan of Pudong can be divided into three phases. The first was the start-up stage (1991 to 1995). Priority was given to the overall planning of the new district and the construction of infrastructural facilities to create a conducive environment for attracting foreign investors. At the same time, four functional zones were initiated to exploit the full benefits of the preferential policies granted by the central government. On 1 January 1993, the Pudong New Area Administration Commission was established to oversee the management of the new district and further enhance the investment environment.

The second phase is the development stage (1996 to 2000). The plan for this period is to improve the infrastructure and functional zones further so as to achieve a fundamentally complete economic base in Pudong. The final phase is labelled as the full scale stage (2001 to 2020 or more). The aim of this final stage is to transform Pudong into a modern model of an export-oriented, multifunctional, international centre in the 21st century.

DEVELOPMENT STRATEGY: SYNERGY BETWEEN PUDONG AND SHANGHAI

Pudong is not a special economic zone but a strategic and bold project under the Municipality of Shanghai. In developing Pudong, Shanghai hopes to regain the leading position in China's economy. Pudong is strategically located and is well poised to make Shanghai a hub of international trade. Given the congested area of Puxi, the old city of Shanghai, there was no choice but to start up a new business district on the large east bank farm lands. Pudong is relying on Puxi's strength in trade, finance, technology, management and an abundant, excellent quality, workforce to trigger its growth. Shanghai is the wealthiest city in China and it has a very strong economic foundation. Thus, it is a sound plan for Pudong to form an integral part of Shanghai's development strategy. The synergistic relationship between Pudong and Puxi is vital to the renaissance of Shanghai's economy.

ECONOMIC PERFORMANCE

Since the formal declaration of the development of Pudong on 18 April 1990, the Pudong New Area has grown rapidly. Annual GNP grew from RMB 6 billion in 1990 to RMB 7.1 billion in 1991. Since 1991, GNP has grown consistently in double digit terms from 19.2% in 1991 to a peak of 79.3% in 1993. This high rate of growth was sustained in 1994 with a 77.4% increase over 1993. For 1995, GNP was RMB 35 billion (see Table 5–1).

For the period 1996 to 2000, growth is projected to be 24% per annum. Pudong's GNP is expected to be between RMB 55 billion and RMB 60 billion in 1997, and to reach RMB 100 billion by the year 2000. This forecast is not overly optimistic but is well within reach, given the increasing commitments from foreign investors.

TABLE 5–1
Pudong's GNP: 1991 to 1995

Year	1991	1992	1993	1994	1995
GNP (RMB billion)	7.1	9.1	16.4	29.1	35.0

Source: Pudong New Area Administration Statistics.

The Trend of Foreign Investment

Foreign investors are increasingly looking to Pudong as a prime location for investment (see Table 5–2). Table 5–3 shows that the top investors are from Hong Kong (53.6%) and Japan (9.6%). The bulk of investment has been in the manufacturing and real estate segments. Total foreign investment in Pudong amounted to US$8.5 billion at the end of 1995.

TABLE 5–2
Foreign Investment in Pudong: 1991 to 1995

	1991	1992	1993	1994	1995
Foreign Direct Investment (US$ b)	0.1	1.3	1.7	2.6	2.8
Number of Projects	170	704	1,628	2,663	3,316

Source: Pudong New Area Administration Statistics.

TABLE 5–3
Sources of Foreign Investment in Pudong

Hong Kong	53.6%
U.S.A.	7.1%
Japan	9.6%
Canada	2.7%
U.K.	6.7%
Singapore	2.3%
Taiwan	2.7%
Others	15.3%
TOTAL	100.0%

Source: Pudong New Area Administration Statistics.

Examples of notable transnational corporations that have invested in Pudong over the last five years include DuPont, Alcatel, the Tokyo-based Mori Building Company, Yaohan Food Department Store, General Motors and Mobil. With the presence of these world-class companies, Pudong soon will be transformed into a hub of global economic activity.

INFRASTRUCTURE CONSTRUCTION

According to the Pudong New Area Administration, RMB 25 billion has been invested in building infrastructural facilities. Ten major projects included in the first phase of infrastructure development that have been completed to date are the Nanpu bridge, Yangpu bridge, inner ring road (Pudong section), Yanggao road reconstruction project, Waigaoqiao harbour area, Waigaoqiao power plant, sewage discharging project, Lingqiao water plant, Pudong gasworks (II) and a telecommunication project.

The Nanpu and Yangpu bridges each have six lanes of traffic and were completed in 1991 and 1993, respectively. The inner ring road, with a total length of 8 kilometres, connects the roads via the two bridges. The completion of the main road system makes access from Puxi relatively convenient. Yanggao road, which is 24.5 kilometres in length, was constructed in 1992 and it is the main route linking north and south Pudong. It also is linked to the Nanpu and Yangpu bridges.

Waigaoqiao port, with an area of 0.5 square kilometres, was opened in 1993. It is located on the southern bank of the mouth of Yangtze river. There are 78 wharves, of which 32 can accommodate ships with a displacement of 10,000 tonnes. In 1994, Pudong had an annual port handling capacity of 67 million tonnes, representing 46% of Shanghai's total capacity.

The Waigaoqiao phase one power station provides a total of 5 million kilowatts of electricity. The Lingqiao phase one water plant is operational and its daily water output is 400 to 600 thousand tonnes. The second phase of the Pudong gasworks was put into operation in 1991. It has the capacity to supply two million cubic metres of gas per day. The public utilities in Pudong, thus, are more or less in place for handling businesses operations.

The sewage discharge plant was completed two years ahead of schedule. It can dispose of 1.4 million cubic metres of waste daily. The telecommunications project provides 350 thousand lines of telephone exchanges and, at present, sufficiently caters to firms in Pudong.

After four years of reform and development, infrastructural facilities in Pudong have improved tremendously and the business environment is ripe for foreign investment. A basic urban framework has been formed and integrated with the town network of Puxi. There are adequate traffic links for easy access between the west and Pudong. Together with the 2 square kilometres of Liujiazui's financial centre, the Bund, and the 4 square kilometres radius of Nanjing Road, the entire plot of land has turned into the central business district of Shanghai. The 28 square kilometres of Liujiazui and the adjacent 30 square kilometres of Puxi are the centre of commerce.

It is estimated that the urban area of Shanghai will stretch from the Huangpu river to cover 400 square kilometres of Puxi and 200 square kilometres in Pudong. Far from being a hindrance to the overall development of Pudong, the Huangpu river serves as a strategic "water corridor" in promoting tourism, culture and recreation. The "Oriental Pearl" television tower and the Opera House in Liujiazui are spectacular landmarks situated by the river. Pudong ended the first stage of development on an upbeat note. Without doubt, Pudong has the basic facilities in place to spring into the next lap of economic growth.

Progress of Phase II Infrastructure

In a continued effort to sustain the rapid momentum of development, Pudong has embarked on the second phase of infrastructure development with a total investment commitment of RMB 94.9 billion. The infrastructure development is scheduled for completion by the year 2000. The ten projects in the pipeline are listed in Table 5–4.

Based on discussions with officials from the Economic and Trade Bureau of Shanghai Pudong New Area and the Shanghai Pudong New Area Administration, there is a crucial need to find alternative means of financing the rapid infrastructure development. However, the projects involved are capital intensive and do not provide immediate prospects for gain. Therefore, one financial mechanism which is currently being explored is the build, operate and transfer (BOT) scheme. The authorities have engaged the services of international consultants such as Coopers & Lybrand to look into how the BOT scheme can be administered and the opportunities opened up to investors.

TABLE 5–4
Phase II Infrastructure Projects

Project	Estimated Cost (RMB billion)
Pudong International Airport	11.0
International Telecommunication Centre	8.0
Container Terminal	4.7
Subway Line No. 2	10.0
Pudong New Area LRT Line	7.2
Waigaoqiao Power Station Phase II	11.6
Outer Ring Road	22.0
Water Supply and Drainage System	9.6
Huangpu River Crossing Project	4.5
East China Sea Natural Gas Project	6.3

THE DEVELOPMENT OF FOUR KEY FUNCTIONAL ZONES

The development of Pudong is planned around four key functional zones. Distinguishing characteristics of these four zones are contrasted below.

Liujiazui Finance and Trade Zone

Liujiazui is located on the other side of the Huangpu river, facing the Bund. It is often referred to as the "golden area" and it is divided into three centres, namely the financial centre, the trade and commerce centre, and the municipal administration centre. The zone is being built to be the centre of east Shanghai with activities focused on finance, trade and commerce. The zone covers an area of 6.8 square kilometres. The section along the banks of the Huangpu river is characterised by sightseeing and cultural recreation. Some of the landmarks in this area include the "The Fortune World" – a building complex for finance, commerce, and tourism, an opera house and a concert hall.

Jingqiao Export Processing Zone

Jingqiao Export Processing Zone is located in the central part of Pudong New Area. The zone is 11 kilometres from the downtown area of the city and its total area is 9.5 square kilometres. The zone is divided between an industrial area (5.8 square kilometres) in the east, an administration and service area as well as residential area (3.7 square kilometres) in the west.

The industrial area mainly caters to manufacturing, bonded warehouses and comprehensive trade. There are essentially three characteristics for projects in the area: they are capital intensive investments (averaging US$1.2 million); they are high-tech projects such as aviation engineering, bioengineering and telecommunications related projects; and they cater to export and processing functions. Some of the companies that have already set up facilities in the area include Nokia Telecommunications, Digital, Tiancifu Bioengineering and as well as Shanghai IBM ATM Company.

The residential area consists of villas, apartment buildings, complexes for commerce, restaurants, and sports and entertainment facilities. The administration authority and education facilities are also being built in the area.

Waigaoqiao Free Trade Zone

Waigaoqiao Free Trade Zone, at the estuary of the Yangtze river, is twenty kilometres away from the city. The zone is the biggest free trade zone (FTZ) in China. To date, 1,400 Chinese and foreign enterprises with a total investment of US$2.2 billion have been established in the zone. Of these, 70% are foreign funded firms. The zone is separated into two parts; the north part is a bonded storage area and the south part is a management centre and export-oriented processing area. A residential area occupying 84 hectares is being built. Developments in the residential area include hotels, shops, clubs and other facilities catering to the needs of businessmen in the zone as well as providing for commercial, cultural and educational services.

The zone is the first multifunctional FTZ in mainland China consisting of three areas earmarked for bonded storage, a trade management centre and an export-oriented manufacturing area. The bonded storage is spread over 38 hectares of land and connects the east side of the port area and the power plant in the north. The northern section is storage area and the southern part is an export-oriented manufacturing area. Administration offices, customs and other facilities are located near the entrance to facilitate goods clearance.

The trade management centre occupies a total area of 24 hectares. This area is earmarked for office buildings, commodity exhibition halls, banks, post office, telephone exchange, restaurant and customs examination offices. The export-oriented manufacturing area accounts for about two thirds of the total area of the FTZ (220 hectares). A road running from north to south connects all the sections in the area. The area is connected to the northern management centre, the bonded storage area and the port area by an overhead bridge. Service facilities, goods storage, transportation and other auxiliary services have been established to cater to the needs of businesses in that area. In short, all the three areas within the Waigaoqiao FTZ are well interconnected to facilitate business transactions.

Zhangjiang High-tech Park

This area covers 17 square kilometres. The park has been earmarked for industries that fulfil at least some of the following general criteria:

(i) transfer and acquisition of international advanced technology and know-how;
(ii) infusion of sizeable domestic and overseas capital and investment;
(iii) development of Shanghai into the national multifunctional economic, trading and financial centre;
(iv) significant expansion of international trade and export; and
(v) supplementation, coordination and integration of industries between Pudong and Puxi.

Examples of some industries which will be highly encouraged in this zone include: energy and transportation (such as power plants, transformer facilities, centralised thermal supply facilities, the development, transportation, storage and processing of oils and natural gas), postal and telecommunications facilities, information technology (such as communication equipment, computers, office automation and microelectronic components), pharmaceutical science, bio-medical technology products, and industries related to aerospace and space sciences.

Infrastructural support for all the four key development zones covers electricity, telecommunications, water supply, sewage, drainage, heat energy, coal, gas and roads. Land on which these facilities are available is commonly known as "nine supplies and one levelling". "Nine supplies" refer to the facilities mentioned above while "one levelling" refers to the levelling of the ground. In comparison, other areas in the vicinity only have "three supplies and one levelling". Investors should thus be prepared to pay a premium for these facilities as disruptions to the business support facilities are minimised, enabling them to focus on actual business operations.

Complementary Role of the Four Key Functional Zones

The four zones have taken shape with structures designed to group together businesses with specified functions to optimise resources resulting from economies of scale. Therein lies Pudong's comparative advantage given the stiff competition from new development areas around Shanghai. From discussions with the authorities in Pudong, it is apparent that the purpose of zoning the whole area of Pudong is to facilitate its development concurrently and, thus, enable the zones to compliment each other at the same pace.

Zhangjiang High-tech Park has been created to provide a premium industrial park for nurturing advanced technologies. This clustering of the frontier industries enables intensive collaboration in research and development, or the forming of strategic alliances for manufacturing and marketing new products. Jingqiao Export Processing Zone serves as a centre for export and processing functions. Industries here are benefiting from the readily available cheap labour and the abundance of raw materials.

Waigaoqiao FTZ facilitates entrepot trade in the region. The finished goods imported are allowed to be sold in the domestic Chinese market provided that they are essential import substitutes. A further advantage is the availability of cheap labour within the zone. The role of Liujiazui is to provide the necessary financial services to fuel industrial growth and to compliment the existing banking and financial industry within the Bund.

Pudong will become significant for China's economy when all these zones are fully developed. Nevertheless, the progress of the subzones, for example Waigaoqiao FTZ, may not be moving at the rapid pace initially intended. While there is great potential in the four zones, much more capital as well as aggressive promotion of investments are needed before the zones can realise their full potential and become a dynamic, integrated and multifunctional business hub.

PREFERENTIAL POLICIES

Pudong is the pet project of China's central government and has its full assurance and support. Pudong New Area is the first central Chinese plan that was conceived without the consultation or involvement of foreign expertise. Compared to the other development zones, the powerful political backing of Pudong will ensure that Pudong continues to grow and prosper at a phenomenal rate. The preferential policies accorded to Pudong are tantamount to, and in some cases surmount, those of the SEZs. The key policies which apply to Pudong New Area are highlighted below:

(i) Foreign investors are allowed to operate tertiary industries such as supermarkets and department stores. In 1993, the State Council approved the largest supermarket in Shanghai, the Yaohan Co. Ltd., a Sino-Japan joint venture and such projects are continuously being developed.
(ii) The securities exchange in Shanghai is permitted by the central government to issue both A and B shares for the development of Pudong.[1]
(iii) The largest FTZ in China, the Waigaoqiao FTZ is located in Pudong. Enterprises within this zone enjoy further special policies. These include duties and licence exemption, permission to establish international trade institutions with both foreign and domestic investors, permission to retain all foreign exchange by the enterprises themselves and free circulation of foreign currencies.
(iv) Foreign ventures are allowed to establish financial institutions such as banks and insurance companies.
(v) To facilitate trade and stimulate foreign investment, the central government has granted the Shanghai municipal government special

---

[1] A shares are allocated only to domestic investors while B shares are open to foreign investors.

powers to approve manufacturing and non-manufacturing projects, as well as grant import and export rights to enterprises in the Pudong New Area.

(vi) Foreign investors engaged in projects such as ports, airports, railways, highways, power stations, telecommunications, transportation and other essential infrastructure projects pay 15% income tax. Enterprises in operation for more than 15 years are exempted from the enterprise income tax for five consecutive years from the first profit making year and are granted a 50% tax reduction for the subsequent six to ten years.

Foreign investors engaged in industrial production projects pay 15% enterprise income tax. Enterprises in operation for more than ten years are exempted from the enterprise income tax for two consecutive years from the first profit making year and are granted 50% tax reduction for the subsequent three to five years. Technologically advanced enterprises may pay the enterprise income tax at the reduced rate of 10% for the next three consecutive years after the period of tax exemption and reduction.

Wholly foreign-owned, or Sino-foreign joint venture banks, and other financial ventures are exempted from income tax for the first year and are granted 50% tax reduction for the subsequent second to third year. Those with paid in capital of more than US$10 million, and in operation for more than ten years, pay the reduced tax rate of 15%.

(vii) There are additional policies for Pudong that have received "in principle" approval from the state council. Equipment, raw and auxiliary materials, vehicles and other articles imported by foreign funded enterprises to be used in production operations, as well as office supplies, are exempted from both customs duties and value added tax. Goods produced by the foreign funded enterprises should be mainly geared towards export. A portion of products may be sold in the domestic market, provided that these goods are import substitutes. Prior approval has to be obtained from the department in charge. In the bonded area of Waigaoqiao FTZ, wholly foreign-owned trade agencies are allowed to engage in entrepot trade, that is, import raw material and spare parts for foreign funded enterprises in the region for production within the region, and then re-export the end product.

For enterprises in the area with Chinese investment, including investments in enterprises in other regions within China, differential policies can be adopted in line with the industrial policies of Pudong New Area. Enterprises that conform with the industrial policies of Pudong, and that are beneficial to the development and opening up of Pudong, can receive preferential treatment in the form of income tax reduction. Also, the term for land lease in the form of "paid-transfer of land-use-right" is between 50 to 70 years. Other regions in China only have land lease terms of between 30 to 50 years.

(viii) Preferential policies exist for profit remittance and reinvestment. If foreign investors remit their share of profits out of China, then the remittance is exempt from income tax. Other foreign funded enterprises, for a period of no less than five years, can receive a refund of 40% of the enterprise income tax paid on the reinvested amount by foreign investors of their share of profits. Investors who reinvest their profits to set up export enterprises, extend export enterprises, or set up technologically advanced enterprises, can get a full refund of the enterprise income tax paid on the reinvested amount for no less than five years.

IMPLICATIONS AND OPPORTUNITIES FOR FOREIGN INVESTMENT

Based on discussions with local government and other accumulated information, several aspects of doing business in Pudong are worth highlighting. These include the following:

(i) forms of business ventures;
(ii) issues affecting the attractiveness of foreign investments;
(iii) opportunities for small and medium size foreign enterprises (SMEs);
(iv) opportunities for investing in tertiary industries; and
(v) opportunities for multinational corporations (MNCs).

Forms of business ventures

China offers three basic forms of business ventures to foreign investors: (1) the equity joint venture (EJV); (2) the cooperative joint venture

(CJV); and (3) the wholly foreign-owned enterprise (WFOE). The EJV has the advantage of clear guidelines and comprehensive legislation to govern it, but some investors find the rules too rigid and consider it suitable only for medium and large firms with the objective of long-term investment. The CJV is perceived as being more flexible, but more risky due to the lack of adequate legal backup, and suitable only for smaller-scale, short-term investments. Generally speaking, the difference between an EJV and a CJV is clear-cut in theory, but in practice it can be become very ambiguous and thus confusing.

Major Issues Affecting the Attractiveness of Foreign Investment

(i) ***Unfriendly Regulatory Environment:*** The Pudong New Area Administration is reputed to be difficult to approach by foreign investors. City officials have a tendency to disregard small investments. In addition, investors have to contend with the long documentation processing and approval time taken by many different authorities. It was disclosed in a meeting with a manager from an investment company that his document was stamped more than 100 times by various government departments in order to get the business registered. So, an investor often needs to put up with the red tape and is frustrated with the general lack of efficiency. In reality, it is not only what you know but, also, who you know that will get your business off the ground.

(ii) ***Overpriced Land***: Land prices rose sharply in 1993 and 1994. They reached as high as US$190 per square metre at one point. Since then land prices have decreased. However, the market rate of land prices is being synthetically inflated by real estate developers who buy up land in bulk and resell it later, at exorbitant prices to foreign investors. *Business China* (October 1995) reported that the Pudong Administration further contributed to the soaring prices by attempting to break the leases of companies, in order to lease the land again at higher market values. Such bad experiences have scared investors, who increasingly have alternative sites to choose from. One of the best alternatives is Songjiang, a county level zone one hour's drive outside of Shanghai.

(iii) ***Lack of Funds for Infrastructure Development:*** The infrastructure construction is progressing rapidly and it involves heavy capital outlays. The government is facing a financial constraint in meeting demand. This lack of funds will mean delays in infrastructure development and will undoubtedly retard Pudong's long-term growth. As mentioned earlier, the BOT scheme is currently being explored to overcome the shortage of capital.

(iv) ***Inadequate Public Transport:*** The present links between Pudong and Puxi are insufficient to accommodate the ever-increasing volume of traffic between the two locations. The long travelling time has hindered most Shanghainese from working in Pudong. The dilemma is that most Shanghainese cannot afford a car and housing in Pudong has yet to be fully developed. More tunnels, subways and better public transport are badly needed to ease the traffic congestion.

(v) ***Escalating Wages:*** Labour costs have become a significant component of total operating costs. Wage increases are further compounded by a double digit inflation rate. Unskilled labour fetches around RMB 1,500 per month. Wages of managers, supervisors and skilled workers also have risen in tandem with the costs of living. The salaries (including basic salaries, bonus, allowances and so forth) of Chinese employees in foreign funded enterprises are to be no less than 120% of the salaries of local state-owned enterprises at the initial stages of the joint venture.

Investors should not be too taken in by the apparent cheap labour in Pudong as compared with labour costs in other Asian countries. It is important to take into consideration the many welfare items such as insurance, medical, housing, retirement and other costs. So, overall labour costs can be much higher than might be expected. For example, it is compulsory to take up endowment insurance for all Chinese employees and the insurance premium should be 30% of their gross salaries. The housing foundation fund will require 15 to 20% of their gross salaries on top of the 2 and 5% salary rated payments for the increased housing price subsidy and the public fund, respectively.

(vi) ***Low Standard of Work Efficiency***: Most Chinese workers are relatively slow in absorbing the positive work attitude in improving business efficiency. Employees from state-owned enterprises, in particular, bring with them a mentality of the "iron rice-bowl" and lack motivation for better job performance. This, unfortunately, leads to problems of quality as well.

(vii) ***Choice and Compatibility of Local Partners:*** The rule of thumb for choosing a partner in a strategic alliance and managing the relationship as observed in many successful business practices is applicable here. Even more critical, is the realisation and cementing of the relationship. There are, however, a few areas of concern that require careful attention. First, in the case of equity joint ventures, both parties should agree on the paid up capital that is required for expansion needs which may span over five to ten years. Secondly, it is advisable to choose the type of investment that gives the most rapid possible payback as opposed to targeting for longer term payback. Earnings should be reinvested in the business to the maximum extent. Thirdly, in the absence of a good current legal framework, the joint venture agreement should be made as comprehensive as possible, especially in the area of dispute and conflict resolution. It is important to note that a contract drafted in very general terms will simply give rise to misunderstandings at a later date.

The above caveats are grounded on several findings. To begin with, local financing is not freely available due to the absence of a supportive financial infrastructure. This is evidenced by the current restrictions on bank lending and the relatively slow development of the Shanghai Stock Exchange.

As a result of these constraints, a local Chinese partner may find it difficult to raise needed equity to meet funding requirements for further expansion. This same Chinese partner will be wary about changing the equity composition of the joint venture, especially if it means that participation is reduced to a minority shareholder (under 30%). These concerns arose from discussions with existing multinationals that had joint ventures and included the Hua Fei-Philips joint venture which maintains a presence in Nanjing, Pudong and many other locations.

On the issue of dispute resolution between joint venture partners, there appears to be a consensus among multinationals that it will depend on the issues at hand. In the absence of strict laws that support contractual obligations, foreign businesses are well advised to review and anticipate possible areas of conflict and state the most equitable and expeditious methods for resolving them in the joint venture agreement. While this may be a daunting task, it is a necessary one.

(viii) ***Access to the Chinese Domestic Market:*** If the intent of foreign business is to tap the growing domestic market (aside from taking advantage of the relative low production cost), then these intentions have to be made clear at the application stage. While there are no specific prohibitions on domestic sales, based on feedback received during discussions with the local authorities, it appears that the ratio of exports to domestic sales for many joint ventures currently located in Pudong is about 70% and above. Potential investors who intend to tap the domestic market are well advised to make their intentions known clearly in the feasibility study covering a five-year projected period of operation.

(ix) ***Firm Political Support:*** The one factor, however, that may swing a potential investor to locate in Pudong is the "apparent favourable treatment and commitment" that the central government places on Shanghai as the "Dragon Head" of economic development. Relative to other development locations in China, the central and local governments will spare no effort in creating the best possible conducive business environment to attract multinational businesses, particularly those suited to the types of development in the four key areas of development in Pudong. The unfailing political backup is the most important consideration for investors, in view of the recent austerity drive by the Chinese government in tightening monetary policy in China.

Opportunities for Small and Medium Enterprises

In a privileged interview with the Economic and Trade Bureau of Shanghai Pudong New Area, opportunities available for SMEs were explored. A summary of this discussion and the critical issues that were raised are presented below.

One aspect deals with land cost. Despite the relatively high land cost within the Pudong area (US$100 per square metre to US$250 per square metre), SMEs can consider land parcels on the periphery of the development zones which are currently priced from about US$20 per square metre to US$100 per square metre. These flattened land parcels are equipped with water facilities, road linkages and electricity supply comparable to that within the four key development zones. These peripheral areas lie on the fringes of the development zones, are connected by good roads and are within a 25-kilometre radius of Pudong's development zones.

A second aspect that SMEs can look into is the possibility of setting up joint ventures with town and village enterprises (TVEs) which currently number around 4,000 in Pudong. TVEs are becoming predominant in China's economy. These TVEs are actively looking for joint ventures with foreign businesses in the food, printing and consumer related products industries for export as well as the domestic market. Details of specific areas can be obtained from the Economic and Trade Bureau of Shanghai Pudong New Area (ETB). The Pudong Chamber of Commerce can also assist in identifying suitable partners for foreign SMEs. The relatively easy access to the huge, ready domestic market provided through partnerships with TVEs is an added advantage over WFOEs. Another preference of SMEs for joint ventures over WFOE is to have a Chinese partner to lead the venture through the bureaucratic maze which is frustrating and time consuming.

In addition, MNCs need a capable and reliable supporting industry to function effectively. Thus, one long-term and high growth potential for SMEs is to identify and select niche areas to complement and support large-scale growth industries that are being undertaken by large multinationals and high-tech industries. Examples of these include the provision of precision tools and machinery spare parts.

The spin-offs for SMEs in riding on the back of these high growth industries of foreign multinationals promise sustainable long-term growth. This potential is made even more attractive by the proximity of peripheral land parcel sites that are affordable to SMEs on the outskirts of Pudong.

Finally, the process of setting up joint venture businesses can be simplified by appointing an approved agent which practically provides a "one-stop" application service. For an agent fee of 3% of the proposed investment, foreign businesses can entrust the task of applying for necessary business set up clearance to legitimate agents who are essentially approved attorneys in Pudong. A list of legitimate agents is provided by the ETB. An investor will discover that using a Chinese consultant will prove to be far more beneficial and cost effective than trying to carry out this process alone.

Opportunities for Multinational Corporations

Pudong provides a strategic location for multinational firms to set up their operational headquarters, research and development centres or manufacturing bases. The excellent infrastructure support, availability of a highly skilled workforce such as graduates from Shanghai Jiao Tong University and Fudan University, and good public utilities sharpen Pudong's competitive edge in challenging other newly industrialised nations in the region (South Korea, Taiwan or Singapore) as an ideal site for relocating the operations of MNCs.

Opportunities for Tertiary Industry

Secondary industry is the prime engine fuelling Pudong's growth. This, in turn, has a spill-over effect on tertiary industry. Over the past few years, the industrial structure has been rationally adjusted. The tertiary industry has developed most rapidly and its value increased from 20.1% of GNP in 1990 to 28.9% in 1993. Thus, there are ample opportunities for doing business in the tertiary industry in Pudong. As stipulated by law, the minimum start-up capital required for tertiary industry businesses is US$100,000. Small investors with capital constraints, may well find their niche in such businesses because of lower start-up costs and faster payback.

CONCLUSION

All of the main indicators show that Pudong's economy has taken off rapidly and that it will go on expanding. Pudong is well positioned to succeed as a global business hub that is deemed to supersede Hong Kong in the near future. The success of Pudong will create a dynamic domino effect on the economic development of the entire Yangtze river basin industrial belt. To appreciate its impact on China's overall growth, the entire Yangtze river belt includes seven provinces plus Shanghai Municipality, and it will contribute 45% of the overall GDP in China by the year 2010. Pudong is set on becoming an economic powerhouse in the north of China.

In concluding, opportunities for foreign business abound for both small and large corporations. How well foreign companies take advantage of and manage the challenges that Pudong offers will determine the extent to which they can derive long-term and sustained returns on investment in China. Therefore, more important to foreign investors than any static list of niches, is the ability to spot new trends and growth opportunities in Pudong. In searching for business opportunities in the fastest growing economy in Asia, the proverbial expression "it is the early bird that catches the worm" may prove to be rewarding.

REFERENCES

Cheng Qizhong, "Seven Major Changes in Four Years in Pudong, Shanghai", *Economic Reporter* No. 6, 1994, pp. 33–5.

Goodman David S.G. and Gerald Segal, *China Deconstructs: Politics, Trade and Regionalism,* Rutledge, London, 1994.

Lianhe Zao Bao, 19 October 1995, p. 24.

Lianhe Zao Bao, 20 September 1995, p. 23.

Pudong Academy of Development, *Report on Development of Pudong 1991–94,* Shanghai People's Publishing House, 1995.

Shanghai Pudong New Area Administration, *Investment Environment and Development Prospect,* 1993.

South China Morning Post, 13 March 1995, p. 7.

The Economist Intelligence Unit, *Business China*, 16 October 1995.

Ya Zhou Zou Kang, 30 July 1995, pp. 37–45.

Yang Mu, John J. Williams and Cao Yong, "Resurrecting Shanghai in the 21st Century: The Shift in China's Regional Economic Strategies", *China Business Review,* December 1995, pp. 11–29.

"Yangtze Belt to be World's Largest", *China Daily* Volume 15, No. 4652, 9 December 1995, p. 2.

Zhang Zhong Li and Zhang Dao Geng, "Pudong Development and the Establishment of Shanghai's Position as the Centre of Trade", *Journal of Asian Economics,* Vol. 6, No. 2, 1995, pp. 279–89.

Zhao Qi Zheng, "Pudong's Development with a world Prospect", *Journal of Asian Economics,* Vol. 6, No. 2, 1995, pp. 275–8.

Zhong He, "Image of Pudong", *Economic Reporter* No. 4, 1994, pp. 29–32.

Chapter 6

The China–Singapore Suzhou Industrial Park

BY
NG Yi Pin
TAN Chee Kiong

INTRODUCTION

THE CHINA–SINGAPORE Suzhou Industrial Park (CSSIP) is a unique project initiated by the top leaders of the Singapore and China governments. The vision is to develop a Chinese township with Singapore characteristics; a township with an efficient, pro-business environment, governed by transparent and predictable policies. The township will be an integrated complex on a 70-square-kilometre site incorporating an industrial park, commercial centres, social facilities and recreational amenities.

The development is two-pronged. The hardware/physical development will be spearheaded by an international consortium of companies from the private sector while the software/administrative development (economic and public policies) will be transferred from the Singapore government.

In view of the heavy emphasis placed on this township development by all levels of government and the private sector, in both Singapore and China, this chapter examines the main competitive edge provided by the township. In addition, the chapter presents some view points on the complementary aspects of Shanghai given its close proximity to Suzhou.

THE CHINA–SINGAPORE SUZHOU TOWNSHIP

The idea of developing a Singaporean-style township in China was broached in 1992 by Chinese leader Deng Xiaoping. While on tour to cities in southern China, he commented that "Singapore enjoys good social order and is well managed. We (China) should tap on their (Singapore) experience and learn how to manage better than them". To bring this idea to fruition, three agreements were signed on 26 February 1994, to formalise the China-Singapore Suzhou Township.

The first agreement is at the highest level of government in China and Singapore. Both governments pledged support for the township. Vice-Premier Li Lanqing of China and Deputy Prime Minister Lee Hsien Loong of Singapore are jointly chairing a China–Singapore Joint Steering Council which is responsible for all major issues relating to the adaptation of Singapore's economic and public administration experience to the Suzhou Township (the software "transfer"). The council will meet annually to discuss the progress of the township and related issues.

The second agreement is between Jurong Town Council, the representative agency of the Singapore government, and the Suzhou municipal government. This agreement was signed at the local government level (working committee level) and concerns the software transfer agreement.

The third agreement is between Singapore-Suzhou Township Development Pte. Ltd., an international consortium undertaking the development of the township, and the Suzhou municipal government. It deals with key commercial terms offered by the Suzhou government to foreign investors. These include land prices, tenure of land use rights, preferential policies, investment activities and the provision of basic infrastructure facilities. More importantly, investors will be offered preferential terms comparable to, or better than, those of the economic and technological development zones (ETDZs) in China's coastal cities. Detailed background and statistical information about the Township is given in Appendix 6–1.

The Competitive Advantages of CSSIP

The main competitive advantages offered by CSSIP can be traced to Suzhou's location, Singapore's software technology and the high level of commitment to the project. These advantages are described as follows:

(i) ***Suzhou's Strategic Environment:*** Suzhou is located at the intersection of China's two main economic development belts, namely the coastal region and the Yangtze river delta. Suzhou, 80 kilometres west of Shanghai, is well linked by expressways, railways and waterways to the major cities in China. To make Suzhou even more accessible by road, two new highways will be completed in 1996. One is to the north of the industrial park, linking Nanjing to Suzhou to Shanghai, and the other is to the south of the industrial park, linking Suzhou to Shanghai's Hongqiao International Airport. These highways will reduce travelling time and provide for a more pleasant journey.

Shanghai is widely referred to as the "Dragon Head" of the Yangtze river delta and some authors have referred to Suzhou as the supporting neck of the dragon river (Yang *et al.,* 1995). It is this neck that links Shanghai and the Western world to the Yangtze river delta market as well as to the entire Yangtze river basin. Hence, in terms of geographic location, the industrial park is located in one of the best possible places in China. Table 6–1 summarises the economic status of Suzhou relative to the total Chinese economy.

TABLE 6–1
Economic Status of Suzhou Relative to China

Resource	Percentage Contribution to China
Land Area	0.09%
Population	0.48%
GDP	1.7%
Financial Revenue	1.1%
Exports	5.0%
Foreign Investment	6.0%

In addition to its geographical advantage, Suzhou also has an established domestic market as well as an industrial base which gives it one of the highest industrial outputs in China. Besides

CSSIP, Suzhou is also home to four state level development zones. The city's GNP has registered an annual average growth of above 20% since 1978 thus giving the residents one of the highest levels of purchasing power among the coastal cities of China. The good supply of human resources and high literacy rate, together with Suzhou's picturesque waterways, lakes and temperate climate, makes Suzhou an ideal place to set up a township in China.

(ii) ***Singapore's Software:*** The "software transfer" is a unique feature and major advantage of the township project. The aim is to propel the township to international standards by creating an environment that is pro-business, governed by transparent and predictable policies, and administered with Singaporean-style efficiency. The township is more than just an industrial project. It aims to contribute towards the economic growth of Suzhou as well as providing a better quality of life for the population. Similarly, investors get the best of both worlds: the vast potential associated with China's economic growth, and the effectiveness and efficiency of a Singapore-style township.

To assist investors, township representatives will help to file the proper documentation for approval. The approval process will be simplified to make it as pro-business as possible. Mr. Chew Whye, Deputy Chief Executive Officer of China-Singapore Suzhou Township Development Pte. Ltd., joked, "to build a factory and start a business in Shanghai, you (the investor) need 168 approval stamps from the different authorities. Here, you need only one." The Suzhou Industrial Park Administrative Committee has been empowered by Beijing's state council to approve projects. Unlike other committees, whose approval authority is capped at US$30 million, this committee's authority has been extended to project sizes with no upper limit.

The sharp contrast in development style between this township and a typical industrial park in Shanghai's Pudong area is clearly visible. In Shanghai, there are many massive tall new buildings in various phases of construction. This is especially obvious in the Pudong New Area. However, the quality of the road infrastructure lags behind the buildings. In one industrial park, the steam carrying pipes are laid above ground level. In order to provide utility services to buildings on different plots of land, the pipes are arched across the roads.

In contrast, there are fewer buildings in the CSSIP. The road network, with all the utilities tucked deep underground, are well developed and lined with street lamps and plants. To ensure good roads, special machinery was brought in to lay the pipes nine metres deep underground. This is to ensure that soil movement and the transport of heavy equipment will not be constrained in the future. Because the industrial park is sitting on ex-farmland, additional effort was put in to remove the imperious top soil before raising the entire area by about 0.9 metres. This extra height is to guard against flood waters. In addition to the transport infrastructure, the township has also invested in hydro plants to guarantee the supply of power, steam, hot water and electricity for firms in the township. This heavy investment in infrastructure not only underscores the commitment of the developer to the park, but it also demonstrates the commitment of the two governments to make the park a success.

Citing an analogy, Mr. Zhang Xinsheng, Mayor of Suzhou, parallels the township with the lotus flower. The township is not just an industrial development; economic and social needs have amalgamated to form a new model for township development. Like the lotus, neither the leaves nor the flower can flourish without the other. Most important are the invisible roots, which in this case are the software factors that make Suzhou township differentfrom other township developments.

The emphasis is on software and this commitment was reiterated by Mr. Lee Kwan Yew, Senior Minister of Singapore. Mr. Lee said: "There is no secret in a McDonald's hamburger. But McDonald's keeps a certain standard and reputation that no other hamburger has been able to match. This (the industrial park) is our first McDonald's abroad. Service the investor, draw him in and give him the support he needs so that news will spread. Then better investors will come in. That is the way we built up Singapore."

(iii) ***Government to Government Commitment:*** One of the risks of investing in any developing country that is starting to open up is the political risk. In this area, the open commitment and support shown by the leaders from both countries has reduced this risk to a minimum. At the highest level of government in Beijing (the central government level), the joint steering council for the township development serves as a forum to discuss any issues that need direction. At the working level, issues can be addressed at the joint working committee which is co-chaired by the mayor of Suzhou and the chairman of Singapore Jurong Town Corporation. The level of commitment to the success of this township is best captured by the endorsements given by the leaders of both countries. A few excerpts are listed in Table 6–2.

TABLE 6–2
Sample of Government Endorsements for CSSIP

Statements	Authority
Singapore enjoys good social order and is well managed. We should tap on their experience and learn how to manage better than them.	Chinese Leader Deng Xiaoping, 1992.
The development and construction of the Suzhou industrial township has established a new model for Sino-Singapore cooperation.	Chinese President Jiang Zemin, 1994.
Singapore hopes the township will yield concrete fruits soon after its operation and it is willing to make joint efforts towards this end with the Chinese side.	Singapore Prime Minister Goh Chok Tong, 1994.
We can let the whole world know that our cooperation in this (Singapore–Suzhou township) project has been fruitful.	Chinese Premier Li Peng, 1994.
We can guarantee that the agreement we have reached with China about Suzhou will be honoured.	Singapore Senior Minister Mr. Lee Kwan Yew, 1994.
China is ready to cooperate with Singapore and make the (Singapore–Suzhou township) project a success.	Chairman of China's National People's Congress. Qiao Shi, 1994.
The agreement on the joint development of Suzhou industrial park bears significance even to China's cooperation with other countries. The park is open to the world and it welcomes investors from other countries to join in the project.	Chinese Vice-Premier Li Lanqing, 1994.
Both governments emphasised that the Suzhou industrial park is the priority for cooperation between China and Singapore, and that the two countries should focus their energies on making it succeed.	Deputy Prime Minister Mr Lee Hsien Loong, 1995.

Source: Various editorial excerpts from *The Straits Times*, 1992 to 1995.

VIEWPOINTS ON THE TOWNSHIP

Suzhou and Shanghai: Competition or Complementary

Due to the geographical proximity of Shanghai and Suzhou, there is competition between the two locations for the same investment dollar. Even if both cities do not wish to compete, it is unavoidable for investors interested in this region not to look at the industrial parks in both cities. Both cities are aware of this competition as well as the complementary economic potential of the two regions.

With the rapid growth over the last few years, land and labour prices in Shanghai have escalated. The cost of prepared land for industrial park development in the Pudong New Area is about US$138 per square metre as compared to US$60 per square metre in Suzhou. Labour cost in Suzhou is less than one-half of what it is in Shanghai. Because of these economic factors, Mayor Zhang Xinsheng thinks that Shanghai is moving towards higher value added service industries and developing into a centre for international trade, commerce and finance.

On the other hand, Suzhou can compliment Shanghai by developing into a lower cost manufacturing base, a place for leisure, and a tourist and recreational destination. More importantly, Mayor Zhang envisions Suzhou as the front door to the vast Yangtze river delta hinterland as well as the business centre for trade entering the China market. Mr. Zhao Dasheng, Deputy Director of Suzhou Industrial Park Administrative Bureau, expressed the same sentiment: "It is not a matter of going after the same investment dollar but, rather, how can the two places work together to bake an even larger cake?"

The idea of a complementary relationship between Shanghai and the Suzhou township seems well conceived but a few points should be highlighted. Shanghai and Suzhou can each be regarded as large enterprises. In addition to their core business, many conglomerates such as GuoMai Communications, Panda Electronics and Baoshan Iron and Steel General Works have their own restaurants, canteens, housing, hairdressers and so forth. Baosteel even operates a four-star hotel. Thus, many large state-owned enterprises historically have stressed self-sufficiency.

Shanghai and Suzhou will need to break away from the self-sufficiency model and plan a complementary and interdependent relationship. According to Mr. Zhao, there is no official forum or coordinating committee between Shanghai and Jiangsu Province on this township development issue. Tax dollars earned in Shanghai are separated from the township. Hence, the level of incentive between Shanghai and Suzhou for the development of the township will be different.

An example of the differences in priority for infrastructural development can be observed when travelling on the Hongqiao airport road out of Shanghai towards Suzhou. You know that you have left Shanghai and reached the border of Suzhou when the two-lane, unmarked road suddenly connects with the international-style four-lane highway that is lined with streetlights. Developments in Shanghai will affect the township. Instead of waiting for economic forces to guide the development of the two regions, the four governments involved (Suzhou, Jiangsu, Shanghai and Singapore) need to coordinate the economic development of the entire region.

Compared to most other coastal cities of China, the land and labour costs in Pudong New Area and the Singapore-Suzhou Industrial Park are higher. In Qingdao, a major coastal city in Shandong province, the cost of prepared land for industrial park use is only US$40 per square metre. Like Suzhou, Qingdao also offers many advantages including access to markets as well as supply sources in the north-eastern region of China. Shandong province, together with Suzhou, were designated as the only two potential areas of development by the Singapore government. A Singapore–Shandong business council was established and a Memorandum of Understanding (MOU) was signed between the two governments in 1993.

The economic differential between Suzhou and Qingdao is more complementary than competitive. China's market is very large and can be divided into different regions. Suzhou serves mid-eastern China while Qingdao serves the north-eastern China market. The Shandong government and a private developer from Singapore have entered into a joint venture to develop an industrial park in Qingdao, although on a smaller scale than the Suzhou industrial park.

Preferential Policies and World Trade Organisation Membership

China's efforts over the past few years to join the World Trade Organisation (WTO) has raised some concern, especially for state-owned enterprises within China. Another disturbing factor is the ninth five-year plan calling for equal tax policies for all regions within China. There is concern about how these two changes will affect the development of the township. Mayor Zhang believes that these two changes will not affect the township as much as other locations in China for two reasons.

First, even though the township is now enjoying preferential terms comparable to, or better than, the ETDZs in China's coastal cities, the main strength of the township is not derived from these policies. Instead, the competitive edge of the township comes from its geographical location, the government-to-government commitment and Singapore's software.

Secondly, most foreign enterprises establish operations in China with an aim to lower their production cost and/or to distribute goods in the China market. But they are not familiar with the market. The Suzhou township is designed to meet these needs by providing an investment environment which incorporates international regulations and business practices.

Strengths and Weaknesses

Mr. Zhao candidly pointed out several areas of concern as well as some positive aspects surrounding the township. Some common problems faced by investors include RMB exchange, labour and costs. On the exchange issue, most of the foreign investment is in U.S. dollars but there is a real shortage of RMB. This situation is unlikely to ease until changes in fiscal policy are made by the central government. This is not expected to happen until 1997.

Turning to labour, supply is sufficient but the skill level is inadequate. To prevent high turnover in companies, labour contracts are drawn up for three years. Over the long term, the problem should abate somewhat because the township is operating a skill development centre. Finally, the cost of setting up operations is increasing. This is to be expected but the rate of increase has been faster than anticipated. This escalation of costs is attributed to the high rate of investment in the park.

The positive factors concerning the development of the township are several. First, most of the businesses that have to acquire farmland for development face the problem of resettling the farmers. Suzhou has very fertile land and there was some fear initially that they would be unwilling to move. As farmland is reverting from the farmers to foreign investors for profit, this issue must be handled cautiously. Actually, the resettlement of farmers has been much smoother than anticipated. An attractive package has been offered to the farmers including a replacement house and monetary compensation as well as retraining for work. In fact, there were farmers asking when they would become eligible for resettlement and whether the process could be done more quickly. However, Mr. Zhao is concerned that as the township becomes more established, farmers may realise that the value of their farmland has risen and, therefore, they may demand a better compensation package. This could happen in about five years' time and, thus, it is not an immediate concern.

Another positive factor is that attracting investments for the township has been very successful. In the first quarter of 1995, the committed investment was US$0.9 billion. By the third quarter of 1995, when Singapore's Senior Minister Lee Kwan Yew visited the township, the committed investment had grown to US$1.5 billion. The amount of committed investment was over US$2 billion by the end of the forth quarter of 1995. Considering the fact that the township was formalised in February 1994, when there was nothing but farmland, the township is actually having problems preparing sufficient land for sale. This suggests that Singapore's software is important and that the industrial park must be doing something right to gain investors' confidence in such magnitude.

Finally, construction of the Hongqiao airport road and other infrastructures are progressing faster and more smoothly than expected. At one point, the Chinese partnership in the township was having financing problems. However, this issue has been solved. The only remaining problem is insufficient manpower to keep up with the rate of development. But this is considered positive because the township wishes to attract highly qualified workers from around the region to supplement the population base.

CONCLUSION

The CSSIP is a new experience as well as a new model for cooperation between China and Singapore. A lot of attention is focused on the project, both from within China and the rest of the world. The township's rate of development is fast, and the rate of investment which is being committed to the township is also very high. The main competitive advantages of the township are strategic location, "software transfer" from Singapore and the government-to-government commitment.

The Singapore "software transfer" plus the country's commitment to the project should be sufficient reasons alone for any investor to take a closer look at the Singapore–Suzhou Industrial Park. The basic infrastructure for the start-up area has been completed and many of the factories are expected to start production by the end of 1996. The market condition in China is very dynamic and early investors in the township are likely to reap considerable additional benefits for being first movers. The main challenge facing the township is in the area of economic cooperation between Singapore, Suzhou, Jiangsu and Shanghai. Given Singapore's experience, it should not be a problem to recreate the Singapore miracle in Suzhou.

APPENDIX 6–1
The Township

The township is located on a 70-square-kilometre site east of the ancient city of Suzhou and it will be developed eastward in the direction of Shanghai. When fully developed, the township will be able to support a population of 600,000 and provide employment for more than 360,000. Several Singapore governmental agencies, including the Urban Redevelopment Authority, Jurong Town Corporation and the Housing and Development Board have been involved in the master planning of the site. Expected to attract US$20 billion in investments, the township will be developed in four phases of about five years each. Each of the phases will comprise industrial, residential and commercial developments. An initial area of 2 square kilometres was available to investors from the end of 1994. Residents, both expatriate and local, will enjoy a full range of modern social facilities at their doorstep within the township. These will include schools, hospitals, supermarkets, golf courses and even a marina.

---

* Much of the information in this appendix has been synthesised from township statistics and data extracted from the Singapore–Suzhou Township 1994 investment booklet.

TABLE 6A–1
China-Singapore Suzhou Township Land Use Statistics

Land Use	Phase 1 Area (ha)	%	Phase 2 Area (ha)	%	Phase 3 Area (ha)	%	Phase 4 Area (ha)	%
Industrial	315	27	525	32	1,560	44	2,400	38
Commercial	53	5	40	2	55	2	148	2
Residential	310	27	470	29	655	19	1,435	23
Public Facilities	72	6	155	9	205	6	432	7
Open Space and Recreation	145	12	140	9	260	7	545	9
Waterbodies	50	4	80	5	210	6	340	5
Infrastructure	225	19	230	14	585	16	1040	16
Subtotal	1,170	100	1,640	100	3,530	100	6,340	100
Golf Course/ Resort	350	–	–	–	–	–	350	–
Grand Total	1,520	–	1,640	–	3,530	–	6,690	116

The township welcomes the following industries: automobile parts and accessories; machinery and light industries; precision engineering; chemical; pharmaceutical and healthcare; electrical and electronics; food; and supporting industries.

Geographic and Demographic Data

Suzhou is situated between Shanghai to the east and Lake Tai to the west. It is a municipality of Jiangsu province on the eastern coast of China. There are already three economic and technological development zones (ETDZs) in the province, namely Lianyungang, Nantong and Kunshan. The Singapore-Suzhou Township is about 80 kilometres from Shanghai (see Table 6A–2 for some comparative data).

TABLE 6A–2
Geographic and Demographic Data

	Size	Population
Jiangsu Province	100,000 square kilometres	68.4 million
Suzhou Municipality	8,500 square kilometres	About 6 million
Suzhou City	178 square kilometres	Under 1 million
Singapore-Suzhou Township	70 square kilometres	About 600,000 (projected)

Infrastructure

(i) ***Air Links:*** Shanghai's Hongqiao International Airport is 80 kilometres away. The Hongqiao Airport Road is completed and travel time is about one hour.

(ii) ***Expressways:*** State highways 204, 312 and 318 provide links to major cities such as Shanghai and Nanjing. The Shanghai–Suzhou stretch of the Shanghai-Nanjing expressway will be completed in 1996.

(iii) ***Rail:*** The national Beijing–Shanghai railway serving passengers and freight passes through Suzhou. Jiangsu's largest freight train hub, Baiyangwan, is nearby.

(iv) ***Ports and Waterways:*** Shanghai is the main port, handling 70% of Suzhou's exports. The remaining 30% passes through Zhangjiagang, an established riverport with container facilities along the Yangtze river. Zhangjiagang can accommodate ocean-going vessels of up to 25,000 dwt and it is linked to Europe, the U.S., the Mediterranean, Japan and Hong Kong.

The other Yangtze river ports serving Suzhou are Liuhe, Qiyagang and Changshu. The new Changshu port, capable of handling vessels up to 30,000 dwt, is being developed by a Singapore-led consortium. A new port at Liujiagang is being planned which will help reduce the dependency on Shanghai. The Beijing-Hangzhou Grand Canal links Suzhou to major cities like Nanjing, Shanghai and Tianjin.

(v) ***Telecommunications:*** There is direct international connection to more than 150 countries. Facsimile, pagers, mobile telephones, telegrams and telex facilities are available.

Labour Costs

An average worker earns about RMB 500 per month (US$58). However, it is customary in China for employers to provide benefits including housing, festive bonuses and insurance. The total package is estimated to be about US$100 per month.

Economic Indicators

With a per capita GDP of RMB 8,315 (US$970), Suzhou City ranks second among major Chinese coastal open cities. It had a GDP of RMB 52.6 billion (US$6.2 billion) in 1993.

Projected Infrastructural Requirements

The projected basic utilities required are summarised in Table 6A–3. Infrastructure developers are invited to undertake the following projects.

TABLE 6A–3
Projected Basic Utilities Required
(in thousands)

	Phase 1 (5 yrs)	Phase 2 (8 yrs)	Phase 3 (10–12 yrs)	Total
Electricity (million watts)	0.3	0.5	1.2	2
Water (cubic metres/day)	58	90	190	338
Sewage (cubic metres/day)	49	76	160	285
Gas (cubic metres/day)	132	268	400	800
Telephone (lines)	53	89	140	282

(i) ***Electricity:*** Construction and maintenance of power generation plants for distribution to end-users and power distribution networks.
(ii) ***Water:*** Construction and maintenance of water treatment works, water intake structure, water transmission and distribution networks.
(iii) ***Sewage:*** Construction and maintenance of sewage treatment plants, sewage pumping stations, sewers and pumping mains.
(iv) ***Gas:*** Construction and maintenance of gasworks, gas storage tanks, gas transmission and distribution networks.
(v) ***Heating and Cooling Systems:*** Construction and maintenance of hot water and chilled water plants, and steam distribution networks.

Utility Services

(i) ***Electricity:*** This is supplied by the Suzhou Power Supply Bureau. An initial capacity of 5,000 KW will be increased to 105,000 KW by the end of 1996.
(ii) ***Water:*** There was an initial capacity of no less than 10,000 cubic metres per day. However, this was increased to 30,000 at the end of 1995.

(iii) ***Sewerage:*** This is serviced by the Chengdong Sewage Treatment Plant with a daily treatment capacity of 3,000 to 5,000 tonnes. It was increased to more than 15,000 tonnes in early 1996.
(iv) ***Gas:*** The initial capacity is 30,000 cubic metres per day from June 1996. Canistered LPG for domestic and commercial use will also be available.
(v) ***Telecommunications:*** As of January 1996, there are 10,000 lines.

Labour and Employment

More than 60% of the workforce of Suzhou City are employed in the industrial and services industries. It has good supply of human resources from its ten universities and colleges, 61 scientific research institutes, 81 vocational institutes and nine adult education institutes.

(i) ***Employment:*** Employees may be hired openly from schools and institutes, or through an employment bureau in the township. Specialist personnel who are not available in the locality can be employed from other areas. The probation period is usually between three and six months.
(ii) ***Dismissal:*** Foreign funded enterprises may dismiss employees for poor performance and violation of company rules. They may also dismiss personnel made redundant by changes in business operations. When taking action against an employee, the labour union should be consulted and the appeal of the employee concerned should be heard.
(iii) ***Wages:*** Foreign enterprises are free to determine the wages of employees which are generally at least 20% higher than those offered by local enterprises.

In Suzhou, an average worker earns about RMB 500 (US$58) per month. However, the total wage package amounts to about US$100 per month after including items such as insurance, housing subsidy, festive bonuses, medical and other welfare benefits.
(iv) ***Work Hours and Leave:*** Government regulations stipulate maximum work hours of 8 hours per day and 44 hours per week. Companies must implement the prevailing leave system of China. Wages are to be paid for public holidays.
(v) ***Employee Insurance:*** Foreign enterprises are to contribute 25% of each Chinese employee's wage towards a retirement insurance fund.

Investment Criteria

The following criteria are to be observed when establishing manufacturing operations in the township.

(i) ***Building Criteria:*** To ensure a minimum quality standard of factory buildings in the township, a minimum investment of US$250 per square metre on Gross Floor Area (GFA) is required.

(ii) ***Investment Period:*** An investor is required to complete his development within a two-year time frame. Extension of this time frame will be considered on a case-by-case basis. During this construction period, the allocated land can only be used for construction activities and not as open yards, sheds or just for storage purposes.

Investors who purchase land and do not carry out any construction activities within the stipulated time frame will face penalties.

(iii) ***Plot Ratio Criteria:*** A minimum plot ratio of 0.4 is to be met based on GFA.

(iv) ***Land Use Right Certificate:*** This certificate will be given subject to compliance with all of the investment commitments and the proper land usage.

(v) ***Other Controls:*** Investors are also required to comply with all planning, safety, environmental and other regulatory controls on planning and design imposed by the relevant authorities.

Tax Incentives

(i) ***Local Income Tax:*** Foreign-funded enterprises within the township are exempt from local income tax up to the end of year 2000.

(ii) ***Repatriation of Profits:*** Foreign investors within the township may repatriate profits abroad free of the 10% withholding tax.

(iii) ***Custom Duty and Value Added Tax:*** Foreign-funded enterprises may import for their own use building materials, production and management facilities, production fuel, raw materials, spare parts, a reasonable number of vehicles (excluding cars) and articles for office use without paying customs duty and value added tax. Unless otherwise covered by state regulations, products manufactured within the township and directly exported are exempt from export tax and value added tax. Machinery, equipment and other building materials required for the construction of infrastructural amenities in the township are exempted from customs duty and value-added tax.

Personal articles brought into the country for setting up homes are exempted from customs duty and value added tax.

(iv) ***Property Tax:*** Foreign-funded enterprises within the township that purchase newly constructed buildings for their own use are exempted from property tax for five years from the date of completion of construction or the date of purchase.

(v) ***Tax Rebate:*** Foreign investors engaging in manufacturing within the township who reinvest the profits can obtain a 40% rebate on income tax. Those who reinvest profits in an export-oriented or high technology enterprise within a business period of not less than five years, can obtain a full rebate of the income tax paid on the amounts reinvested.

(vi) ***Other:*** There are a number of preferential tax rates that are applicable to different types of operations. These tend to change periodically and it is recommended that interested investors update the relevant tax information with the Suzhou Township Authority.

Prepared Land

Manufacturers who wish to set up operations in the Singapore-Suzhou Township may build their own factories. The available lease periods are: residential, 70 years; industrial, 50 years; and commercial, 40 years. Prepared plots of industrial land of various sizes, serviced by roads and utilities, are available for companies who wish to build their own factories.

REFERENCES

Chen Quiping, "Suzhou Seeks Niche in World Market", *Beijing Review*, 29 August to 4 September 1994, pp. 9–15.

Chew Whye, Deputy CEO of the China-Singapore Suzhou Township Development Pte. Ltd. Presentation on the Development of the China-Singapore Suzhou Industrial Park from the Developer's Perspective held at the Zhu Hui Hotel, Suzhou, 8 December 1995.

Fernandez Warren, "13 New Investors to Pump in $429m in Suzhou", *The Straits Times,* 28 August 1995.

Fernandez Warren, "Success of Suzhou Vital to Singapore's Good Name: SM", *The Straits Times,* 28 August 1995.

Li Lan, "Suzhou Industrial Park: Transferring Which Experiences from

Singapore", *Lian He Zhao Bao,* 31 October 1995.

Singapore-Shandong Business Council, "*Singapore-Shandong: Forging the Link*", Singapore, 1994.

Singapore-Suzhou Township Development Pte. Ltd., "*Singapore-Suzhou Township*", Singapore, 1994.

Suzhou Foreign Investment Administrative Commission, "*Suzhou Investment Guide*", China, 1995.

Third Dragon Development Pte. Ltd., "*Qingdao Shandong Singapore Sapphire Industrial Park*", Singapore, 1995.

Yang Mu, John J. Williams, and Cao Yong, "Resurrecting Shanghai for the 21st Century: the Shift in China's Regional Economic Strategies", *China Business Review*, December 1995.

Zhang Xinsheng, Mayor of Suzhou, Presentation on the Development of the China–Singapore Suzhou Industrial Park from the Suzhou Municipal Government's Perspective held at the Zhu Hui Hotel, Suzhou, 8 December 1995.

ECONOMIC SECTOR ANALYSES

Chapter 7

The Banking Structure and Financial Aspects of Doing Business in Shanghai

BY
Alicia CHEUNG Wai Lai
LEE Teck Meng
POH Chwee Heng
YEO Leng Tiong

INTRODUCTION

CHINA'S IMPRESSIVE ECONOMIC growth and huge potential market of 1.2 billion consumers are strong attractions for many foreign investors. With the increasing number of investors and foreign businesses interested in doing business with China, one of the major bottlenecks foreign companies face when they do business in China is "finance".

China is in a state of flux, with rules and regulations being revised frequently to cope with changing to a market economy. The feeling of change, and its accompanying uncertainty, is indelibly felt in Shanghai, with the Chinese government's emphasis on the Pudong economic zone. Chinese cultural factors, the evolving government structure and legal framework, as well as the "infamous" Chinese bureaucracy, make "finance" a complicated matter. Nevertheless, finance remains an indispensable part of doing business and, in order to be able to operate successfully in Shanghai, an understanding of China's financial system and, in particular the banking structure, is crucial.

This chapter has three objectives. first, it presents a detailed study of China's financial system, paying particular attention to the banking system in Shanghai. Second, it highlights the financial services offered by Chinese and foreign banks in Shanghai, as well as the financial aspects of doing business in Shanghai. Third, it examines current and future trends in Shanghai and the financial impact that these may have on businesses.

CHINA'S BANKING SYSTEM[1]

Structure of China's Banking System

The main thrust of China's recent banking reform is to set up a strong and independent central bank and commercialise the banking system. China's banking system comprises the People's Bank of China (PBC), specialised banks,[2] commercial banks, foreign banks, local credit cooperatives; and various other quasi-official, unofficial and private financial institutions (see Figure 7–1).

FIGURE 7–1
Structure of Banking System

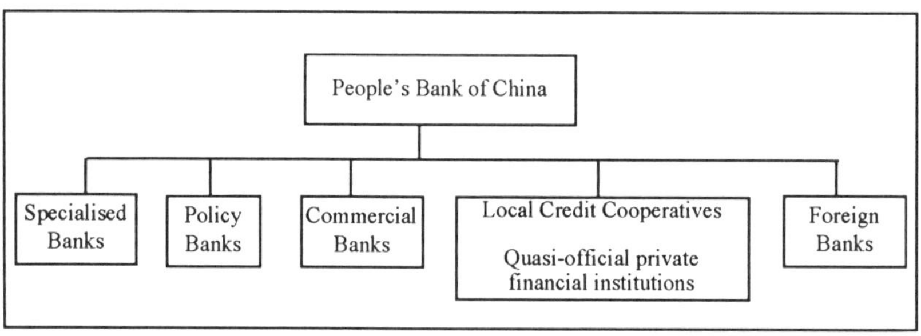

Under the Chinese banking law reform of 1978 the entire banking system was removed from the control of the Ministry of Finance and given more autonomy. The PBC became responsible for the banking

1 Liu Zi Liang, Deputy Director of Pudong administration and Ma Jia Nan, Manager of Pudong administration, Tel: 878 1759 (interviewed 15 December 1995).

2 These comprise the Bank of China, the People's Construction Bank of China, the Agricultural Bank of China, and the Industrial and Commercial Bank of China.

system, and its president gained ministerial rank, reporting directly to the state council which is the country's highest administrative body. The Bank of China (BOC) subsequently gained a status almost equal with the PBC, being allowed to report directly to the state council. Officially, the PBC retains supervisory authority over all banking activity, including the BOC, and bureaucratic turf battles between the two major banking entities have resulted.

BANKING IN SHANGHAI

People's Bank of China

The PBC was established by the Chinese Communist Party in 1948 to serve as the country's central bank. Within the context of a planned economy, the PBC functioned as a rubber stamp organisation charged with doling out the funds allocated to enterprises by the government. Because the government controlled the fiscal appropriation, the PBC's role in financial policy matters was severely limited.

During the 1980s, the government resolved to limit its intervention in the economic sphere and particularly in the financial sector. It allowed the PBC greater autonomy to actually manage the financial system. In 1986, the law reaffirmed the PBC's role as the central bank and defined the duties of the bank in relation to the government. The PBC decreased its role as a direct lender.

The primary duties of the PBC were shifted from the micro level to macro level operational and policy concerns. These include the following.

(a) Research and propose laws and guidelines governing financial activities.
(b) Implement and administer the laws governing banking activities.
(c) Regulate issuance and circulation of currency.
(d) Manage interest rates on deposits and loans.
(e) Control credit to state enterprises.
(f) Manage foreign exchange and gold reserves.
(g) Regulate the establishment, merger and dismantlement of banks and financial institutions.

The PBC is playing a crucial role in the transformation of China's banking system into a market driven sector. The PBC is attempting to pattern its operations after central banks in developed capitalist nations such as the U.S.A. and Japan.

Foreign Banks

Foreign owned and joint venture banks have been allowed to operate again in China since the economic reforms began in the late 1970s. The number of foreign bank branches and representative offices has grown dramatically since the late 1980s. There were 33 foreign bank branches and several joint venture finance institutions operating in Shanghai at the end of 1995. In August 1993, Citibank announced that it would relocate its China area headquarters from Hong Kong to Shanghai, and other major banks are expected to follow suit. This move reflects a growing conviction that Shanghai will emerge as the country's prominent financial and business centre during the ensuing decade, especially for domestic business.

Foreign banks in Shanghai concentrate their activities on trade finance and cash settlement of stocks traded on the Shanghai exchange, but many hope to have access to a more open renminbi market in the near future, which would give them added scope for doing business in China. Bankers speculate that this liberalisation of the financial markets will be driven by China's desire to participate in the World Trade Organisation (WTO).

Regulations on foreign financial institutions in Shanghai cover foreign banks incorporated in Shanghai or operating there as branches of overseas parent organisations, Sino-foreign joint venture banks and Sino-foreign joint venture finance companies. Typically, a basic criterion for operating a bank in Shanghai is the establishment of a representative office for a minimum of three years. Foreign banks' allowable activities in China are somewhat limited, but the scope of their authorised business, geographic as well as functional, is expected to expand as China's economy becomes more fully integrated with that of the rest of the world.

Policy and Specialised Banks

(i) ***The Bank of China***: Designated to handle virtually all international banking operations as the overseas agent for the PBC and the state council. The BOC is responsible for the following roles:

(a) All foreign trade transactions.
(b) International inter-bank, RMB and foreign currency deposits and loans.
(c) International remittances.
(d) Foreign exchange and gold.
(e) Participate in international loan syndications.
(f) Issue government bonds and securities.
(g) Foreign investments.
(h) Provide consultancy services to international and domestic clients on investment in China and overseas.

(ii) ***The Industrial and Commercial Bank of China*:** Created in 1983 to takeover PBC credit operations, the Industrial and Commercial Bank of China (ICBC) is the largest and most influential, specialised and commercial bank in China. Its main functions are to provide the following services in urban areas:

(a) Accept savings deposits from, and provide working capital to individuals and enterprises.
(b) Provide payroll management services for state enterprises.
(c) Operate securities, trust and real estate businesses.
(d) Issue credit cards.
(e) Deal with foreign exchange matters in the special economic zones.

(iii) ***The Agricultural Bank of China*:** Established in 1979 to finance rural farm and business activity, and to facilitate the production and distribution of agricultural products. The Agricultural Bank of China (ABC) is the second largest specialised bank in China. It serves the same functions in rural areas as the ICBC does in urban areas.

(iv) ***The People's Construction Bank of China*:** Created in 1954 to handle government investments in large capital construction projects. The People's Construction Bank of China's (PCBC) main functions are the following:

(a) Settle allocations and administer loans for large-scale capital and technological construction projects.
(b) Hold and regulate investment funds of state enterprises.
(c) Supervise the financial aspects of approved construction projects.

Commercial Banks

(i) ***The Communications Bank of China***: Re-established in 1987, resurrecting an entity that had been dormant for more than 30 years. The Communications Bank of China's (CBC) main functions are:
   (a) Support the modernisation of the economy through the development of domestic and foreign enterprises in China.
   (b) Deal in both RMB and foreign currency deposits and loans.
   (c) Operate the securities market.

Inter-bank Market

The inter-bank market includes a network of commercial banks, specialised banks and a small number of non-bank dealers and brokers. These firms buy and sell foreign exchange. By 31 December 1994, 26 cities were linked up with the Shanghai National Foreign Exchange Centre (SNFEC) which had a membership of 303 financial institutions, 89 of which were foreign investment financial institutions. Both the interbank market and the swap centres are under the management of the SNFEC.

The swap centre is a place where the simultaneous purchase and sale of foreign currencies with RMB is made. This is where foreign banks and non-bank financial institutions buy and sell RMB. While domestic enterprises engage in foreign currency transactions in the inter-bank market, foreign investment enterprises, including joint ventures and wholly foreign owned enterprises, are only allowed to use the swap centres for foreign currency swapping. By the end of 1994, about 80% of all foreign currency transactions were conducted through the inter-bank market which finalised US$40.8 billion in transactions since the SNFEC was set up in April 1994. Among the total transactions completed, 95% were U.S. dollar-RMB trades and 5% were Hong Kong dollar-RMB exchanges.

The inter-bank market will allow the lending and borrowing of local RMB funds between domestic banks on an overnight basis and a short term basis of up to one year. Foreign banks are not allowed to take part because they are banned from doing RMB business. This ban may be lifted by the end of 1996.

Clearing and Settlement in Shanghai

(i) ***Domestic Clearing:*** There is only RMB clearing in China and it is regulated by the PBC. For RMB, the PBC makes a distinction between payments below RMB 200,000 and above RMB 200,000. For payments below RMB 200,000 made within Shanghai, cheques are processed through the "same city RMB clearing system" which was set up in May 1994. Not all local banks are members of this system, so it is in the interests of potential account holders to find out a bank's status.

For payments above RMB 200,000, local Shanghai banks must give the payment instruction to the RMB electronic clearing centre to pay from their accounts held with the Shanghai branch of the PBC. The Shanghai branch of the PBC conducts settlements by netting all payment instructions each day. These netted settlements are then netted through their RMB accounts with the PBC to their respective head offices.

If payment is made to another city, then special arrangements must be made with each bank, even though cross border payments have been made "straight through" since May 1994. The procedure follows a system whereby the issuing bank clears a cheque through the receiving bank's Shanghai branch, which will then transfer the funds via its nostro[3] account to the ultimate beneficiary. Unfortunately, a transaction is rarely this smooth.

(ii) ***International Clearing:*** Traditionally, there has not been a settlement system for foreign currency. The National Foreign Currency Clearing System (managed by the PBC, Shanghai branch) was set up in May 1994. The responsibility of this system is to settle all U.S. dollar, Japanese yen and Hong Kong dollar payments. Given its recent development, little is known about the effectiveness of this system.

New Foreign Exchange System

Foreign currency transactions, including cash, securities and bonds, deposits and remittances, are centralised and controlled by the State Administration of Exchange Control (SAEC) and its branch offices. The major features of exchange control in China are summarised below.

(i) Foreign currency borrowing by a foreign investment enterprise

---

3 A nostro account is a clearing account that is maintained with a correspondent or clearing bank where the bank is not a direct clearing member of a local clearing house.

(FIE) is required to be registered with the SAEC or its branch offices.

(ii) Export proceeds of FIEs, or receipts from sources outside China, are required to be transferred into China. No foreign exchange receipts are to be kept with, or lent to, anyone outside of China without the approval of the SAEC.

(iii) FIEs may sell, through the local foreign exchange adjustment centre, their surplus foreign exchange at the market price or buy with RMB the foreign currency they need, subject to availability.

(iv) Repatriation of profits after tax, dividends and capital in foreign currency is permitted if a FIE has sufficient foreign currency deposits with the BOC.

(v) The foreign personnel of FIEs may remit their after-tax salaries and other legitimate income abroad.

(vi) FIEs may open, with the approval of the SAEC, a foreign exchange account with a bank abroad.

FINANCIAL ASPECTS OF DOING BUSINESS IN SHANGHAI

Banking Services[4]

(i) ***Bank Accounts:*** All foreign businesses must set up an account with either the BOC or another foreign exchange authorised bank through which they must channel all foreign exchange related business. These accounts are characterised as either fixed or current accounts. Fixed accounts are for set terms, usually three, six, 12 or 24 months, and they pay interest at either fixed or floating rates. Demand transaction accounts are characterised as either current, which pay no interest, or deposit, which pay a floating rate of interest on account balances. These accounts must be maintained in an approved foreign currency, usually the U.S. or Hong Kong dollar, Japanese yen, Deutsche Mark, or British pound. Special arrangements can be made for RMB accounts. Currently, only Chinese banks can operate RMB accounts.

(ii) ***Deposits:*** Foreign exchange certificates were abolished in early 1994 and both individual and corporate residents now can open

[4] Pei Yigen, *Corporate Banking*, ABN AMBRO Bank, Shanghai Branch, Tel: 63299303 (interviewed on 8 December 1995).

RMB accounts. But since foreign banks are not authorised to handle RMB transactions, RMB accounts must be opened at local banks. Current account deposits are non-interest bearing while interest rates on RMB deposits range from 3.15% for ordinary deposits to 17.1% for eight-year time deposits. A 20% withholding tax is levied on the interest earned.

Both residents and non-residents can open foreign currency deposit accounts. These accounts can be opened at Chinese local banks as well as branches of foreign banks. However, opening a non-residential deposit account depends on the bank's judgement. Generally speaking, foreign currency deposit accounts consist of ordinary and time deposits, and the interest rate varies according to each bank.[5]

As part of the foreign exchange reforms which started in 1994, the *Provisional Foreign Currency Account Control Law* was promulgated and enforced on 2 April 1994. Under this law, foreign-owned enterprises must obtain authorisation for investment from the Ministry of Foreign Economic and Trade Cooperation and they must receive a business licence after registering at the State Administration for Industry and Commerce. Furthermore, they must register their foreign currency at the State Administration of Exchange Control and they must receive a "foreign currency registration certificate". After undertaking the foreign currency registration, foreign currency accounts can be opened at a bank, and receipts and payments can be done within the limit of the balance prescribed in the "foreign currency registration certificate". When this limit is exceeded, inspection and ratification by the State Administration of Exchange Control is then required. It should be noted that off-shore deposits by firms are not allowed.

(iii) ***Transactional Banking:*** China should not be considered a single payment country. The payment system is still very underdeveloped, making cross-province payments difficult, if not impossible. Cheques that are issued in a company's back office can only be for payees who maintain an account in the same city. A cheque must be drawn in a city where the cheque will be cleared. For customers in other cities, special arrangements must be made between the bank of the issuer and the bank of the receiver. These arrangements are not

---

5 *Asia Handbook*, Bank of Tokyo, 1995.

easy, and it often takes days of negotiations before a bank grants approval. Book-to-book transfers in RMB are also difficult in China and they are reported to take five days on average.

(iv) ***Balancing Requirements:*** FIEs are required by law to ensure that their foreign currency revenues cover their hard currency expenditures so that the two net out and create no foreign exchange obligation for China. Under certain circumstances, balancing requirements can be waived for joint ventures. For instance, joint ventures that manufacture technologically advanced products, for which there is high demand in the Chinese domestic market, may be allowed to sell their products in China without regard to balancing requirements because of strategic needs and because onshore production effectively acts as import substitution, cancelling out foreign exchange that they would have lost anyway.

(v) ***Currency Conversion:*** The PBC announced on 21 November 1994 that foreign exchange certificates would cease to be circulated as of 1 January 1995. Pricing, collection, payment or settlement of accounts within China must be made in RMB. Currently, only domestic banks can provide RMB facilities, while foreign banks and financial institutions are restricted to doing only foreign currency business.

Financing Activities[6]

(i) ***Trade Finance:*** The financing of trade transactions in China is a relatively straightforward matter. The Chinese banks have extensive correspondent relations with foreign banks and generally follow international payment procedures. Foreign bank branches set up in China further ease the settlement of international trade, which takes place through any of the following methods: open account, advance payment, collection, guarantees, documentary credit, countertrade and large-scale export finance.

Open accounts and advance payments are relatively simple methods of settlement whereby either the buyer or seller gives credit to the other and settlement takes place through direct payment. These methods are used by Chinese corporations mostly in the trade of foodstuffs, particularly in trading with Hong Kong. Because the

---

[6] Information gathered through interviews with the Bank of Tokyo, Pudong Branch, December 1995.

extension of credit is involved, these methods are normally accepted only if trust exists between the transacting parties.

The BOC offers cross-border factoring which could soon become a more commonly used financial technique for Chinese sales to foreign importers. Foreign buyers seem more and more reluctant to go to the trouble and the expense of opening up letters of credit for purchases of Chinese goods and they would rather trade on "open account" terms.

Another relatively common method of trade settlement used in China is the exchange of title documents against payments through banks, known as collection. As this payment method might require the supplier to extend some credit, Chinese suppliers usually accept this method only if they have long standing relationships with foreign buyers and regard them as creditworthy.

The majority of Chinese exporters demand payment by letters of credit "at sight", normally confirmed and irrevocable. Indeed, the majority of China's trade is undertaken through these documentary credits. Orders made through Hong Kong middlemen or associated companies outside the People's Republic of China are commonly financed by back-to-back letters of credit, transferable letters of credit or letters of credit opened against a guarantee issued by the associated organisation in the People's Republic of China.

Although documentary credit is the most commonly used method of trade financing, China does not formally subscribe to the Uniform Customs and Practices for Documentary Credits (UCP 500) that govern such transactions internationally (China is not a member of the Paris-based International Chamber of Commerce (ICC) which formulated these rules). However, in November 1994, some 164 Chinese banks and institutions mentioned that they were in the process of signing up with ICC and the UCP 500.

For suppliers and buyers, the main attraction of letters of credit is that they guarantee payment and receipt of title from an independent party (a bank) if commercial and shipping documents are presented in accordance with the letters of credit, regardless of the underlying contract. This is called the "autonomy principle", and it is fundamental to the law governing letters of credit and the smooth flow of international trade. Since China is not yet legally bound by the UCP 500, however, the autonomy principle is not always assured.

Incidents of delays in payments are still occurring. However, Chinese banks are becoming more concerned with their international reputation and, therefore, they are taking such measures as increasing the number of well-trained people on their staffs. The Bank of China requires its bills officers to comply strictly to the UCP 500.

As a rule, exporters seek to minimise their risk when the issuing bank of a letter of credit is in a distant country and unfamiliar to them. The advising bank in the exporter's home country is commonly asked to add its confirmation to the letter of credit to take over the exporter's risk. Chinese banks, however, do not allow foreign banks openly to confirm their letters of credit. Chinese banks make documents under letters of credit payable at their own counter. So, technically speaking, documents are only found to be in order after being checked by the issuing Chinese bank.

(ii) ***Investment:*** Before a foreign bank agrees to extend a loan to a project in China, it naturally evaluates the risk involved and the viability of the project. To do so, the bank scrutinises the profitability of the project, the future cash flows and the environment in which the project is to operate.

Such information is easily obtainable in industrialised countries where the legal and administrative framework is well developed. In China, however, the situation is different. The legal system is not well defined, and official policies and procedures are traditionally surrounded by a sense of "secrecy". Many regulations are labelled as *nei bu*, or internal, and therefore they are not disclosed to foreigners.

For these reasons, specific financing structures and procedures have been developed in the People's Republic of China. These different structures are briefly described in the following paragraphs.

(iii) ***Guarantees and On-lending:*** So far, the most common structure for financing larger capital projects, whether joint ventures or not, has been a foreign loan guaranteed by a Chinese entity of considerable strength and repute, or by the foreign investor's partner. Also common are loans that are borrowed by a Chinese bank, or financial institution, which subsequently on-lends the proceeds to the end-user.

In these structures the foreign lender's risk, legally speaking, involves not the project but the guarantor or on-lender. A thorough examination of the quality of the Chinese guarantor is of extreme importance since local guarantors have failed to honour their commitments in the past. While the fact remains that foreign lenders will have difficulty in finding a reliable Chinese guarantor, the new *Guarantee Law* that was passed and became operational in October 1995 should improve the legal status of loans guaranteed by mortgages or other securities. The Chinese institutions that may issue guarantees are limited under Chinese rules. In 1991, the SAEC appointed seven Chinese institutions[7] that can have the authority to automatically grant SAEC approved foreign exchange guarantees.

In recent years, there has been a proliferation of other Chinese entities obtaining ad hoc approvals for international fund raising activities, including state-owned companies and provincial state organisations or China International Trust and Investment Corporations (CITI). All these guarantors must be approved by SAEC, which acts to control and monitor foreign exchange exposure. Even then, only a few guarantors are acceptable to foreign financial institutions. Foreign companies should be careful to determine that the guarantee is issued by an institution's head office (which is authorised to do so), rather than at the local level.

(iv) ***Syndicated Loans:*** Loans to, or guaranteed by, the approved Chinese entities often take the form of syndicated loans with participation by a number of foreign banks. These loans vary in size from US$10 to US$20 million, for which a club deal with three or four banks is formed, or up to as much as US$200 to US$400 million, for which a syndicate of 20 to 40 banks is required.

In these structures, a People's Republic of China bank or CITIC is often involved. By virtue of its establishment in China, the Chinese financial institution is in a position to obtain legal title (on behalf of the foreign bank syndicate) to any collateral on assets located in China. The term of such loans varies from five to ten years, although the banks prefer to limit it to seven years. The loans normally carry a floating interest rate at the London inter-bank offer rate or the Hong Kong inter-bank offer rate plus a flat margin.

Most China loan syndications have been put together in Hong Kong which, in this respect, is China's offshore financial centre.

---

7 Industrial and Commercial Bank of China (ICBC), Agricultural Bank of China (ABC), Bank of China (BOC), People's Construction Bank of China (PCBC), Bank of Communications (BOCOM), CITIC Industrial Bank and China Investment Bank (CIB).

The large number of foreign banks established in Hong Kong, the financial infrastructure with lawyers and accountants, and its proximity to China make it a natural location for this purpose.

(v) ***Other Financing Structures:*** The structures described above have generally been successful but they are by no means the only financing structures used for deals in China. In fact, the way larger projects are funded has been changing in recent years as guarantees have been increasingly hard to obtain.

(a) ***Limited Recourse Financing:*** Borrowers and lenders have been turning to limited recourse financing for the funding of larger projects. These are deals in which the money is lent on the principle of a project generating cash flows. In the past few years, a couple of projects, mainly in the energy and infrastructure sectors, have been on a build-operate-transfer (BOT) basis. The foreign company or consortium will build and operate the project for a specified period of time after which the entire project will be transferred to the Chinese government. In the BOT structure, the foreign bank has to look more closely at the project's inherent viability and weigh it against possible project risks.

(b) ***Leasing:*** Leasing has been fairly popular with smaller Chinese companies that cannot afford to buy expensive machinery and equipment. Leasing companies in China (over 50 companies have already been established), several of which are joint ventures with foreign banks, can buy the equipment and lease it to a factory while keeping legal title. After the lessee has met its obligations, it can buy the machinery for a nominal fee. The absence of a developed secondary market for equipment is said to hinder leasing on a wider scale, making it a relatively unexplored area on China's financial map.

(c) ***Equity/Bonds:*** Another way of raising capital is through issuing equity. The Chinese equity markets are moving closer to becoming a viable source of financing for FIEs which have the option to issue B shares on the Shanghai and/or Shenzhen stock exchange, or H shares in Hong Kong, but conditions for listing remain restrictive. The B shares on the former exchanges can only be purchased by foreigners. The central authorities continue to dictate which companies are allowed to issue and list shares. The issuance of corporate bonds by FIEs remains relatively uncommon.

Joint ventures can also issue local bonds. Requirements for the issuance of these bonds are that the company must have operated for a certain number of years as determined by the local authorities, that the interest rate must be lower than the prevailing rate for loans and that placement must be by, or through, the Bank of China. Such regulations make bond issues unattractive and, hence, there are only a few instances of corporate bond issues.

(d) ***RMB Financing*:** Local currency financing, of course, is of great concern to foreign companies operating in China. While in many cases the local partner of a joint venture takes care of RMB financing, in some cases, the foreign partner has to deal with this issue. Normally, the PRC banks can provide short- and long-term RMB loans (against certain claims on a joint venture's assets). When lending to FIEs, the Chinese banks are careful about evaluating a project's viability and they demand appropriate (foreign bank) guarantees.

Occasionally, FIEs have rolled over short-term RMB loans from the Bank of China or other commercial banks and used them for short-term purposes. The foreign partner in a joint venture can sometimes borrow RMB from the Chinese partner.

To overcome the occasional reluctance of local banks to provide RMB loans, joint ventures or their foreign banks sometimes deposit foreign exchange with a local bank as security for the loan. This structure is officially called a "foreign exchange secured RMB loan". Thus far, its use has been limited because local banks cannot exceed certain RMB loan quotas even though foreign exchange security deposits are made. However, this practice has been suspended as of the later half of 1995 due to a directive from the PBC.

FUTURE TRENDS

The Shanghai-based China Foreign Exchange Trade System started in April 1994 as part of the plan to make the renminbi fully convertible. Pressures from both domestic and foreign investors are expected to push the authorities to accelerate the liberalisation of the renminbi and to introduce more currency trading products on the Shanghai forex market. Such moves will create liquidity and provide foreign investors with a hedging tool for their dealings in China. With the easing of foreign exchange regulations by the PBC, FIEs can also look forward to the increased easing of forex transactions.

There is also a trend towards the creation of more joint banks similar to that of the China International Capital Corporation joint venture by Morgan Stanley and CPCB. China is looking to joint venture with other international banks to gain experience in project financing and investment banking. Such a practice will invariably lead to more emphasis being placed on service quality and a more sophisticated range of banking products and services by Chinese banks. Banks operating in the Pudong area will become "one-stop" convenience centres for business needs. Increasingly, banking secrecy is becoming recognised as an important banking issue.

New methods of raising infrastructure capital that are becoming popular include the use of project funding, project bonds and so forth, as well as funding through the International Finance Corp using syndicated loans. There will be more listings of infrastructure related companies on foreign exchanges, but this is likely to be relatively small. The PBC has indicated that, in time, it will merge the credit co-operatives into commercial banks serving the outlying areas. FIEs in outlying areas are likely to benefit from such a move.

Shanghai is in a process of continual change, and rules and regulations are constantly being revised. Although there has been a gradual improvement in both the domestic and international clearing systems, FIEs must still understand the mechanics of fund flows in China's banking system and make adjustments accordingly in cashflow projections to cater to delays in fund transfers. For the short term, FIEs should continue learning to work within the confines of the banking system.

REFERENCES

Asia Handbook, Bank of Tokyo, Tokyo, 1995.

Pei Yigen, *Corporate Banking*, ABN Ambro Bank, Shanghai, 1995.

Chapter 8

Shanghai's Real Estate Market: The Investment Climate

BY
Catherine LIM
Caroline SIM Poh Lee
Celine TEO Su Ming
Vincent YEK Tiew Chan

INTRODUCTION

AFTER NEARLY 45 YEARS of isolation from the outside world, Shanghai is now being repositioned to regain its past glory as one of the major financial and trade centres in Asia and to become a hub for finance and trade in north-east Asia. To achieve this goal, the Chinese government has introduced far-reaching policies to build Shanghai into a world-class economic, financial and trade centre and to foster new economic growth in the Yangtze river and delta[1].

Covering an area of 6,431 square kilometres, the Shanghai Municipality has a residential population of about 16 million and three million mobile people from other cities and overseas. The Shanghai region generates 20% of the country's gross national product. The 1995 growth in foreign investment in the Shanghai region alone is estimated to be about 77%.

1 The Mayor of Shanghai, Professor Xu Kuangdi, reportedly said: "If we look at the next ten or 20 years, the most important thing for this world is China's very rapid economic growth. To support such [expected] large amounts of economic activities, some city will become the new financial centre to distribute the money, [and Shanghai is the one]" (*Asiamoney*, September 1994, p. 46).

Shanghai is being portrayed as the head of a splendid, powerful dragon with its tail in Sichuan province and its segmented body in the six provinces along the Yangtze river basin.[2] Shanghai's strategic and central location on China's eastern seaboard, and its key role in the economic development of the Yangtze river delta combined with the development of the central and northern parts of China, make Shanghai particularly appealing to foreign investors. Secondly, Shanghai's historic reputation as a major financial centre in Asia has enjoyed international recognition among foreign enterprises and it is the Chinese government's intention to revive the city's past glory. Furthermore, foreigners also have an historic attachment to this city. To date, more than 135 transnational companies have set up operations in Shanghai.[3]

A third reason for the emphasis on Shanghai is that the Chinese government, keen to fulfil leader Deng Xiaoping's vision of building Shanghai into one of the world's economic, financial and trade centres as quickly as possible thereby fostering new economic growth in the entire Yangtze river area, has introduced far-reaching policies to develop the city (Yang *et al.,* 1995). The inter-bank money market, the commodity futures exchange, and the Shanghai Securities Exchange, representing China's central stock market, have been established and are growing significantly.

A fourth reason is that several former mayors of Shanghai, such as Jiang Zemin, Zhu Rongji, Huang Ju and Wu Bangguo, are among a handful of the most powerful people in the central government. Thus, there is a preference on the part of the central government to develop Shanghai.

Lastly, the infrastructure in Shanghai makes it one of the better developed cities by far. Shanghai is well linked to other major cities in China and other countries by road, rail, waterways and air. In the 1990s, Shanghai has achieved remarkable progress in terms of infrastructure development. Billions of RMB have been spent developing highways and bridges linking Puxi and Pudong, the city's two main divisions on each side of the Huangpu river. Shanghai's commitment to improve its

---

2 This view was put forward by Mr Zhu Zhengyuan, Economic and Commercial Counsellor, Embassy of People's Republic of China, at a seminar conducted by Nanyang Technological University in August 1995.

3 See *The Straits Times*, "MNCs to Help Shanghai to Become Financial Centre", 27 October 1995 and *Asian Business*, "Beijing Stifles Shanghai Dream" which analyses how Beijing's potential political moves might affect Shanghai, October 1995.

infrastructure will continue to support future economic development and growth.[4] Appendix 8–1 outlines a list of major infrastructure projects in Shanghai.

To support Shanghai's economic achievements and to further achieve its goals, buildings and infrastructure of international standard are needed. Thus, there has been a surge in office, residential, industrial and retail property development since 1990. Puxi, the traditional core commercial district, faced pressures of overcrowding. To ease the problem, the government earmarked the Pudong area for economic development. Progress in this new area has already gained momentum and the Shanghai government is promoting the area aggressively.

Given these developments, this chapter examines the investment climate in Shanghai's real estate market. It highlights the problems faced by developers and potential investors in real estate development and reviews market conditions in various property sectors in Shanghai. A brief summary of taxation issues is included. The chapter concludes with a summary of our views and opinions, and provides some recommendations and advice to potential investors.

PROBLEMS FACED BY REAL ESTATE INVESTORS

Foreign investors who are keen to invest in real estate development projects in Shanghai must first understand the legal issues related to their investments, and the legislation enacted to regulate the real estate industry.

Land in China is the property of the state and is administered exclusively by the state on behalf of the people. Under this concept, freehold land is not available. Private individuals and organisations only may be granted land use rights. These are transferable by way of sale, exchange and gift. The state may grant the right of land use to enterprises, cooperatives, work units or individuals, and will ensure that land is used in accordance with state plans.[5]

In China, the State Land Administration is the highest administrative authority that governs the management of land in the country. It is

---

4 See *Bangkok Post*, "Modernised Shanghai to Emerge by 2020", 26 October 1995.

5 "Land use rights" refer to rights granted by the state to use land for a fixed period of years. The term "lease" is used in major legislation promulgated in 1990 on land use rights when referring to the secondary market (i.e., resale market).

concerned with the broad management of land and policy-making. Its functions include organising central land use planning; preparing and enforcing policies, laws and regulations; arranging for land registration, statistics and investigations; coordinating matters relating to land administration; settling disputes and dealing with illegal occupation of land. Various land administration bureaux established in the provinces, districts, cities and autonomous regions implement these policies while the lower levels of regional governments make the detailed implementation regulations.

In Shanghai, the two main authorities are the Shanghai Municipal Land Administration Bureau, which deals with matters relating to leaseholds granted or assigned for value, and the Shanghai Municipality Real Property Registry, which is responsible for registering all types of land dealing activities. In line with the central government's aim of regaining Shanghai's position as a commercial and financial centre, the city has been allowed to develop its own local legislation governing land and property transactions. Shanghai has 14 items of property legislation, the largest number of local property laws and regulations after Shenzhen and Guangzhou.

From interviews conducted with foreign developers and property consultants, it is clear that real estate investors in Shanghai face several problems. These can be categorised into legal issues and development issues.

LEGAL ISSUES IN REAL ESTATE INVESTMENT

The more significant legal issues that concern most developers and property consultants are as follows.

(i) ***Issues Related to the Implementation of Real Estate Legislation and Provisions:*** The Chinese government enacts legislation and provisions on an ad hoc basis and in a reactive manner. In China, unlike in the common law system where legislation is amended to reflect change, old and new legislation coexist side by side. Legislation and statutory provisions are drafted to meet current situational needs regardless of what has been implemented in the past. This has caused confusion as to which legislation and/or provision prevails at any point in time.

(ii) ***Difficulty in the Enforcement of Legislation:*** A second difficulty faced by foreign investors relates to the enforcement of legislation. For example, foreign investors are welcome to invest in property in Shanghai and those who develop residential buildings enjoy favourable terms in the granting of land use rights.[6] Provisions stipulate that only specific project development companies are allowed to be established in the form of equity joint ventures, cooperative joint ventures or wholly foreign-owned enterprises. However, recent developments indicate that this restriction is being relaxed. Foreign developers now are allowed to obtain long-term property development licences. However, the Chinese government could withdraw these licences by enforcing the provisions mentioned above, which are still in force.

Consider another example. The Shanghai government has implemented a provision which requires all tenants and landlords to register their tenancy agreements with the Registry in order to legalise the arrangement. An unregistered tenancy agreement is not legally enforceable and the landlord and tenant are liable to legal action by the government. In practice, the majority of landlords and tenants do not register their status and the government has not done much to enforce these provisions. Foreign investors find it disturbing because local companies are not willing to pay for the registration.

(iii) ***Problems with the Enforcement of Mortgages:*** To attract foreign property investors, the Shanghai government realised the need to implement regulations for real property mortgages to enable secured lending to take effect. It implemented the *Shanghai Municipality, Real Property Mortgage Procedures* in August 1994. These procedures have a wider definition for "mortgagor" and "mortgagee" when compared to local mortgage legislations in other areas of China. In other areas of China, a foreign bank without a registered branch in that locality would not be able to register a mortgage over real property within that locality. Shanghai appears to be the only locality that allows a foreign mortgagee, without any formal establishment in China, to register a mortgage. Third party mortgages also can be created. In practice, local banks are reluctant to accept

---

6 *Using Foreign Investment in Developing Commodity Housing for the Domestic Market Tentative Provisions,* Shanghai Municipality, 28 December 1993.

mortgages related to real estate. Appendix 8–2 provides a comparison of mortgage provisions among the major provinces and cities in China.

Investors face enforcement problems because mortgage contracts cannot be executed in foreign countries that have no diplomatic relations with China, or commercial representation within China. In addition, mortgage contracts must be in writing and in the Chinese language.[7] Even if there is a foreign language version, only the Chinese version will be regarded as accurate. Therefore, it is advisable that the mortgage document sets out the agreed terms between the parties as clearly as possible, because enforcement of mortgages has not been tested to any great extent to date. Frequently, foreign investors in real estate are caught by this provision, as the meaning of contract terms in English or some other language may change when translated into Chinese.

Although the provisions require the mortgage contracts to be registered within 30 days of execution with the Shanghai Municipal Real Property Registration Office, the local Land Administration Bureau and the local Building Administration Department, registrations of mortgages are not widely practised in China. Unregistered mortgages are ineffective against third parties. Nonetheless, enforcement priority between competing mortgages will be determined in accordance with the date of registration at the Registry. If more than one mortgage is registered within the prescribed period, then priority will be determined based on the date of creation of each mortgage.[8]

(iv) ***Lack of Legal Protection for Investors Against Errant Developers:*** Another problem faced by foreign investors is the lack of legal recourse against errant developers and in situations where the developers go bankrupt. In the event of abortive developments, especially when developers go bankrupt, there are no legal provisions providing legal recourse to investors. In China, there are no proper and adequate bankruptcy laws to protect the creditors and buyers of the development should this event occur. The Chinese government is expected to draft a comprehensive set of bankruptcy laws in 1996.

---

7 *Real Property Mortgage Procedures*, Article 20, Shanghai Municipality, 11 August 1994.

8 *Registration of Transfers for Value of Leaseholds Implementing Rules*, Article 7, Shanghai Municipality.

Foreign investors in the Shanghai property market are advised to understand the various laws governing their investments and affecting their business ventures. The *Shanghai, PRC Land Administration Law Implementing Procedures* ("Land Administrations Procedures"), which came into effect on 1 May 1994, is a fundamental piece of legislation providing a substantive legal framework that allows Shanghai to regulate its property market. Its aims are to control land grants so that land utilisation will comply with urban master plans and to impose more stringent legal liability provisions, with a view to reducing abuses and malpractices.

Although there are three methods of obtaining land grants – by agreement, tender invitation or auction – leaseholds for commercial projects only can be obtained by way of tender or auction. This introduces the market mechanism which aims to ensure that a proper value for the land is obtained. In the past, land was granted by a process of agreement among government officials, resulting in prices far below market prices. Upon expiration of the term of use specified in the grant contract, the state will acquire ownership of the leaseholds of buildings and other attachments to the land without compensation. If the land user needs to continue using the land, then he may apply for an extension of the land grant six months prior to its expiration. If a land user fails to develop and utilise the land in accordance with the terms set out in the land grant, then he is subject to penalties ranging from the imposition of fines to the confiscation of illegal income. Appendix 8–3 outlines the leasehold terms for various types of properties in China.

Indeed, Shanghai does have a substantive legal framework for the development of real estate property. Land reform in Shanghai is already one of the most sophisticated in China. However, further developments are needed in the existing legal framework to streamline the legislation to ensure that the real property market in Shanghai continues to prosper.

ISSUES FACED IN THE DEVELOPMENT STAGE

Investors, especially foreign developers, face another set of problems during a project's development and construction stage. These are discussed below.

(i) ***Delays in Resettlement of Dwellers:*** The experience of foreign developers shows that resettlement of dwellers proves to be the most difficult part of their project development. Delays of more than six months are not unusual; in some cases, projects are delayed by more than one year. The Chinese government imposes deadlines for the completion of the projects when granting leases to foreign developers. Resettlement delays force developers to rush development in order to meet their deadline. In the process, developers incur huge cost overruns. In view of this, foreign developers are advised to negotiate for a longer development period, and for the local government to handle the resettlement issue. In practice, some foreign developers found that even enlisting the help of the local government did not eliminate this problem.

(ii) ***Lack of Quality of Local Building Raw Materials:*** The quality of the local building materials often fail to meet the international standards and specifications required by foreign developers. Thus, it is difficult for buildings to qualify as premium and grade "A" buildings. As a result, it is not easy to attract foreign multinational corporations as buyers. Developers who import raw materials, increase their costs substantially, partly because of the 4–6% tariff on imported materials.[9]

(iii) ***Low Labour Productivity:*** Foreign developers often find that labour productivity in China is so low that, despite the fact that the cost of labour is so cheap, the overall cost of their development is much higher than budgeted. In addition, with the lack of adequate construction machinery in China, due to the high tariffs on such machinery, foreign developers find it difficult to replace labour with machinery to reduce cost overruns. In fact, most foreign developers end up relocating skilled senior and middle management staff from their home country to China in order to reduce their dependency on local labour.

(iv) ***Importance of Proper Connections with Relevant Authorities:*** Foreign developers often find that their projects are delayed because of the number of approvals required before they can commence development. The number of approvals is said to be around 50 to 60 from different levels of local and state government, and from differ-

---

9 Note that there is talk that Beijing will abolish the duty-free import of equipment. See *Business Times*, "Tax-free Equipment Imports to be Stopped", 1 November 1995 and *Business Times*, "How Tax Changes Will Affect Foreign Firms in China", 6 November 1995.

ent authorities and bureaux, such as the Planning Bureau and the Shanghai Land Administrative Bureau. Moreover, most foreign developers lack the necessary connections or *guanxi* that would speed up their application approvals.

There is a misconception that *guanxi* implies spending excessively on entertainment and gift-giving. In fact, *guanxi* here implies that developers need to network with local authorities, so that the latter can assess the developer. It would be unwise for a foreign developer to resort to gift-giving and lavish entertainment. Such action would not bring them any benefits and approvals obtained via this avenue are vulnerable to confiscation.

SHANGHAI PROPERTY MARKET CONDITIONS

Given the geography of Shanghai and its present business concentrations, Puxi is likely to emerge as the commercial district. Puxi comprises three main districts namely, Huangpu, Luwan and Jing'an. These are where major office concentrations are found. In 1990, the Chinese government earmarked Shanghai Pudong as an extension of the main business area, to relieve pressure on Puxi. Pudong New Area is situated on the east bank of the Huangpu river. It has experienced heavy development and it is the fastest growing area of Shanghai. The master plan separates Pudong into four major development zones: Lujiazui Finance and Trading Zone, Waigaoqiao Free Trade Zone, Jinqiao Export Processing Zone, and Zhangjiang Hi-tech Park. The Lujiazui Zone, which is opposite the Bund, is designed to be an extension of the CBD in Shanghai Puxi. It is designated especially for finance and trading activities.[10]

OFFICE PROPERTY MARKET

Demand for office space in Shanghai has outpaced supply since 1991. In 1994, the annual take-up increased to approximately 400,000 square metres. Thus was evidenced by the sharp decline in vacancy rates from over 25% in 1991 to virtually zero by the end of 1994. In 1995, the estimated annual take-up was over 580,000 square metres. The number of

---

[10] See *South China Morning Post*, "Chartered in Pudong Talks", 28 October 1995.

foreign investment companies maintaining a presence in Shanghai has continued to increase but at a considerably lower rate than the 50% growth recorded in 1994. Growth in demand will continue in 1996 but at a slower rate than in 1995.

The surge in demand has spurred a wave of office construction throughout the city. The grade "A" office inventory in Shanghai shot up to 847,900 square metres by the end of 1995, as compared to 227,900 square metres of gross floor area at end of 1994. In 1995 alone, some 620,000 square metres of office space (all grades) were completed and an additional 1 million square metres of new office space is slated for completion before the end of 1996. By the end of 1997, the city's office inventory is projected to increase eight-fold if all projects meet the completion dates currently promulgated by developers. However, we project that, in reality, some of these projects (about 20 to 30%) are likely to be delayed.

Though annual absorption of office space for the next three years is projected to remain in the range of 600,000 to 680,000 square metres (for all grades), given the optimistic projections of China's economic growth, the anticipated large new supply over the same period will push vacancy rates levels above 20%. Appendix 8–4 contains the list of office buildings that will be completed over the next few years.

Shanghai's grade "A" office inventory will double by the latter part of 1996. Vacancy rates are heading towards 12% in Puxi, and in excess of 15% in Pudong, by mid-1996. The 1.2 million square metres of new space will push the vacancy rates above 20% by the end of 1996. With a further rise in vacancies inevitable in 1996, rents are expected to decline by at least 10 to 15% over the next 12 months to mid-1997. Further declines are expected in the range of 12 to 15% per annum for the subsequent two years, given the impending supply (1.6 million square metres by 1997). However, the fall in rents will be dampened if project completions are postponed and staggered over a longer period, which may well be the case.

In the city's traditional core CBD area (Huangpu district), new supply is estimated to be less than 15% of the anticipated total new supply; more than 40% of the potential new space is located in Pudong. The balance of 60% comes from the recently developed areas outside Huangpu district and the fringe areas. Table 8–1 summarises the estimated annual new supply and take-up for office space (all grades).

As a result of the imbalance in the annual demand and supply, rents and capital values have begun to decline since mid-1995, following the same pattern as Guangzhou and Shenzhen. Monthly rentals have retreated by about 5 to 8%, to an average of US$70 per square metre of net floor area. Capital values of grade "A" office space are pre-selling at US$2,400 to US$3,150 per square metre on gross floor area in Puxi and at US$1,450 to US$1,950 per square metre in Pudong (see Appendix 8–8 for a definition of terms).

The increase in new supply, leading to greater availability, has provided tenants with a real choice in terms of location and occupancy costs. As a result, some tenants have moved out of high rent buildings. Vacancy levels for grade "A" space have risen to around 5%. For example, Roche Pharmaceutical recently relocated from the Shanghai Centre, where monthly rents are about US$90 per square metre, to the less prestigious Coal and Science Building with a monthly rent signed at US$36 per square metre.

TABLE 8–1
New Supply and Annual Take-Up of Office Space in Shanghai (Pudong and Puxi)

Year	New Supply (square metres)	Annual Take-Up[a] (square metres)	Annual Excess/(Deficit) (square metres)
1994	390,000	400,000	(10,000)
1995	710,000	640,000	70,000
1996	1,200,000	660,000	540,000
1997	1,020,000	680,000	340,000
1998	575,000	680,000	(105,000)

[a] Assumes that all projects can be completed as scheduled and based on an optimistic estimation of economic growth.

Source: Compiled from research reports from Colliers Jardine, Jones Lang Wootton and articles from *South China Morning Post.*

The impending new supply over the next three to four years and the falling rents will continue to apply substantial downward pressure on the capital values of office space, which are projected to decline at a rate of between 10 to 12% annually over the next few years. However, office properties located in the prime Huangpu district and next to the proposed MRT station will face smaller declines in their rents and capital values. Nonetheless, in promoting and developing Shanghai into a financial and commercial centre, the government may introduce more investment incentives to attract foreign investments to the city. This will generate more demand for properties and ease the downward pressure on the capital values and rental rates in the medium to long term.

RETAIL PROPERTY MARKET

Overall demand for retail space in Shanghai, especially from international retailers, has softened since the second half of 1994 but the demand for both street front stores and upper class department stores in prime locations, such as Nanjing Road and Huaihai Road, remains relatively strong (see Figure 8–1). Prime rentals have been stable at US$160 to US$370 per square metre per month throughout 1995. Partly due to the austerity programme imposed by the Chinese government, the purchasing power of local businessmen and wealthy individuals has been constrained. The increase in retail sales in Shanghai over the past two years has just matched the inflation rate in the city.

FIGURE 8–1
Trends for Annual Rents and Capital Values for Prime Office Space

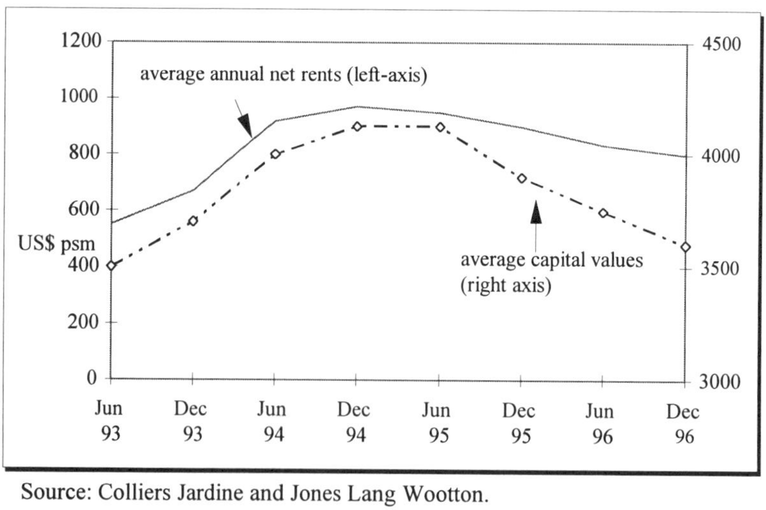

Source: Colliers Jardine and Jones Lang Wootton.

At the end of 1995, the stock of joint venture retail floorspace amounted to more than 500,000 square metres, a 100% increase over

1994. Some 300,000 square metres of retail space are estimated to be completed in 1996. New areas for retail centres are emerging. They include Xujiahui in Xuhui, Lujiazui in Pudong, Sky City in Zhabei and Yuyuan in Nanshi district. The prime Nanjing and Huaihai areas are continuing to consolidate and they will remain as the prime CBD precincts. In the Huaihai Zhong Road area, several large retail centres are being developed by Hong Kong developers. Table 8–2 shows some of the major retail developments in Shanghai.

Approximately one million square metres of retail property is scheduled for completion before 1998. The Shanghai No. 1 Yaohan development in Pudong, a ten-storey shopping centre with a total retail space of about 150,000 square metres, was completed in January 1996. Henderson Land Development will develop a commercial-cum-residential project with a total gross floor area of 86,100 square metres along Nanjing Xi Road.

TABLE 8–2
Some of the Known Major Retail Development Projects in Shanghai

Development Project	Completion Date	Gross Floor Area (square metres)
Yaohan Nextstage	January 1996	150,000
Tianfu Building	Mid-1996	12,040
Shanghai Bao'an Tower	Mid-1996	23,820
Shui On Building	Second Half 1997	30,000
Shanghai Central Plaza	Second Half 1997	139,350
Shanghai Square	First Half 1998	34,430
New World Square	End 1996	74,253
LandMark	End 1997	32,000

Source: Compiled from *the South China Morning Post*, Colliers Jardine and Jones Lang Wootton reports.

Rents for prime CBD retail space in Shanghai are beginning to show signs of softness, partly due to the austerity programme, the sharp growth in supply and slower tourist and business traveller arrivals.[11]

[11] This latter phenomena is expected to be temporary. According to *The Straits Times*, 25 April 1996, Beijing is expanding its airport in anticipation of 35 million arrivals per year by 2005 from the present 15 million arrivals. With Shanghai destined to be the new centre of economic and industrial activity in all of China, business traffic

With more supply coming onstream, the rents and capital values for prime CBD retail are expected to decline by about 5 to 10% during 1996. The declines will vary according to their locations within the CBD. Downward pressure will continue during 1997, when more supply is released. Prime CBD retail space can now be rented for US$275 to US$375 per square metre per month on net floor area. Capital values for prime CBD retail space are currently between US$20,000 and US$25,500 per square metre of gross floor area for ground floor space.

HOTEL PROPERTY MARKET

Demand for hotel rooms was strong from 1990 to 1994 as a result of the sharp recovery of international inbound business travellers and tourists after the Tiananmen Square incident cooled off. The growth in demand was not matched by a corresponding increase in the number of hotel rooms, which resulted in occupancy rates rising sharply to about 77% by the end of 1993. By mid-1994, occupancy rates began to decline, partly due to a drop in the tourist and business traveller arrivals and the austerity programme implemented by the government.

The tension between Taiwan and China led to a decline in visitors from Taiwan in 1995. In addition, the number of visitors from Hong Kong and Macau also declined. On the other hand, "non greater China" visitors, who accounted for 83% of all arrivals, actually increased, especially business visitors. The city's booming exhibition industry partly accounts for this trend. During 1995, in addition to the East China Fair, Shanghai hosted an increasing number of economic promotion events, together with trade exhibitions for the automobile industry, instrumentation, telecommunications, computers, building materials, jewellery, fashion, photography and art. These activities have supported hotel occupancy rates and, hence, room rates.

At the end of 1995, Shanghai had about 28,000 hotel rooms for foreign visitors, spread among seven five-star hotels, 11 four-star hotels and 33 three-star hotels. In order to meet the growth in demand experienced over the past ten years, hotels have expanded their operations. The supply of new hotel rooms increased by over 10% per annum in the pe-

---

will rise sharply and, therefore, supply and demand forces in the real estate and rental markets will move to new equilibrium levels over the next five years.

riod from 1985 to 1990, and more than four-fold between 1984 and 1994. The tight supply of hotel rooms is likely to continue until new hotels come on stream in 1996, including the Shanghai New Asia Changcheng, the Shanghai New Asia Plaza and the New Asia Tomson Hotel in Pudong, and in 1997 (see Table 8–3 for details).

TABLE 8–3
Projected Supply of Hotel Rooms in Shanghai: 1995 to 2000

Project	Hotel Rating	Year Opening	Number of Rooms	Location
New Asia Tomson	5-Star	1996	494	Pudong
Shanghai New Asia Changcheng	3-Star	1996	286	Shanghai Rail Terminus
Shanghai New Asia Plaza	3-Star	1996	262	Shanghai Rail Terminus
East Jin Jiang	5-Star	1997	500	Pudong
Shangri-la	5-Star	1998	450	Pudong
Shangri-la	5-Star	1998	500	City Centre
Jin Mao Mansion	5-Star	1998	400	Pudong
Shanghai Lujiazui Finance and Trade Zone Devt. Co. Ltd.	4-Star	1998	300	Pudong
Jin Ma Property Co.	5-Star	1998/99	450	Pudong
Shanghai Lujiazui Finance and Trade Zone Devt. Co. Ltd.	4/5-Star	1999	400	Pudong

Source: Compiled from *South China Morning Post* and reports from Colliers Jardine and Jones Lang Wootton.

At December 1995, the daily rate for a standard room, inclusive of the 10 to 15% service charge, averaged US$200 to US$265 in five-star hotels, US$185 to US$220 in four-star hotels and US$110 to US$130 in three-star hotels. Current rates are 5% higher than six months ago. The Hilton Hotel in Huangshan Road, Jing'an, is quoting the highest tariff in Shanghai at US$287.50 per night for a standard room. However, with new openings in 1996 and 1997, rates for five-star hotels are expected to correct by 5 to 10%. On the other hand, room rates for three- and four-star hotels are projected to remain relatively stable, with only some minor corrections.

RESIDENTIAL PROPERTY MARKET

The rapid economic development in Shanghai City, the influx of a mobile population, including expatriates, and the rapid replacement of older residential properties by commercial properties are factors that continue to generate demand for residential properties. Annual take-up for residential properties grew from about 200,000 square metres in 1993, to 780,000 square metres in 1994 and 900,000 square metres in 1995. Demand for middle and low cost apartments is high.

In 1995, 1.34 million square metres of new residential floorspace approved for overseas sales was completed in Shanghai. The estimate for 1996 is 530,000 square metres. Of the residential developments under way, approximately 60% are in Puxi, but none are located within the Huangpu CBD area. Major residential completions during 1996 will include the Mayfair Tower (11,000 square metres) in Jing'an district and the International Apartment Building (23,000 square metres) in Hongkou in the north of the city.

Residential rental levels have peaked in Puxi as both developers and potential tenants anticipate the impact of the impending new supply. Monthly rentals for the best apartments are expected to remain at an average of US$60 per square metre per month. In 1996, vacancy rates for apartments are projected to rise and, therefore, rentals are expected to slide, especially for buildings in peripheral locations with inadequate amenities and poor management services. A two-bedroom prime apartment with 100 square metres commands about US$1,250 to US$1,550 per month, while a three-bedroom apartment (150 square metres) can a fetch a monthly rental of about US$1,900 to US$2,350.

At the end of 1995, capital values for prime apartments showed signs of weakness. Although they were valued at US$1,900 to US$2,800 per square metre, developers offered discounts ranging from 5 to 15%, depending on payment terms. Villas close to the inner ring road were valued at US$2,600 to US$2,800 per square metre. Luxury apartment yields are currently in the 15 to 20% range, but they are expected to soften over the next 18 months because capital values and rents may fall by 10 to 15% due to supply excess.

Foreign investors are also active in local residential developments where land and building costs are lower. The Man Po Group of Hong Kong intends to invest US$200 million to develop a residential complex at the junction of Yanan Road and Zhenning Road. By February 1995,

Shanghai's domestic housing renovation scheme had registered foreign investments of US$8.5 billion.

INDUSTRIAL PROPERTY MARKET

Gross industrial output in Shanghai was RMB 62.75 billion (US$7.56 billion) at 1990 constant prices for the first quarter of 1995, up by 10% over the same period for 1994. Shanghai has been successful in attracting foreign and local industrial companies to its major industrial zones. To date, there are about 1,600 companies in the Waigaoqiao Free Trade Zone (Waigaoqiao) with a total investment in excess of US$2.5 billion. Waigaoqiao has more than 300,000 square metres of factory space completed, of which 35% has been sold. An additional 260,000 square metres were completed in the Jinqiao Export Zone (Jinqiao) of which 65% has been sold. Over the next two years, a further 200,000 square metres of industrial space is expected to be completed in Waigaoqiao.

Factory space in Jinqiao and Waigaoqiao is currently valued at an average of US$330 per square metre of gross floor area and US$320 per square metre, respectively. Warehouse space averages US$490 per square metre in Waigaoqiao. In addition, there are more than 200,000 square metres of serviced industrial land available for sale at prices averaging US$100 per square metre in Waigaoqiao. In Jinqiao, industrial land is going for US$70 to US$97 per square metre, a slight decline from over a year ago.

Developers in Pudong and property consultants are optimistic about the future of the rental market. This is largely attributed to the fact that many end-users, especially foreign companies and investors, are hesitant to purchase due to concerns over the capital gains tax on property and land imposed in January 1995. Annual rentals for factory space in Jinqiao and Waigaoqiao are relatively stable at US$45 per square metre while factory rentals at Zhangjiang Hi-tech Development Zone average US$60 per square metre. However, industrial rents in the Caohejing High-tech Industrial Park and the Minghang Economic and Technological Development Zone are relatively soft, averaging US$60 and US$34 per square metre per annum, respectively. Capital values for industrial properties in these two zones range from US$220 to US$320 per square metre.

Two foreign joint venture industrial developments, the Shanghai

Malu Industrial Park in Jiading and the Super Ocean Industrial Town in Pudong, are currently under construction. Phase one of the Shanghai Malu Industrial Park, which has 19 industrial buildings of 27,000 square metres gross floor area, was completed in the first quarter of 1995. This industrial space is selling at US$480 per square metre, 40% higher than local industrial developments. Prices at Super Ocean Industrial Town range from US$338 to US$530 per square metre, depending on the type of industrial building. Appendix 8–5 provides a comparison of the rental and capital values of various types of properties among the major cities in the Asia Pacific region.

TAXATION IN SHANGHAI

In Shanghai, foreign investors may invest in the property market in the form of equity joint ventures, contractual joint ventures or wholly owned foreign enterprises. At present, the main taxes applicable are an enterprise income tax, a business tax, a land value added tax and a real estate tax. These are summarised in Table 8–4. Appendix 8–7 contains a summary of the various taxes applicable to real estate development in Shanghai.

Tax Implications for Foreign Companies Undertaking Construction Projects in China

With the surge of economic activity in the property sector, PRC enterprises have increasingly engaged foreign companies to undertake property construction projects in China. Foreign companies that are engaged in these construction projects usually provide the project design services, project management services and project construction works.

If the foreign company has a permanent establishment in China, the income which it derives from the provision of the above-mentioned services would be subject to business tax and enterprise income tax. Tax exemptions, however, are available under certain tax treaties concluded between China and other countries. Under these treaties, the income derived from a project in China by a foreign company incorporated in another country that has a bilateral treaty with China, would not be subject to enterprise income tax if the project continues for a period, or aggregate periods, of not less than six months within any 12-month period. In these circumstances, the foreign company is not considered to have a permanent establishment in China. The assessment of the tax liability is based, essentially, on the source of income, and the nature and duration of the service provided.

TABLE 8–4
Main Taxes Applicable to Foreign Investors in Shanghai

Type of Tax	Tax Rates
Income tax	Investors are required to pay income tax comprising 30% national income tax and 3% local income tax.
Business tax	For construction and construction related works, a 3% business tax is computed on its gross turnover. For transfer and leasing of land use rights and buildings the business tax is 5% of gross turnover.
Stamp duty	Construction and project development contracts: 0.05% of the contract value. Real estate leasing contracts: 0.1% of its leasing value. Transfer of titles : 0.05% of the contract value.
Deed tax	Buyers of real estate properties are subject to 6% of transfer price deed tax. However, if the buyer is an overseas Chinese, or a resident of Hong Kong or Macau, and the price is in foreign currencies, then the rate is only 3%.
Real estate tax	The applicable rate is 1.2% based on the residual value of the real estate, or 12% based on the rental value of the real estate.
Real estate value added tax (or capital gains tax)	Depending on the increased value of the real estate being disposed of, the tax rate could range from 30% to 60% on the increased value. Appendix 8–6 provides details of this tax.

Project Design Services

Foreign companies engaged in the provision of project design services may enjoy tax exemption for offshore income. Offshore income is derived from design services such as the preparation of plans and drawings performed outside China. A foreign company is considered to have a permanent establishment in China if the design plans and drawings are prepared partly or wholly within China. In such cases, the gross income derived from the project minus the offshore income is subject to business tax at a rate of 5% and the onshore income is subject to enterprise income tax at a rate of 33%.

The capacity to provide proper documentation of costs and expenses is essential to the accurate computation of taxable income. In the absence of proper documentation, a deemed profit rate of 15% on the gross onshore income may be applied by China's tax authorities. Other pitfalls to avoid are the failure to expressly provide in the terms of the contract for the fee chargeable with respect to services performed outside of China, and documentation which does not properly distinguish between the services performed within and outside of China. In the face of such uncertainties, or ambiguities, both the income earned inside and outside of China may be combined for the purposes of tax computation.

Project Management Services

Business tax at a rate of 5%, and enterprise income tax at a rate of 33%, are payable on gross revenue and taxable income derived from the provision of project management services within China. Again, a foreign company may be saddled with an onerous tax burden if proper documentation of costs and expenses are not maintained and its taxable income cannot be assessed with accuracy. In such a case, a deemed profit rate of 10% may be applied in the computation of taxable income.

Construction Services

Business tax at a rate of 3%, and enterprise income tax at a rate of 33%, are payable on gross income arising from a construction project. If taxable income cannot be determined accurately for some reason, say, due to inadequate documentation, the foreign company may be deemed to earn taxable income equivalent to 10% of its gross income.

From the above, it can be seen that proper tax planning is essential before the commencement of any of the above construction projects in China. If China's tax bureau is unable to distinguish the different types of income derived from the different categories of services performed in different jurisdictions, it may elect a form of tax computation that results in the highest tax payable.

Proper distinctions should be made between revenue earned from services performed inside and outside of China in the terms of the contract. A foreign company may also wish to consider appointing independent contractors for services that are to be performed in different jurisdictions to facilitate the provision of proper documentation for the purposes of tax computation. This may help to ensure that the foreign company's tax liabilities are kept within acceptable levels.

CONCLUSION

Foreign investors are cautioned to carefully consider the following issues before investing in real estate in Shanghai:

(i) Market conditions do not favour short-term investments over the next one or two years. This is especially so in the office and residential property markets, where rents and prices are anticipated to decline further. Foreign investors, therefore, should position themselves for long-term investments, and time their entry accordingly. Market conditions suggest that a correction is in order; thus, a waiting strategy is appropriate.

(ii) As in any real estate transaction, the location of the project is very important for future capital appreciation and for rental purposes. Shanghai is no different, and foreign investors should conduct research to gain sufficient knowledge of the Shanghai market before making investment decisions.

(iii) Foreign developers should establish networks with local government authorities, and understand the approval process and legal environment both in Shanghai and at state level. This would help to reduce the risk of delays and project management risks.

(iv) Foreign developers should position their products to meet foreign investor demand, notably from Hong Kong, Taiwan and South-east Asia, as local purchasing power is still low.

(v) Individual investors in property are advised to study the reputations and track records of developers to avoid problems relating to completion and workmanship.

Finally, investors need to remember that the principle of *caveat emptor* prevails, that is, let the buyer (or investor) beware.

APPENDIX 8–1
Infrastructure Projects in Shanghai

Name of Project	Total Investment (RMB)	Date of Completion
Completed infrastructure projects		
Nanpu Bridge	820 million	19 Nov 1991
Yangpu Bridge	1.33 billion	23 Oct 1993
Yanggao Road Extension	800 million	Dec 1992
Waigaoqiao New Harbour Zone	620 million	30 Oct 1993
Pudong Gasworks Phase II	212 million	June 1991
Waigaoqiao Power Plant	3 billion	1993
Linqiao Water Works	189 million	1994
Sewage Drainage Project	1.35 billion	1993
Ventilating project	11.5 million	1992
Inner Ring Road (Pudong)	230 million	20 Nov 1993
Subway Line 1 (Puxi)	2.4 billion	April 1995
Under planning and/or construction		
Pudong International Airport	11 billion	
International Telecoms Centre	8 billion	
Container Terminal	4.7 billion	
Subway Line 2	10 billion	
Hongqiao-Pudong LRT	7.2 billion	
Waigaoqiao Power Plant II	11.6 billion	
Outer Ring Road	2.2 billion	
Water Supply and Drainage	9.8 billion	
Three other LRT Lines	N/A	

Sources: *Report on Development of Pudong*, Pudong Academy of Development, *Business Times, Straits Times and China Daily.*

APPENDIX 8–2
A: Comparison of Real Estate Mortgages

	Guangzhou	Beijing	Shanghai
Legislation	*Guangzhou Municipality, Administration of Real Property Mortgage Procedures,* 6 June 1990 (57 Articles).	*Beijing Municipality, Administration of Real Property Mortgage Procedures,* 20 April 1994 (42 Articles).	*Shanghai Municipality, Administration of Real Property Mortgage Procedures,* 22 August 1994 (66 Articles).
Securities over which mortgage may be created	Article 6: (1) urban State leaseholds (2) buildings (3) valid pre-sale contract	Article 5: (1) State-owned leaseholds (2) buildings (3) other real property rights	Article 6: (1) leaseholds (2) buildings (3) future real property rights (4) other real property rights
Mortgage contract	Article 21 (1–11): Contents stated.	Article 15 (1–6): Contents stated.	Article 19 (1–19): Contents stated. Article 18: Mortgage contract must be signed in a country with which China has diplomatic relations or where it has a representative trade office.
Registration	Article 25: Within 30 days of notarisation if signed in China or within 60 days if signed overseas.	Article 17: Within 30 days of signing of mortgage contract.	Article 38: To be registered within 30 days of it becoming effective if signed in China; within 60 days of it becoming effective if signed abroad.
Effective date of mortgage	Not stated.	Not stated.	Article 22: Date of notarisation if signed in China; date of authentication if signed in foreign country.

APPENDIX 8–2 (cont'd)
A: Comparison of Real Estate Mortgages

	Guangzhou	Beijing	Shanghai
Enforcement of mortgage	Article 37: (1) auction (2) assignment (3) others Article 45: Proceeds for distribution. Article 49: Party at fault to be liable.	Article 26: (1) sale (2) auction (3) other disposal Article 31: Proceeds from disposal. Article 35: Mortgage not valid if not registered.	Article 37: (1) auction (2) assignment Article 55: Distribution of proceeds from disposal. Article 58: Mortgagor liable if property is disposed of without authority.
Legal liability	Article 52: Mortgagor not liable for *force majeure.*	—	Article 60: Mortgagor not liable for *force majeure.*

Source: *China Property Review*, Vol. IV. No. 6, 1995.

B: Comparison of Real Estate Mortgages

Special Economic Zones	Zhuhai	Xiamen	Fujian Province
Legislation	*Zhuhai SEZ, Administration of Real Property Mortgage Procedures,* 13 December 1992 (56 Articles).	*Xiamen SEZ, Land Management Rules,* 28 January 1994 (49 Articles).	*Fujian Province, Mortgage Loans Rules,* 29 December 1992 (63 Articles).

APPENDIX 8–2 (cont'd)
B: Comparison of Real Estate Mortgages

Special Economic Zones	Zhuhai	Xiamen	Fujian Province
Mortgage	Article 43: Real property may be mortgaged. Article 45: Prepurchased property may be mortgaged.	Article 32: Leaseholds plus structures	Article 6 (1)–(9): House, leaseholds, foreign currency, bills of lading, deposit receipts, other property.
Mortgage contract	N/A	Article 32: Written mortgage contract.	Article 22 (1)–(10): Contents listed. Article 23: Insurance by mortgagor.
Registration	N/A	Article 32: Within 15 days from date of signing.	Article 28: Land to be registered with state land bureau; ships with transport department.
Effective date of mortgage	N/A	N/A	N/A
Enforcement of mortgage	Article 47: Property to be disposed of if mortgagor defaults.	Article 33: Terms of mortgage shall not exceed terms of leaseholds.	Article 42: Auction, assignment and sale. Article 46: Treatment of proceeds.
Legal liability	N/A	N/A	Article 50–60: Mortgagor liable. Article 54: Where mortgagor fails to disburse loan as agreed, mortgagee may require early repayment.

Source: *China Property Review*, Vol. IV. No. 6, 1995.

APPENDIX 8–3
Leasehold Terms for Various Land Use in China

Type of Land Use Granted	Maximum Leasehold Term	
	China	Singapore
Residential	70 years	99 years, 999 years* and freehold*
Industrial	50 years	
Educational, Scientific, Technological Cultural, Public Health or Sports	50 years	
Commercial, tourist or recreational	40 years	
Comprehensive development	50 years	

* Lease terms of 999 years and freehold are no longer being given for new land sold by the Singapore government.

APPENDIX 8–4
Supply of Grade "A" Office Space in Shanghai City

Year	Building Name	Developer	Gross Floor Area ('000 square metres)		Accumulated Office Supply ('000 square metres)
			Total Space	Office Space	
Grade A Office Space in Huangpu District					
1985	Union Building	Jin Jiang Group	30	21	
1993	Guang Ming Building	N/A	30	18	
1994	Central Place	Fortune Capital	17	16	

APPENDIX 8–4 (cont'd)
Supply of Grade "A" Office Space in Shanghai City

Year	Building Name	Developer	Gross Floor Area ('000 square metres)		Accumulated Office Supply ('000 square metres)
			Total Space	Office Space	
	JF News Tower	Jie Fang Daily	31	22	77
1995	Manhattan Plaza	Asia Commercial	11	4	
	Shanghai East Ocean Ctr	Winsor, etc.	25	18	
	ChunShen Jiang M.	Shanghai Chunshenjiang	17	11	
	Shen Jin Bldg	Shanghai Ye Jiang	36	30	140
1996	Shanghai Landmark Plaza	HK Radiant	40	2	
	Novel Plaza	Novel Enterprise	28	14	
	Shanghai Business Centre	New Huangpu	28	20	
	Harbour Ring HP Centre	Harbour Ring	13	11	
	Fu Shen Li Building	N/A	42	21	
	New World Complex	N/A	160	48	
	Harbour Ring Plaza	Harbour Ring	57	42	
	Financial Square	Shanghai Jin Shun	29	21	
	Central Plaza	Shun Tax	45	42	361
1997	Shanghai King City	Shanghai Henli	200	116	
	World Trade Tower	Shanghai Chang Xin	47	35	
	No. 53 Jinling Road	Shanghai New Huangpu	24	11	523
1998	DBS Land Complex	DBS Land	98	39	
	Sinar Mas Complex	Sinar Mas	146	73	635

APPENDIX 8–4 (cont'd)
Supply of Grade "A" Office Space in Shanghai City

Year	Building Name	Developer	Gross Floor Area ('000 square metres)		Accumulated Office Supply ('000 square metres)
			Total Space	Office Space	
Grade A Office Space in Lujiazui, Pudong					
1995	Yin Du Building	People's Bank of China	32	22	
	Tomson Fin. Building	Tomson Group	53	27	
	Yu An Mansion	N/A	38	26	75
1996	Shanghai Int'l Fin. Bldg	Wan Guo Securities	100	88	
	China Merchant Tower	China Merchants	58	41	
	Construction Mansion	Construction Bank	67	39	
	Chuan Bo Building	China Shipping	48	37	
	Nextage Shanghai	Yaohan	145	13	
	Suncome Liauw's Mns.	Liauw's Group	47	22	370
1997	New Shanghai Int'l Tower	CITIC, Bank of China	54	35	
	World Finance Building	Shanghai World Constr.	87	57	
	Shanghai World Fin. Ctr.	Forest Overseas	106	60	
	China Insurance Mns.	China Insurance	64	48	
	Union Square	Jin Zhao	90	68	
	C.R. Times Square	China Resources	81	57	695
1998	B O Communications Building	BO Communications	80	56	
	Pudong Int'l Fin. Building	Bank of China	120	90	
	Jin Sui Building	Agricultural Bank	49	26	
	Yuan Dong Building	Industrial Bank of China	42	30	
	Jin Mao Building	N/A	274	112	1,134

APPENDIX 8–4 (cont'd)
Supply of Grade "A" Office Space in Shanghai City

Year	Building Name	Developer	Gross Floor Area ('000 square metres)		Accumulated Office Supply ('000 square metres)
			Total Space	Office Space	
2001	Mori Building	Mori Group	250	125	
Grade A Office Space in Jing'an District					
1990	Shanghai Centre	Kerry, AIG, Kajima, etc.	185	24	24
1995	Universal Mansion	Hong Lung	45	19	43
1996	Pacific Plaza	K. Wah	93	47	
	Shanghai Concord Plaza	Pacific Concord	307	98	
	Jiu An Plaza	N/A	27	–	188
1997	Jing An Centre	Ming Xin	40	10	
	OCBC Centre	OCBC Properties	60	45	
	MeiLongZhen Plaza	Hutchison Wh.	92	40	
	Hang Lung Centre	Hang Lung, CVIC	200	120	
	CITIC/ Swire House	CITIC Pacific, Swire	102	82	
	Henderson Complex	Henderson	75	25	
	Tong Ren Building	Shanghai Four Seasons	12	12	
	New Times Square	Asiatic	15	8	
	Eastlake Building	Fujita Corporation	25	15	545
1998	Shangri-la Centre	Kerry Properties	155	34	
	Lucky Target Square	Lucky Target	70	58	637

N/A - not available

Source: Sanwa Bank, compiled from "Shanghai to See Surge in Office Space", *South China Morning Post*, 8 November 1995.

APPENDIX 8–5
Comparison of Rents and Capital Values Among Major Cities

A: Comparison of Rents and Capital Values for Prime CBD Office Space

City	Annual Net Rents (US$ Per Square Metre)		Capital Values (US$ Per Square Metre)	
	Sept 1995	Sept 1996[F]	Sept 1995	Sept 1996[F]
Bangkok	167 – 238	167 – 238	1,793 – 2,191	1,793 – 2,191
Beijing	777 –1,059	699 – 953	4,400 – 4,900	3,960 – 4,410
Guangzhou	636 – 822	572 – 739	3,096 – 4,008	2,786 – 3,607
Hong Kong	1,072 – 1,462	997 – 1,360	13,624 – 21,501	12,670 – 19,996
Ho Chi Minh City	420 – 600	420 – 540	N/A	N/A
Jakarta	125 – 200	125 – 200	1,900 –2,500	1,850 – 2,500
Kuala Lumpur	173 – 220	173 – 216	2,386 – 2,585	2,307 – 2,505
Shanghai	764 – 1,044	687 – 990	3,420 – 4,400	3,078 – 3,960
Singapore	608 – 734	631 – 773	14,735 – 18,135	14,735 – 18,513
Sydney	179 – 392	212 – 463	2,267 – 6,045	2,645 – 6,422
Tokyo	511 – 1,534	476 – 1,432	16,043 – 38,103	15,041 – 36,097

N/A - not available

[F] Forecast values

Source: Colliers Jardine Research, *Asia Pacific Property Trends Supplement September Quarter 1995 Survey*, November 1995.

APPENDIX 8–5 (cont'd)

B: Comparison of Rents and Capital Values for Prime CBD Retail Space

City	Annual Net Rents (US$ Per Square Metre)		Capital Values (US$ Per Square Metre)	
	Sept 1995	Sept 1996[F]	Sept 1995	Sept 1996[F]
Bangkok	335 – 1,171	335 – 1,171	3,984 – 7,968	3,984 – 7,968
Beijing	2,040 – 3,120	1,836 – 2,886	N/A – 10,450	N/A – 10,450
Guangzhou	1,284 – 3,120	1,156 – 2,808	5,151 – 13,050	4,635 – 11,745
Hong Kong	3,675 – 13,366	3,675 – 12,965	52,688 – 62,266	52,688 – 62,266
Ho Chi Minh City	480 – 720	480 – 720	N/A	N/A
Jakarta	420 – 1,500	480 – 1,800	2,400 – 3,500	2,400 – 3,500
Kuala Lumpur	591 – 1,181	591 – 1,146	6,423 – 13,698	6,423 – 13,005
Shanghai	1,788 – 4,056	1,609 – 3,853	N/A	N/A
Singapore	2,675 – 3,448	2,675 – 3,448	22,669 – 30,225	22,669 – 30,225
Sydney	944 – 1,417	972 – 1,426	25,387 – 30,223	27,201 – 32,490
Tokyo	920 – 1,841	818 – 1,841	20,054 – 35,095	18,049 – 35,095

N/A - not available
[F] Forecast values
Source: Colliers Jardine Research, *Asia Pacific Property Trends Supplement September Quarter 1995 Survey*, November 1995.

APPENDIX 8–5 (cont'd)

C: Comparison of Rents and Capital Values for Prime Industrial Space

City	Annual Net Rents (US$ Per Square Metre)		Capital Values (US$ Per Square Metre)	
	Sept 1995	Sept 1996[F]	Sept 1995	Sept 1996[F]
Bangkok	57 – 96	61 – 102	398 – 717	398 – 717
Beijing	50 – 100	50 – 100	410 – 440	410 – 440
Guangzhou	24 – 60	24 – 60	238 – 383	238 – 383
Hong Kong	197 – 247	207 – 259	2,088 – 2,645	2,088 – 2,645
Ho Chi Minh City	N/A	N/A	N/A	N/A
Jakarta	31 – 100	37 – 111	264 – 450	290 – 510
Kuala Lumpur	70 – 89	72 – 90	716 – 835	716 – 835
Shanghai	40 – 60	40 – 60	236 – 362	236 – 362
Singapore	237 – 275	244 – 284	5,265 – 6,669	5,827 – 6,950
Sydney	76 – 87	79 – 94	642 – 944	680 – 982
Tokyo	304 – 405	253 – 405	4,091 – 5,164	3,880 – 4,913

N/A - not available
[F] Forecast values.
Source: Colliers Jardine Research, *Asia Pacific Property Trends Supplement September Quarter 1995 Survey*, November 1995.

APPENDIX 8–5 (cont'd)

D: Comparison of Rents and Capital Values for Prime Three-bedroom Residential Apartments

City	Annual Net Rents (US$ Per Square Metre)		Capital Values (US$ Per Square Metre)	
	Sept 1995	Sept 1996[F]	Sept 1995	Sept 1996[F]
Bangkok	96 – 153	96 – 153	2,231 – 3,506	2,231 – 3,506
Beijing	720 – 864	684 – 820	3,120 – 3,520	2,964 – 3,344
Guangzhou	168 – 252	151 – 228	1,241 – 1,777	1,116 – 1,599
Hong Kong	489 – 714	489 – 714	9,014 – 10,541	9,014 – 10,541
Ho Chi Minh City	600 – 696	600 – 696	N/A	N/A
Jakarta	176 – 453	149 – 386	1,984 – 3,555	1,786 – 3,199
Kuala Lumpur	134 – 195	121 – 175	1,592 – 2,417	1,496 – 2,272
Shanghai	504 – 768	456 – 684	2,750 – 3,400	2,337 – 2,980
Singapore	223 – 249	223 – 249	5,616 – 6,178	5,616 – 6,178
Sydney	123 – 213	126 – 227	2,342 – 4,836	2,418 – 4,987
Tokyo	303 – 967	287 – 919	7,320 – 14,038	7,320 – 14,038

N/A - not available

[F] Forecast values

Source: Colliers Jardine Research, *Asia Pacific Property Trends Supplement September Quarter 1995 Survey*, November 1995.

APPENDIX 8–6
Real Estate Value Added Tax: A Summary

On 27 January 1995, the long awaited implementation rules for the real estate value added tax were released by the Chinese authorities, providing a number of clarifications concerning how the value added tax is to be implemented. The basic unit to be considered in the evaluation of real estate value added tax is the cost of real property. All work units and individuals who derive revenue from the assignment of land use rights in state-owned land, and the structures on such land or other attachments, are subject to payment of this tax. This value added tax is commonly known as a capital gains tax. This tax is levied in accordance with the value added as a result of the transfer of real estate at the following progressive tax rates:

Scope	Rate
On that part of increased value that does not exceed permissible deductions by 50%	30 %
On that part of increased value that exceeds permissible deductions by 50% but less than 100%	40 %
On that part of increased value that exceeds permissible deductions by 100% but less than 200%	50 %
On that part of increased value that exceeds permissible deductions by 200%	60 %

To compute the capital gains tax in real estate investment, investors can deduct the following expenses:

(i) expenses incurred for obtaining land use rights;
(ii) land development cost;
(iii) cost of constructing new buildings or valuation of old buildings;
(iv) tax in connection with the resale of property; and
(v) other deductions determined by the Ministry of Finance.

Capital gain is determined by reducing income by the allowable expenses from the assignment of the property. In the case of individuals, the rules provide for exemption from, or reduction, of this tax, depending on the length of residence in their residential accommodation.[12] Any

[12] Article 12 of *Implementing Rules for the Real Estate Value Added Tax.*

individual who, as a result of changing his place of work or in order to improve his living conditions, assigns residential accommodation that is used by himself, will be exempted from the tax if he has lived in the original accommodation for five or more years. When he has resided in such accommodation for three or more years, but less than five years, the tax will be reduced by 50%. Where revenue is derived in a foreign currency, the amount of the proceeds will be converted into renminbi on the basis of the market rate on which the revenue is received, or on the first day of the month in which it is received, and the amount of tax calculated on the basis of the converted amount.[13]

In addition, the following categories of the real estate transactions are exempted from tax under the implementing rules:

(i) the transfer of real property without consideration such as by way of succession or by way of gift;
(ii) relocation of property by means of sale either due to appropriation by the government or for any other reasons, provided the taxpayer has lived there for more than five years and;
(iii) construction of ordinary standard residential buildings for sale, of which the amount of capital gains does not exceed 20% of the applicable deductions.
(iv) The Ministry of Finance also has issued a tax circular relating to agreements on property development or transfer made prior to 1 January 1994. These agreements may qualify for tax exemptions in the following situations:
    (a) property transfer agreements if made prior to 1 January 1994, regardless of the time of actual transfer,
    (b) in the case of property development agreements made prior to 1 January 1994, or where the capital had already been injected prior to the commencement of the development project prior to 1 January 1994 in accordance with the applicable law, any transfer of the developed property for the first time within a period of five years from 1 January 1994, shall be exempted from this tax. The date for determination is the date the transfer agreement is made.

---

[13] Article 20 of *Implementing Rules for the Real Estate Value Added Tax.*

APPENDIX 8–7
Taxation of Real Property Development in Shanghai

Type of Taxation	Tax Rate	Applies to	Taxable Standard	Taxpayer
Business Tax	5%	Selling of property building and attached structure.	Purchasing income.	Vendor
	5%	Transfer of land use rights.	Transfer income.	Vendor
	5%	Rental.	Rental income.	Vendor
	5%	Agency services.	Serving fee.	Agent
Urban Property	1.2%	Self-occupation.	Capital value of the property.	Property owner
	12%	Rental.	Rental income.	
Stamp Duty	0.3%	Transfer of building and attached structure.	Transaction value of property.	Contracting parties
	0.5%	Construction project's contract for survey and design.	Contract value.	
	0.3%	Construction and installation contract.	Contract value.	
	0.3%	Purchasing agreement.	Contract value.	
	0.5%	Property transfer.	Transaction value of property.	
	0.05%	Contract for loans.	Contract value.	
	1%	Contract for leasing.	Contract value.	
Use of Farm Land Tax	RMB 3–10 psm	Development not for agricultural purposes.	Occupation of the agricultural land.	Land-user
Land Use Tax	RMB 0.5–0.75 psm pa	Land used by enterprises.	Area of occupation.	Land-user
Enterprise Income Tax	33%	Income from real property business.	Profit before tax.	Enterprise

APPENDIX 8–7 (cont'd)

Type of Taxation	Tax Rate	Applies to	Taxable Standard	Taxpayer
Deed Tax	6% 3% 6% 6% 6% 3%	Private treaty. Property mortgage. Free gift. Commodity property for overseas sale. Overseas purchaser and enterprise. Overseas Chinese purchasing with foreign currency.	Transaction value. Value of mortgage. Existing value by valuation. Transaction value. Transaction value. Transaction value.	Purchaser Mortgagee Donee Purchaser Purchaser Purchaser
Land Value Added Tax	30% to 60%	Transfer of land use rights and attached building.	Amount of capital gains. 1) 30% for capital gains not exceeding 50% of the allowance. 2) 40% for capital gains between 50%-100% of the allowance. 3) 50% for capital gains between 100%-200% of the allowance. 4) 60% for capital gains in excess of 200% of the allowance.	Vendor
Urban Maintenance & Construction Tax	7% 5% 1%	Urban area. County and province. Village.	Amount of business tax.	Taxpayer of business tax
Additional Tax for City Education	3%	Urban area, county, province and village.	Amount of business tax.	Taxpayer of business tax

APPENDIX 8–7 (cont'd)

Type of Taxation	Tax Rate	Applies to	Taxable Standard	Taxpayer
Rents	RMB 0.015–0.06 psm pa	Private land for housing in city and town.	Occupied area.	Land-user
Recovering Land Use Tax	RMB 5000 per mu.	Land used for construction in village.	Occupied area.	Occupier
Land Use Fee	RMB 0.5–1.30 psm pa RMB 1 psm	Land used by overseas investor (excluding real property project). Land sales.	Occupied area. Area of vending (RMB 1000 minimum).	Land-user Purchaser
Land Surveying Fee	RMB 560	Land survey and red-line mapping.	RMB 560 per case.	Land-user
Operational Fee for Temporary Re-sumption.	RMB 0.2–5.2 psm per month	Temporary use of land.	Occupied area.	Land-user
Development Fund for Arable Land	RMB 18–30 ('000) per mu	"Use of non-protective arable land, arable land" and major landscaped state-owned land.	Occupied area.	Land-user
Operational Fee for State-owned Land Use	RMB 0.25–1 psm	Excluding city and town.	Occupied area.	Land-user
Land Valuation Fee	1%	Valuation of land.	Capital value of land.	Instructor

APPENDIX 8–7 (cont'd)

Type of Taxation	Tax Rate	Applies to	Taxable Standard	Taxpayer
Registration of Real Property Fee	RMB 50–500	Registration of transfer of land use rights, land use contract certificate, selling of property, pre-sale certificate.	Value of transaction.	Registered owner
Land Use Certificate Fee	RMB 5–20	Collection of land use right certification.	RMB 5-20 per case.	Collector
Exceeding Tender Fee for Private Sales Property	20% 5%	Over 200% in excess of the valuation purchased by organisation. Over 200% in excess of the valuation of the selling price of the property purchased by person.	Amount exceeding valuation of the selling price of the property. Amount exceeding valuation.	Vendor Vendor
Registration Fee of Real Property Ownership Right	RMB 0.25 psm	Registration of the real property ownership right.	Registered gross floor area of the property.	The holder of right to the property
Measurement Registration Fee of the Property	RMB 0.05 psm	Measurement of the property.	Measurement of gross floor area of the property.	Trustee
Valuation Fee of Property	1%	Valuation of the property.	Value of property RMB 10 minimum.	Trustee
Handling Fee for Transfer of Property	1%	Transaction of commodity property. Purchasing of overseas commodity property and high standard domestic commodity property. Inheritance of property.	Transaction value. Purchasing price. Value of valuation.	Both parties Purchaser Inheritor

APPENDIX 8–7 (cont'd)

Type of Taxation	Tax Rate	Applies to	Taxable Standard	Taxpayer
Handling Fee for Transfer of Property (cont'd)		Property as gift. Property as gift.	Value of valuation. Value of property.	Donee Prize winner
Certificate of Property Ownership Fee	RMB 5	Collection of certificate of ownership.	RMB 5 per case.	Registered owner
Registration Fee for Newly Commodity Property	RMB 3	Collection of certificate for new commodity property.	RMB 3 per case.	Registered owner
Handling Fee for Commodity Property	0.8%	Transaction of standard domestic commodity property.	Amount of transaction stated in contract.	Both parties
Registration Fee for New Commodity Property	RMB 0.125 psm RMB 0.25 psm	Registration for newly built commodity. Registration for newly built commodity non-domestic property.	Registered gross floor area.	Developer

psm : per square metre
pa : per annum
mu : metre used
Source: The PRC Property Series. Volume I: Shanghai: 4–5.

APPENDIX 8–8
Glossary

Capital value: The value of a fully leased property under prevailing market conditions.

Rents: Unless otherwise stated, rents refer to the rate at which vacant floorspace would be leased in a prevailing market, excluding maintenance, management, power, other operating expenses, real estate taxes, statutory charges and other outgoings (for net rents). They are not adjusted to take into account incentives.

Definition of premium and grade "A" office space:

	Premium Offices	**Grade "A" Offices**
Location and Size	Core of office district greater than 20,000 square metres net lettable area.	Anywhere in the office district greater than 6,000 square metres net lettable area.
Floor Plate	Greater than 1,100 square metres largely column free.	Greater than 600 square metres largely column free.
Age, Services, Finish	Top quality modern space which is generally a pace setter in establishing rents and includes: the latest or a recent generation of building services; ample natural lighting; good views/outlook; prestige lobby finish; and quality access to/from an attractive street environment.	High quality modern space including: ample natural lighting; good views/outlook; prestige lobby finish; and quality access to/from an attractive street environment.

REFERENCES

"China's Growth Set to Remain Steady at 9% a Year", *The Business Times*, 17 November 1995.

"China: Broad Tariff Cuts Will Offset Tax on Machinery", *The Business Times,* 22 November 1995.

"Foreign Investors in China May Lose Some Tax Perks", *The Business Times,* 28 November 1995.

"Investment in Pudong Jumps 20% to US$13b", *The Business Times,* 24

November 1995.
"MNCs to Help Shanghai to Become Financial Centre", *The Business Times*, 27 October 1995.
"Modernised Shanghai Will Emerge by 2020", *Bangkok Post*, 26 October 1995.
"New Implementing Rules for Land Capital Gains Tax", *China Trade Review,* Ashton–Brooke Asia Publishing Ltd. Vol. 2, No. 2, 1995, pp. 1–3.
"Reduced Tariffs Rates", *China Trade Review,* Ashton–Brooke Asia Publishing Ltd. Vol. 2, No. 2, 1995, pp. 5–7.
"Tax-Free Equipment Imports to be Stopped", *The Business Times*, 1 November 1995.
Asiamoney, September 1994, pp. 45–9.
Chan, E., "Shanghai to See Surge in Office Space", *South China Morning Post*, 8 November 1995.
Chan, V. and, R. Bowker, "PRC Bankruptcy Developments: Law, Policy and the Foreign Investor", *China Law Briefing*, Vol. 1, No. 4, 1995, pp. 8–11.
Chen, Q. and W. Shi, "Re-establishing Shanghai as an International Financial Center", *Beijing Review*, August 15–21, 1994, pp. 14–7.
Clayton, D., "Chartered in Pudong Talks", *South China Morning Post*, 28 October 1995.
Colliers Jardine Research, *Asia Pacific Property Trend*, July 1995.
Colliers Jardine Research, *Asia Pacific Property Trends Supplement September Quarter 1995 Survey*, November 1995.
Jones Lang Wootton Research and Consultancy, *Asia Pacific Property Digest: The Market as at October 1995*, 1995.
Leung, J., "Beijing Stifles Shanghai Dream", *Asian Business*, October 1995, pp. 24–8.
Lu, N. "How Tax Changes Will Affect Foreign Firms in China". *The Business Times*, 6 November 1995.
Pudong Academy of Development, *Report on Development of Pudong 1991–94*, Shanghai People's Publishing House, 1995.
Shanghai Foreign Investment Commission, *Brief Guide of Shanghai Investment*, 1993.
Shanghai Pudong New Area Administrative Committee, *Shanghai Pudong New Area Real Estate 1994,* 1995.
Shanghai Pudong New Area Administrative Committee, *Shanghai Pudong New Area*, 1995.

Tam, W., "Taxation of Foreign Companies Undertaking Construction Projects in China", *China Trade Review*, Vol. 1, No. 9, 1995, pp. 1–3.

Tan, T.H., "Tax Changes May Hurt Beijing's Competitiveness", *The Straits Times*, 6 November 1995.

Walker, T., "Beijing to Keep Tight Grip on Money Policy", *Financial Times,* 11 October 1995.

Wu, Y.W., "The PRC Property Series Vol. I: Shanghai", *Asia Law and Practice*, 1995.

Xu, K., "Shanghai, A City Marching Towards the 21st Century", A public speech given in Singapore in August 1994.

Yang Mu, John J. Williams and Cao Yong, "Resurrecting Shanghai for the 21st Century: The Shift in China's Regional Economic Strategies", *China Business Review*, December 1995.

Yip, K.B., "Governing Mortgage Law Issues Need Careful Attention", *China Property Review*, Vol. IV, No. 6, 1995, pp. 1–6.

Chapter 9

The Yangtze Tourism Delta*

BY
CHOY Kum Luen
LAM Mun Wai
Evelyn LIM
LIM Mui Huang

INTRODUCTION

CHINA'S POPULATION OF more than 1.2 billion means that it has the world's greatest potential for domestic and outbound travel. With its double digit economic growth since 1992, it will definitely be a force to contend with in the next decade.

This chapter presents an overview of the tourism industry in Shanghai and Jiangsu. The focus is on tourism investment opportunities and how Shanghai, Suzhou and Nanjing could synergise their tourism efforts. These three cities located along the lower reaches of the Yangtze river are referred to as the Yangtze Tourism Delta. They form the apexes of a triangle or delta. The information contained in this chapter is culled from published material, interviews and data provided by interviewees.

* We are grateful to Dr. Choo Teck Min, Dr. Cao Yong, the Singapore Tourist Promotion Board in Shanghai, the Jiangsu Provincial Travel and Tourism Administrative Bureau, the Hilton in Shanghai and the Shanghai Municipal Tourism Administration for providing us with information and assistance in compiling this chapter.

BACKGROUND

Administration of the Industry

Tourism in China is overseen by the China National Tourism Administration (CNTA), formerly known as the Travel and Tourism Bureau. Set up in 1964, the bureau was created as a policy making body to direct and control two travel agencies, both headquartered in Beijing and having provincial branches. One was the China Travel Service (CTS) created in 1949 for ethnic Chinese visitors; the other was the China International Travel Service (CITS) created in 1954 for non-Chinese. Business travellers and trade delegations came to China through the relevant trade bureaux, and sports delegations were handled by the relevant state associations.

In 1984, the CNTA was charged with defining the overall travel and tourism policy for the country and then overseeing its implementation. The CNTA, today, has ten departments: general administration; policy and law; planning and statistics; resource development; travel companies and hotel management; general business; marketing and promotion; finance and foreign currency control; personnel, labour and education; and international liaison. Transport (aviation, rail and road) does not come under CNTA control. CNTA officials say that their inability to control this sector is the major problem in their task of coordinating China's travel industry.[1] (However, few national tourist offices in other countries have this control either).

Travel Agencies

Travel agencies in China are licensed according to three categories. Category A ("Grade A" or "first category") agencies can negotiate business with foreign tour operators directly and can handle foreign visitors, overseas Chinese and compatriots. They can also accept foreign currencies and issue visas. Category B agencies cannot conduct business with foreign tour operators directly but can handle foreign visitors, overseas Chinese and compatriots for Category A agencies. Category C agencies can only handle domestic travel by Chinese citizens. Appendix 9–1 enumerates travel agencies by region and category for 1993 and 1994. The big three agencies – China Travel Service, China International

---

1 Economist Intelligence Unit (EIU), *International Tourism Reports,* No. 1, 1995.

Travel Service and China Youth Travel Service – handle more than half of the visitors who use travel agencies[2] in China (see Appendix 9–2).

Category distinctions started to fade from 1991 following the government's strong emphasis on economic growth. Deng Xiaoping's famous saying, "it does not matter if the cat is black or white, as long as it catches mice", was applied to travel agencies. It does not matter what kind of travel agency it is, so long as it "catches" the tourist.

Accommodation

The accommodation sector has shown the greatest improvement, in both quality and quantity, of all the travel industry sectors in China over the last decade. The recovery of inbound business to China after 1990 increased the occupancy and operating revenue of hotels and led to near boom conditions in many centres from 1991 onwards. More information on the accommodation sector is found in Appendix 9–3, "Number of Star-Rated Hotels, 1994"; Appendix 9–4 "Number of Hotels by Economic Type And Capacity, 1994"; and Appendix 9–5 "Number of Hotels, Rooms and Occupancy Rates: 1994".

Travel Restrictions

Access to points in China has widened. In 1982, there were 122 cities or areas open to foreign visitors, but only 30 could be visited without a travel permit. By 1984, there were 148 open cities; by 1990, more than 500 and by 1994, there were 1,068 open cities and areas.

Riots in Tibet in 1987 and 1988 led to restrictions on visits to Tibet. Following further riots in 1989, martial law was imposed in Tibet between March and May 1990. Martial law was also imposed in Beijing, just before the Tiananmen Square incident in June 1989. It was lifted in January 1990.

There have been restrictions on travel from many Asian countries; but these have been steadily lifted, particularly since 1988 and most notably on Taiwanese visitors. In 1987, the Taiwanese government lifted the travel ban on visits to China by its citizens. Malaysia lifted restrictions on its nationals travelling to China in 1990, and Indonesia in 1994.

---

2 EIU, *International Tourism Reports,* No. 1, 1995.

Visits and Receipts

International arrivals in China were a staggering 43.7 million in 1994 (Appendix 9–6). This makes China the world's third most popular destination, after France and the U.S.A. China's total is double the combined number of arrivals in Hawaii, Hong Kong, Singapore and Thailand; the four "biggest" destinations in the Asia-Pacific region. Of the 43.685 million international visitors to China, 5.1821 million were foreigners, 0.1152 million were overseas Chinese, 36.9969 million were from Hong Kong and Macau, and 1.3902 million were from Taiwan. Total receipts from international tourism amounted to US$7.322 billion. Appendix 9–7 shows a breakdown of arrivals from the top tourism generating countries to China.

While international tourism is growing at a steady pace, domestic tourism is developing even faster. The total number of domestic trips in 1994 was 524 million, of which 205 million were by urban residents and 319 million by rural residents. Total revenue generated from domestic tourism was RMB 102.351 billion (approximately US$12.6 billion).

Travel Patterns

The travel patterns of CTS clients give some indication of tourist preferences.[3] CTS's most popular tour routes for long haul markets cover the east of China, namely Beijing, Shanghai, Suzhou (for traditional Chinese gardens), Wuxi (for its lake and picturesque canals) and Hangzhou (a scenic city, known for its West Lake). Tours to Guangzhou and Guilin (China's best known natural beauty spot) are also popular. There is less interest in Xian, the ancient capital of China known primarily for its Qin Dynasty terracotta army. However, this is a popular destination for CITS's foreign clients. CITS's most popular itineraries include Beijing, Xian, Shanghai, Guilin and Guangzhou, with Suzhou, Wuxi or Hangzhou and, sometimes, Nanjing.

For Americans, a Yangtze river cruise, first available in 1982, and since 1994 operated by several new companies, has become increasingly popular. Japanese favour the same spots, but there is greater interest in Confucius's birthplace and the ancient cities of Luoyang and Datong. Appendix 9–8 shows foreign visitor arrivals by city, for the period 1989 to 1993. Arrivals by province in 1994 are shown in Appendix 9–9.

---

3 EIU, *International Tourism Reports*, No. 1, 1995.

CHINA'S TOURISM DEVELOPMENT PLANS: 1996 TO 2000[4]

Growth Targets

During the Ninth Five-Year Plan (1996 to 2000), the goals of the Chinese tourism industry are: an annual growth rate of 8 to 9%, or 8.1 to 8.8 million more foreign visitors a year; an annual growth rate of 7 to 9%, or 11.2 to 12.3 million in the number of organised overseas tourists; and an annual growth rate of 12 to 14%, or 1.02 to 1.12 billion, in the number of domestic tourists. Total tourism income is targeted to increase from RMB 340 to RMB 370 billion (US$45.5 billion), at an annual growth rate of 13 to 15%. Of this total, the overseas visitor receipts will reach US$13 to 14 billion at a growth rate of 10 to 12% per annum and receipts from domestic tourism will reach RMB 223 to RMB 244 billion (US$30 billion), at a growth rate of 14 to 16% per annum.

Development Plans

To realise these targets, China will continue to improve its tourism infrastructure.

(i) ***Accommodation:*** More accommodation facilities will be built in key cities, newly opened zones and new, popular scenic spots. Hotel construction will be controlled in areas where there is already sufficient supply. No construction will be approved in areas with an average occupancy of less than 60%.

Renovation of old hotels, especially the upgrading of one- and two-star hotels, will continue. Hotels for foreign tourists will number approximately 4,000 by the year 2000. Half of the added rooms will be in one- and two-star hotels, to meet domestic demand. Tourist hotels will be encouraged to expand their catering facilities for both guests and local diners.

(ii) ***Attractions:*** The environment of tourist sites will be improved. Guidance will be given on the construction and development of new scenic areas. Attention will be paid to the development of tourist facilities in areas close to cities to meet the growing demand of urban people on weekends. More man-made attractions that provide knowledge and participation opportunities for visitors will be built.

---

4 *Travel China*, Vol. 7, No. 19, 15 to 20 October 1995.

The development plan aims to increase the share of tourist spending on shopping from 20% in 1994 to 25% by the year 2000. Hence, emphasis will be given to improving consumer goods. Under the plan, 200 more enterprises producing tourist commodities will be approved bringing the total number of such enterprises in the country to 500.

The entertainment sector is targeted to contribute at least 5% of the country's tourism earnings. To this end, every tourist city will be required to have at least one medium-sized, or larger, facility for night entertainment, and every key scenic spot will have at least one facility for hosting day time performances.

(iii) ***Investment Opportunities:*** Foreign capital has played a very important role in the rapid development of China's tourism industry. In recognition of this, and to open itself more broadly to foreign investment, the state council, in August 1992, established the first 11 national tourism zones. These are:

(a) Jinshitan, Dalian, Liaoning province.
(b) Shilaoran, Qingdao, Shandong province.
(c) Taihu Lake, Jiangsu province.
(d) Sheshan National Tourism Holiday Resort, Shanghai.
(e) Zhijiang, Hangzhou, Zhejiang province.
(f) Wuyi Mountains, Fujian province.
(g) Meizhou Island, Fujian province.
(h) Nanhu Lake, Guangzhou, Guangdong province.
(i) Yintan, Beihai, Guangxi province.
(j) Dianchi Lake, Kunming, Yunnan province.
(k) Yalong Bay, Sanya, Hainan province.

Tourism investments in these zones will enjoy preferential policies. For instance, foreign-funded enterprises will have a 24% reduction in income tax. Enterprises with a contract period of more than ten years will be exempt from enterprise income tax in the first and second profitable years, and enjoy a 50% reduction in the third, fourth and fifth years.

Foreign funded enterprises in national holiday resorts, as designated by provincial governments, will be exempt from customs duties and consolidated industrial and commercial taxes on building materials, production management, transport and office equipment. This exemption will also apply to imported personal effects and transport used by foreign workers and employees, up to certain limits.

Raw materials, spare parts, machine components and fittings, subsidiary materials and packing materials, which enterprises import to produce touristic commodities for export, will be handled as bonded goods. Sino-foreign joint ventures with category A travel agencies will be allowed to establish locations in the national holiday resorts to handle overseas tourists. Joint venture bus/taxi companies using Chinese-made vehicles will be permitted in these resorts. Foreign currency shops will also be allowed.

Visit China Year 1997

The importance of tourism was emphasised during the 13th National Congress of the Communist Party in 1987, at which it was said that more should be done to expand the tourism industry so as to increase foreign exchange earnings. Several activities have since resulted, such as Visit China Year 1992, China Water and Mountain Tours 1993, China Heritage 1994 and China Folklore 1995. The promotion of China as a resort destination, under the banner "China Resort Holiday 1996" is a major objective for 1996. This will lay the foundation for "Visit China Year 1997".

SHANGHAI

Shanghai, often known as the "Paris of the East", has the appeal of a vibrant, exciting and lively modern city, combined with a unique architectural heritage. It has good communication facilities, and a transportation network which links it with all major cities in China and several foreign capitals. It is the centre of modernisation in China and, as such, is a major attraction to tourists, particularly domestic tourists.

Visits and Receipts

With 1,321,824 overseas visitors in 1994,[5] Shanghai ranked third in China as a tourist destination, after Guangdong and Beijing. Visitor arrivals have

---

5 Statistics Report on China's Tourism Industry in 1994.

grown annually at 10.81% since 1991.[6] It is estimated that on average three million people pass through Shanghai everyday.[7] Most domestic tourists come to Shanghai on group tours to experience modern city life, visit relatives, attend meetings or as part of staff benefits offered by trade unions.[8]

In 1994, 1.66 million trips were made by Shanghainese. This figure, for the first ten months of 1995 was already 1.76 million.[9] Most Shanghainese make short trips to neighbouring cities such as Suzhou, Hangzhou, Wuxi and Nanjing, on holiday or to visit relatives.

In terms of domestic and foreign tourism receipts, Shanghai received US$850 million in 1994,[10] third after Guangdong and Beijing. Accommodation (40.2%), long distance transportation (19.2%), food (13.4%) and shopping (13.4%) accounted for most of the receipts. Sightseeing, entertainment and communications accounted for 1.9, 5.8 and 4.6%, respectively. Average expenditure per overseas visitor was US$643 in 1994. The average length of stay was 3.6 days.

Major sources were non-Chinese foreigners (77.1%), Hong Kong and Macau Chinese (11.8%), Taiwan Chinese (3.8%) and overseas Chinese (1.3%). In 1993, Taiwan Chinese accounted for 17.2% of the market. Numbers dipped in 1994 while foreigners increased by 19.57%.

Of the foreigners, Japanese accounted for the majority (48%) followed by Koreans (9.2%), Americans (8.8%), French (4%), Germans (3.4%), Singaporeans (3.1%), Filipinos (2.8%) and others (20.6%). About 43% were on group tours. However, it is observed by the industry,[11] as well as by the Shanghai Tourism Bureau, that the trend is towards independent travel (FIT). In 1994, the number of FITs was 759,100, an increase of 21.26% over 1993.[12] It is also estimated that the majority of these FITs are business travellers.

---

6 *Shanghai Tourism Today*, brochure by the Shanghai Tourism Bureau, 1995.

7 Interview with Mr. Huang Guang Rong, the Deputy Director, Travel Agency and Hotel Management Department, Shanghai Municipal Tourism Administration in December 1995.

8 Interview with Mr. Huang Guang Rong, the Deputy Director, Travel Agency and Hotel Management Department, Shanghai Municipal Tourism Administration.

9 Interview with Mr. Huang Guang Rong, the Deputy Director, Travel Agency and Hotel Management Department, Shanghai Municipal Tourism Administration.

10 *Shanghai Tourism Today*, brochure by the Shanghai Tourism Bureau, 1995.

11 Interview with Mr. David Wang, Director of Sales and Marketing, Hilton Hotel, Shanghai in December 1995.

12 *Tourism Times*, a publication by the Shanghai Tourism Bureau, 19 February 1995.

Accommodation in Shanghai

Shanghai has 111 tourist hotels (out of 2,995 in all of China), with more than 28,000 rooms.[13] The occupancy rate was about 70.89% in 1994. Twenty-two of the top (in terms of turnover) 50 travel agencies in China are based in Shanghai.[14] Shanghai can be reached by air, rail, land and sea. Shanghai is linked by 170 domestic and more than 20 international air routes making it a convenient gateway to the rest of China, as well as the "Eastern Door" of China to the outside world.

Pudong, the new business metropolis in Shanghai, deserves special mention here. The development of Pudong has been rapid since it began in 1989. By the beginning of the next century, it will have an up-to-date infrastructure, a comprehensive free trade zone, an advanced export processing base and a high class residential area. Besides recreational tourism, "business trip tourism" is being developed in Pudong to take advantage of the large number of businessmen who come to Pudong to conduct business feasibility studies.

Attractions in Shanghai

Major attractions include the world-renowned Bund, the Jade Buddha temple, the Temple of the Town Gods, the Mandarin Gardens, Dr. Sun Yat-Sen's Residence, a Huangpu cruise, the Shanghai Exhibition Centre, Lu Xun's (the writer) residence and memorial, the Yangpu and Nanpu bridges (the world's second and third longest suspension bridges) and the Oriental Pearl TV and Radio Tower (the tallest in Asia, located in Pudong) among others.

Shanghai has two major shopping belts located on Huaihai Road and Nanking Road. The former is more upmarket, while the latter is visited mostly by locals. Shanghai is known for the wide selection, quality and reasonable prices of its consumer goods, compared to other provinces in China. Shanghainese believe Shanghai quality is the best.[15]

Tourism Plans for Shanghai

Shanghai has been known to the world as an important commercial and

---

13 *Shanghai Tourism Today*, brochure by the Shanghai Tourism Bureau, 1995.

14 Interview with Mr. Huang Guang Rong, the Deputy Director, Travel Agency and Hotel Management Department, Shanghai Municipal Tourism Administration.

15 Interview with Mr. Huang Guang Rong, the Deputy Director, Travel Agency and Hotel Management Department, Shanghai Municipal Tourism Administration.

industrial centre. Today, two important pillars in Shanghai's economy are the financial and property sectors. Tourism is gaining recognition and is now regarded as the third pillar.

To add to its urban attractions, Shanghai is busy developing recreational facilities. One such development is the Sun Island Holiday Resort,[16] where work began in August 1995. Located in Qingpu county, 30 minutes' drive from Hongqiao International Airport, it will offer villas, a golf course, horse paddock, archery field, indoor and outdoor swimming pools, bowling lanes, tennis courts, a health club, sauna and KTV facilities. There will also be convention and exhibition halls.

Another recently announced project is the Sheshan National Tourism Holiday Resort.[17] Situated in Songjiang county, which has the only mountain forest in the Shanghai region, Sheshan already has a number of recreation centres and has developed forest tours which attract two million domestic and foreign tourists a year. Plans are being prepared to solicit overseas investment in future resorts.

JIANGSU PROVINCE

Jiangsu province is one of the fastest growing provinces in China, with a land area of 100,000 square kilometres and a population of 70 million. Located along the south-east coastline of China, it has been a tourism resort area since ancient times. The province has many well-known tourist cities, each with distinctive features. These include the historic sites in Nanjing; the classical gardens of Suzhou; scenic Taihu in Wuxi; the cultural city of Yangzhou; the hills, forests, temples and monasteries in Zhenjiang; pottery, caverns, sea of bamboo and tea plantations in Yixing; the ruins of the ancient town of Yancheng in Changzhou; the cultural relics of the Han Dynasties in Xuzhou; the famous historic sites on the Yellow Sea in Lianyungang; scenic spots, skirted by rivers and sea, in Nantong; the famous hills and ancient temples in Changshu; rare animals in Yancheng; the endless plain fields in Huaiyin; and the former abodes of the celebrities in Huai'an. These attractions make up a combination which no other province can match.

---

16 *Culture and Recreation*, a publication by the Shanghai Jin Jiang (Group) Holding Co., 17 December 1995.

17 *Welcome to China, Shanghai*, Vol. 5, Issue No. 5, a publication endorsed by the Shanghai Municipal Tourism Administration, 1995.

Jiangsu's tourism resources are immense, with 346 cultural conservation sites, 75 museums with 800,000 artefacts, four national tourist attractions, nine state attractions, three national gardens, five provincial nature reserves, two national wildlife reserves, seven historic and cultural towns, two national holiday villages, four provincial holiday villages and 10,000 small scenic spots.

There is also tremendous potential in the archaeological sites being discovered in the province. For instance, a Tang Dynasty site is being excavated. In Xuzhou, the terracotta statues are even older than those in Xian. In Xuyi, the largest tomb ever discovered from the Ming Dynasty awaits excavation. An estimated RMB 50 million (US$6.2 million) is needed for the project and it promises to be the best archaeological site in China. Jiangsu has the added advantage of proximity to neighbouring provinces with many scenic spots, such as Hangzhou, the capital of Zhejiang province, and Huangshan.

Nanjing has good transport connections. There are twice daily flights between Nanjing and Hong Kong and three flights a day to Beijing. There are airports in Changzhou, Nantong, Xuzhou and Lianyungang, Changzhou and in Wuxian county, with services to major tourist cities in China. A new international airport is planned for Nanjing, with the first phase scheduled for 1997 and completion in 1998.

Road and rail traffic are heavy in Jiangsu. The Beijing-Shanghai, Shanghai-Nanjing and Lianyungang-Lanzhou trunk railways link the tourist cities within the province. Two double-decked, air-conditioned tourist trains run every day between Nanjing and Shanghai. Highways in Jiangsu radiate in all directions with Nanjing as the centre. Shanghai-Nanjing State Highway 312, Nanjing-Nantong and Nanjing-Lianyungang first-grade highways are open, and the Nanjing-Shanghai Expressway will be completed by October 1996.

A new road bridge is being constructed across the Yangtze river at Jiangying. The Yangtze river, which runs for 390 kilometres through the province from the west to the east, is both an important commercial waterway and, also, an exceptionally interesting water cruise route. At present, there are three deluxe pleasure boats and two hydrofoils offering tourist services.

Visits and Receipts

Tourism in Jiangsu has developed significantly in the last few years.

With 40.9 million domestic and foreign tourist arrivals it ranks as the fifth most popular region in China. Tourism domestic and foreign receipts amounted to RMB 10.8 billion (US$1.3 billion) in 1994, representing an 11% increase over the previous year;[18] again making it fifth, in terms of receipts. Domestic tourism receipts were RMB 200 million (US$24.6 million) in 1994, an increase of 100% over 1993.

Tourism Business

There are 700 tourism enterprises in Jiangsu, including 14 Category A, 47 Category B and 117 Category C travel agencies, 29 tourist factories, and 212 hotels with 20,500 rooms, most of which are small and medium-sized establishments as of December 1995. Hotels with three stars or more number 54. Ten universities offer tourism courses. An estimated 50,000 people work in the tourism industry.[19]

Attractions

Jiangsu has an age-old tradition of producing world famous arts and crafts from each of its cities. Nanjing has its rain flower pebbles, cloud brocade, velvet tapestry, rain flower tea, pressed and salted duck and salted duck gizzard. Suzhou is renowned for its embroidery, sandalwood fans, woodcut New Year's pictures, mahogany furniture and Biluochun tea. Yangzhou has its lacquerware, jade carvings, Yangzhou pickles, Gaoyou salted duck eggs and Jingjiang dried pork. Zhenjiang produces table screens made of white marble, artistic lanterns, table rubbings, traditional Chinese medicine plasters, fragrant vinegar and refined sesame oil. Changshu has its drawn work, green hair turtles and *ormosia* (love pea). Wuxi produces clay figurines, pearls, Wuxi spare ribs, oil gluten and silk cream. Yixing is known for its purple sand pottery, Jun-style pottery, and lily designs. Changzhou makes double-edged and fine-toothed combs and bamboo carvings. Nantong has its tie-dying cloth, indigo printed cloth, kites, Ji Desheng antidote for snake poison and Rugao ham. Deep-fried noodles and straw-woven articles are Huai'an's specialities, while Lianyungang has its shell mosaic pictures and crystal decorations. Finally, Xuzhou is famous for its winter peaches, dehydrated pteridophyte seedlings, crunchy candies and haw jelly and juice.

---

[18] Jiangsu Provincial Travel and Tourism Bureau.
[19] Jiangsu Provincial Travel and Tourism Bureau.

Jiangsu cuisine may not be as well known as that of Guangzhou, in the south, but its Huaiyang cuisine enjoys a higher ranking in China. In recent years, hotels have promoted menus of famous banquets comprising newly created dishes such as Duck banquet in Nanjing, Red Mansion banquet, Qiong Flower banquet and Triple-Head banquet in Yangzhou, and Royal Court banquet of Emperor Qianlong in Zhenjiang, and so forth. Changzhou has applied the principles of traditional dietotherapy to a series of anti-ageing, brain-nourishing, skin-hydrating and anti-cancer meals. Suzhou and Wuxi promote boat dishes. Others include the Eight Immortals banquet in Nantong, Pengzu banquet in Xuzhou and seafood in Lianyungang. These present a great opportunity for gourmet food tours in Jiangsu.

Jiangsu's Tourism Development Plan

Currently, there are three economic technological development zones (Lianyungang, Nantong, and Kunshan), four high technology development zones (Nanjing's Pukou district, Suzhou, Wuxi and Chang-zhou) and eight tourist resort zones in Jiangsu province.

According to the Director of the Jiangsu Provincial Travel and Tourism Administrative Bureau, Mr. Feng Hui Qun, the province has one goal, two initiatives, three strategies and four key points to focus on. In the past, tourism development had always been in southern Jiangsu, south of the Yangtze river, due to the better infrastructure that existed there. Henceforth, the government would like to balance that by opening up opportunities in northern Jiangsu.

Jiangsu's goal is to double international tourist arrivals and quadruple domestic visits by the year 2000. Its two initiatives are for southern Jiangsu to lead the north in its development, and for the city development to filter down to the town and village level, thereby leading to a more balanced development throughout the province. The three strategies encompass:

(i) forward planning and development (the tourism industry is set to exceed the pace of development in other industries);
(ii) involvement and participation at all levels, not just at the governmental level; and
(iii) priority for big-scale tourism development projects which need foreign funds.

The overall aim is the development of a world-class tourism product. Vacation zones and scenic spots are to be developed. Major man-made attractions in the pipeline include the Three Kingdom City in Wuxi, Tang Dynasty, European City, Sui Hu City and Asian City. Three more five-star hotels are to open in Nanjing, namely the Mandarin, International and Jingshan. There will be 11 provincially-built four-star hotels, with at least one or two in each city. Shopping complexes are also on the drawing board. Educational tourism (travel in pursuit of learning), economic tourism (travel for employment and investment) and leisure tourism (travel in pursuit of relaxation and entertainment) are to be highlighted. The provincial tourism plan fits into the national plan, with attention paid to both international and domestic markets.

Outbound Travel

Jiangsu generated about 6,000 outbound Chinese visitors, most of whom travelled to South-east Asian countries. In the past, most travelled on group tours but, today, about 55% are independent travellers indicating a new trend in tourism.

Tourism Investment Opportunities

Mr. Feng identified tourism investment opportunities to be in the areas of large scale hotel construction, redevelopment of existing hotels, tourist attractions, water-borne activities on Lake Taihu or the Grand Canal, and training and development. Suzhou has a water cleaning project which will produce cleaner canals and lakes there, when it is completed in 1998. Highway rest stops, a vital tourist amenity that is now lacking in inter-city travel, are to be built by the highway project developer. Mr. Feng felt that there were enough travel agents in Jiangsu already, given the small market at the moment. It appears that there are not enough golf courses, with three planned in Zhenjiang, Suzhou and Wuxi, in addition to the existing 36-hole and 9-hole courses. Some general information on investment in Jiangsu for potential investors is provided in Appendix 9–10.

Challenges In Tourism Development

Mr. Feng summed up the challenges that the province faces in tourism development as follows:

(i) There is a need for an international airport in Jiangsu. There are 16 international airports in China, but none in Jiangsu. One is being built in Nanjing.
(ii) There is no world-class attraction, although there are many interesting attractions. The old city wall of Nanjing, which is 33 kilometres long, is currently being repaired.
(iii) Lack of funds for development and promotion are common obstacles faced by any developing nation. The tourism bureau is considering the possibility of collecting tourism taxes.

Shopping is a weak link. There are few shopping centres, which are small and scattered, and which duplicate a limited range of merchandise. Tourist shopping centres are being developed and Suzhou's Shi Chuen Street is being developed into a pedestrian mall.

Travel agents complain about the intense competition generated by too many agents competing for a share of a small pie. Jinling Travel cited a figure of 6,000 foreign customers a year, not a big number on any scale.

The tourist coach business is a loss-maker. However, money can be made from inter-city express services because of low coach rental rates resulting from competition in the international tourist market. The cost of vehicles in China is exorbitant.

Other Problem Areas

(i) Travel agencies find it hard to book tourist-class train seats.
(ii) The standard of tour guides is inconsistent and unprofessional. Foreign language ability is a problem.
(iii) There are no travel trade associations to represent the trade.
(iv) Tourist coaches have problems with parking in cities. Underlying "protectionistic" tendencies in each city favour local tour operators.
(v) Profit margins hover around 10 to 12%, according to Jinling Travel, and many travel agencies have closed due to insolvency.

TOURISM IN NANJING

The historic southern capital of China, Nanjing, formerly known as Jinling or "Ning" for short, is the capital of Jiangsu province and ranks first in terms of political, economic and cultural importance. Located on the lower reaches of the Yangtze river, the city, circled by water and hills, has been known since ancient times as the "curling dragon and crouching tiger" because of its strategic importance and natural beauty.

It was the capital city of ten ancient dynasties; hence, its rich historic and cultural heritage. As one of China's four ancient cities (the others being Beijing, Luoyang and Xian), Nanjing is famous for its many archaeological sites, some of which have yet to be opened or discovered.

Nanjing, therefore, has a key role in the development of the tourism industry in Jiangsu. Since the beginning of the sixth dynasty, the banks of the 5-kilometre Qinhuai river, with the Confucian temple as the centre, thrived. Today, the area has become a popular place for sightseeing, shopping, eating and amusement.

Other major attractions include the solemn and magnificent Sun Yat-Sen Mausoleum in the eastern suburbs, the Yangtze River Bridge, the natural moat of the Yangtze itself, the landmark five-star Jinling Hotel towering over the city, Xuanwu lake and Mochou lake, Xiaoling Tomb, the old city walls and other ancient architectural structures of the Ming and Qing dynasties. It is a city laid out on a grand scale, with a splendour and majesty only paralleled by Beijing.

SUZHOU

Located in the south of the Yangtze river delta, Suzhou is bordered by Lake Taihu to the west and Shanghai to the east. In China it is well-known as a historical and cultural city, with a 2,500-year history, stretching back to its inception as the town of Helu in 514 B.C. Suzhou is the leading city in Jiangsu in terms of wealth and economic growth because of its proximity to Shanghai, its famous history and its major attractions. The gardens in Suzhou have achieved worldwide fame, especially the Gentle Wave Pavilion, the Lion Forest, the Humble Administrator's Garden and the Lingering Garden built in the architectural styles of the Song, Yuan, Ming and Qing dynasties.

Geomancers claim that the city is ideally located, with its hills and waters. The city is crisscrossed by water lanes while the outskirts are studded with lakes and pools. Visitors can cruise along the canals on dragon boats, watch the daily activities of those who live and pass by the water and pass under small bridges: scenes that are straight out of Chinese paintings. The old towns of Tongli, Zhouzhuang and Luzhi with their distinctive architecture and lanes paved with slabstones from the Ming and Qing dynasties, still remain intact.

Suzhou's other tourist attractions include a great variety of festivals and other events, particularly the annual silk and tourism festivals, a wide variety of high quality arts and handicrafts, interesting shopping, pearling and fishing activities.

Current Status of Tourism

In 1993, Suzhou's GNP was RMB 50 billion (US$6.2 billion), the third highest of cities in China. It ranked sixth among Chinese cities in terms of tourist arrivals. Within Jiangsu, Suzhou was ranked first, followed by Nanjing and Wuxi, respectively. Suzhou had 6,055 Sino-foreign joint ventures in 1993 with US$5.096 billion worth of contracted investment (tourism and non-tourism related) and US$1.52 billion worth of actual investment in the same year.

In the past, most visitors to Suzhou came in groups. This has changed, and now half of those visiting are independent travellers.[20] In 1994, Suzhou received 300,000 overseas visitors, down from 356,000 in 1993, and six million domestic visitors who spent a total of RMB 400 million (US$49.2 million). Overseas arrivals increased by 9% in 1995 and are expected to grow again in 1996 by 9%. The length of stay increased from 1.02 days in 1994 to 1.92 days in the first half of 1995.[21]

The tourism industry has been growing at an average annual rate of 20%, making it an important industry for the city. There were 134 tourism enterprises and 10,000 people directly employed within the tourism sector. Of the 31 hotels, with a total of 4,594 rooms, 18 were star-rated, including four in the four-star category and 14 in the three-star category. Out of the 48 travel agencies, 14 belonged to categories A and B. There were 15 companies in the coach and boat-chartering business. The Suzhou Taihu National Tourism Vacation Zone (STNTVZ) is the only national resort zone in Jiangsu while there are three other provincial resort zones in Suzhou.

---

[20] Jiangsu Provincial Travel and Tourism Bureau.

[21] Suzhou Travel and Tourism Bureau.

Suzhou Taihu National Tourism Vacation Zone (STNTVZ)

This is a special resort approved by China's State Council. It is located 15 kilometres west of Suzhou city, 85 kilometres from Shanghai airport and 20 kilometres from the Singapore-Suzhou Industrial Township (SSIT). The start-up area of the zone is 11.2 square kilometres. It is well connected by road, rail, air and water. Since its inception in October 1992, some RMB 300 million (US$37 million) has been sunk into infrastructure construction. A 15.8-kilometre long and 40-metre wide tourist highway, a 35,000 KV electricity transformer station, a water supply plant with a daily capacity of 60,000 tonnes, 30 kilometres of inner roads and the 4,348-metre long Taihu bridge have been built. Currently, the rest of the inner roads, two more 110,000 KV transformer stations and a sewage treatment plant, with a daily capacity of 40,000 tonnes, are near completion.

The STNTVZ is set amid the Taihu lake scenic spots, with beautiful natural scenery and abundant natural resources. As the birth-place of the Wu culture, the resort has numerous historical relics and unique folk customs. Visitors to Suzhou Taihu number about one million annually, with an average expenditure of RMB 500 (US$61). However, the majority of the visitors belong to the working class and their average expenditure is only about RMB 80 (US$10) per day.[22]

Table 9–1 lists those investment projects recommended by the STNTVZ Group Company in 1995, each of which can be customised to investors' requirements. The Taihu Resort and Hotel are expected to be operational by the latter half of 1996. A golf course development is also well underway. The construction of a "waterworld" has been completed. Singapore, Hong Kong and Wu county are cooperating on the development of "Wu Cultural City" (see Table 9–1). The authorities are also seeking investors for training and development, and souvenir retailing. Investors are also welcome to propose new projects for which land or other resources will be provided by the STNTVZ authorities.

Interested investors can contact the Foreign Investors' Service Centre, which can provide consultation and turn-key services from negotiation to setting up the business. Its address is:

Taihu Development Mansion 3F, South Renmin Road
Suzhou, Jiangsu Province, P.R. China 215128
Tel: (512) 525 9095, Fax: (512) 525 4168

---

[22] Suzhou Taihu National Tourism Vacation Zone.

TABLE 9–1
Investment Projects in the Suzhou Taihu National Tourism Vacation Zone

Project	Description	Value US$ (millions)	% Foreign Share
Wu Cultural City	Theme Park – combination of ancient civilisation and interactive modern technology.	30	50
Seasonal Park	Flower and fruit garden.	2	–
Central Hotel	4–5 diamond rating; 300 suites and rooms; local style and architecture.	30	70
Family Holiday Villages	A large-scale, mid-level group of holiday villages comprising villas and apartments, with recreational facilities.	2	100
International Vacation Centre	Upmarket villas, apartments, mini-golf course; bowling centre, pool, health club, water sports, etc.	30	100
Children's Holiday Camp	Science Museum, small observatory, picnic camps, playground, military training centre, etc.	2	100
Taihu International Enterprisers' Club	Country club setting with conference facilities, offices, villas and apartments for members.	20	100
Artificial Skiing Park	Year-round artificial snow ski slopes.	10	80
International Conference and Exhibition Centre	High standard conference centre by the lake or on an island, with office buildings.	30	80
Lakeside Department Store	Medium or high-class department store, large supermarket, cafe and parking area.	10	50
Food Processing	Processing and packing of local aquatic animals, vegetables and fruits for local and overseas consumption.	Negotiable	–
Tian Er City Club	Health Club.	10	90
Water Treatment Factory	Water treatment.	10	60

TABLE 9–1 (cont'd)

Project	Description	Value US$ (millions)	% Foreign Share
Dress and Souvenir Manufacture	Production under foreign licence for local retailing – dress, sports attire, shoes, embroidery, tourist souvenirs.	Negotiable	–

Source: Suzhou Taihu National Tourism Vacation Zone Development Group Co.[23]

Unlike other projects, which need approval from the administrative departments of state councils, those in the STNTVZ are approved by the administrative committee of the vacation zone itself. The committee has the right to approve projects up to a total investment of US$30 million.

Besides the STNTVZ, there are numerous other authorities involved with general investment and development in Suzhou. They include the Suzhou Municipal Tourism Administration, People's Government of Wuxian City, Suzhou City Planning Bureau, Suzhou Panmen Tourism Development Company Limited, International Commercial Centre Company Limited, China-Singapore Suzhou Industrial Park Development Company Limited and the Suzhou Suteng Panmen Tourism Development Company Limited.

Suzhou Panmen Tourism Zone

This zone, located just ten minutes from the Singapore-Suzhou Township is not one of the eight tourism zones identified in Jiangsu. The total land area is 14.2 square kilometres. Panmen, with a population of 300,000, also has a history dating back 2,500 years. It has numerous attractions and some of the best parks, gardens and transportation system in Jiangsu.[24] The Old Suzhou City which falls within this zone, occupies about 350 acres of land. The three most important historical buildings are the 800-year-old Ruixian Tower built during the Song Dynasty, the 400-metre ancient city wall and the Humeng bridge.

The zone is being developed in three stages by the Suzhou Suteng Panmen Tourism Development (SSPTD) Company Limited, which is owned by the government. Land leases are for 50 years.

---

[23] *Investment Opportunities of Suzhou Taihu National Tourism Vacation Zone in 1995.*

[24] Publication by Suzhou Panmen Tourism Development Co. Ltd.

(i) Stage one is the development of a 454-room hotel by Pidemco Land of Singapore. This will be managed by Marriot Hotels and will be operational in 1997;
(ii) Stage two is the development of a 3.5-hectare commercial belt with offices and shopping centre covering about 50,000 square metres; and
(iii) Stage three is the development of a 16-hectare cultural theme park, the "Gusu Garden", which aims to improve nightlife in Suzhou city.

Stages two and three are expected to be completed by the year 2000 and should see a projected target of 2.5 million visitor arrivals, including 250,000 foreigners.

Nanjing Pearl Tourism Vacation Zone

Table 9–2 shows a listing of proposed investment projects by the Nanjing Pearl Tourism Vacation Zone company set up to promote investment in the area.

TABLE 9–2
Investment Projects in the Nanjing Pearl Tourism Vacation Zone

Project	Description	Value US$
Integrated entertainment city	Water sports, entertainment	16.0
Central Hotel	3-star hotel	9.5
Zoological Gardens	Attraction	28.5
Cable car project	Transportation	2.6
Water theme park	Water sports	9.2

Source: Jiangsu Travel and Tourism Bureau.

CONCLUSION: A COMPARISON OF THE THREE CITIES

In this section, the strengths, challenges and development issues for each of the three destinations are assessed. These factors have a bearing on the prospects of tourism-related investment in each of the three cities.

Shanghai

With its well-developed infrastructure and extensive transportation links,

Shanghai serves as an important gateway to China for both holiday and business travellers. Its cosmopolitan appeal has also earned it the reputation of being the "face of modern China" and has attracted large numbers of international and domestic visitors. As the country's foremost business and financial centre, Shanghai draws large numbers of business travellers and it is a natural candidate to be a major convention centre in China.

Capitalising on the destination's strengths, Shanghai's Vice-Mayor Gong Xueping, who chairs the newly formed municipal tourism development task force, has suggested that Shanghai should focus on "tourism projects related to business travellers, international conferences and exhibitions, as well as culture, sports and shopping" (*Shanghai Star*, 1995). One problem that Shanghai still faces is a rather high level of air pollution, a by-product of the city's industrial activities, even though there has been much improvement in recent years. Steps are being taken to move the industries away from the central part of Shanghai and out to the peripheral areas.

Another challenge that the destination faces is rising costs that could undermine its competitiveness *vis-à-vis* other regions in the country. For instance, Shanghai hotels record the highest room rates in the whole of China. Shanghai must offer value-for-money tourism services and experiences in order to compete.

While its hotel sector is already more developed than in other regions, the designation of the Sheshan National Holiday Resort and the development of Pudong New Area should generate new investment opportunities in the resort, leisure and accommodation sectors. Its huge population base, with relatively high disposable incomes, makes it a fertile ground for investment. The domestic market for travel and entertainment offers huge potential for investors, within Shanghai itself as well as in the nearby cities. Night entertainment, for instance, is quite lacking in Shanghai.

Suzhou

Located less than two hours' drive from Shanghai, Suzhou's strategic position enables it to be the "back garden of Shanghai". Currently, about 70% of Suzhou's visitors come from Shanghai, a large hinterland with a population of 15 million. The high rate of economic development and corresponding growth in demand for vacations and leisure activities in

Shanghai will continue to benefit Suzhou, which can provide more attractions, leisure and recreational outlets for the Shanghainese. Suzhou can capitalise on the market potential of the Shanghai population as well as the large numbers of foreign visitors that can be funnelled through this gateway, by developing facilities such as attractions and golf courses, that would cost much more to construct in Shanghai. The Suzhou Taihu National Vacation Zone is a recommended venue for such projects.

To fully exploit its business potential, this national vacation zone should target both high spending consumers and the mass market. For the former, products such as golf courses, exclusive country clubs and resorts are possible investment projects. As for the mass market, the focus could be on family entertainment, and recreational attractions and facilities. Development plans should take into consideration the unique characteristics of the place that are worth promoting. An emphasis on providing service quality and value for money would also be important.

Nanjing

Nanjing's rich historic and cultural heritage has given it a variety of impressive attractions that have unique appeal to both foreign and domestic visitors. These attractions are unlike those of Shanghai and Suzhou and, yet, since Nanjing is located a reasonably short distance from the other two cities and is accessible by rail and road, it shares part of the visitor traffic to the other two cities. The completion of the highway between Nanjing and Shanghai will further facilitate the flow of visitors. The new airport, when completed, will also improve the destination's accessibility tremendously and will bring in more visitors from other parts of China, including Hong Kong.

One possible area of development is the souvenir industry. Nanjing could look into producing high quality souvenirs that reflect the destination's rich heritage. There is already a sizeable industry of this nature that engages in the sale of art goods, such as paintings and sculpture, as well as other souvenirs. However, there appears to be much potential in making improvements to product packaging and marketing.

In general, the three destinations have unique strengths and appeal that would attract different visitor market segments and, when combined, would offer a much richer travel experience than any one of them could provide individually. Hence, the destinations are complementary rather than being direct competitors. It would be strategic, therefore, to package these destinations together using Shanghai as the funnel for foreign visitors.

APPENDIX 9–1
Number of Travel Agencies: 1993 to 1994

Locality	Category A		Category B		Category C		Total	
	1994	1993	1994	1993	1994	1993	1994	1993
Beijing	72	23	41	40	174	170	287	233
Tianjin	4	1	10	8	85	79	99	88
Hebei	6	4	13	14	117	64	136	82
Shanxi	1	1	13	10	45	43	59	54
Inner Mongolia	6	3	40	17	52	46	98	66
Liaoning	7	5	28	30	154	203	189	238
Jilin	6	6	22	19	108	62	136	87
Heilongjiang	6	4	19	19	103	111	128	134
Shanghai	19	13	14	13	123	105	156	131
Jiangsu	14	11	45	47	138	117	197	175
Zhejiang	8	7	17	19	189	125	214	151
Anhui	3	3	30	22	123	95	156	120
Fujian	9	9	27	27	149	89	185	125
Jiangxi	4	2	7	12	80	27	91	41
Shandong	9	6	23	14	280	143	312	163
Henan	3	3	19	17	21	82	43	102
Hubei	3	3	13	19	119	88	135	110
Hunan	4	3	25	27	110	80	139	110
Guangdong	34	24	161	166	152	118	347	308
Guangxi	5	4	25	24	106	81	136	109
Hainan	7	4	11	20	116	60	134	84
Sichuan	4	4	21	23	313	111	338	138
Guizhou	3	1	10	11	43	46	56	58
Yunnan	3	2	17	14	230	108	250	124
Tibet	5	2	5	12	26	7	36	21
Shaanxi	7	5	13	15	61	48	81	68
Gansu	3	2	17	18	87	25	107	45
Qinghai	1	1	5	4	16	9	22	14
Ningxia	3	1	5	2	13	7	21	10
Xinjiang	8	7	20	20	66	22	94	49
TOTAL	**267**	**164**	**716**	**703**	**3,399**	**2,371**	**4,382**	**3,238**

Source: China National Tourism Administration, *Tourism Statistics of China, 1994.*

APPENDIX 9–2
Tourists Received by Travel Agencies: 1984 to 1994
('000)

Agencies	1984	1985	1986	1987	1988	1989	1990	1991	1992	1993	1994
CITS*	398.7	468.8	459.3	505.0	231.1	137.8	110.2	488.0	647.0	740.7	810.2
% change on previous year	19.0	17.6	–2.0	9.9	–54.2	–40.4	–20.0	75.9	32.6	14.5	9.4
CTS**	825.8	773.3	595.3	847.7	1,103.9	843.1	1,064.6	1,066.0	962.0	820.2	619.4
% change on previous year	–9.0	–6.4	–22.9	42.3	30.2	–23.6	26.3	0.2	–9.7	–14.7	–24.5
CYTS***	47.4	51.8	79.0	125.3	147.3	99.8	135.2	156.0	150.0	140.4	224.8
% change on previous year	61.7	9.2	52.6	58.6	17.5	–32.2	35.4	15.4	–3.9	–6.4	60.1
Others	738.0	1,066.3	1,437.8	1,524.4	11,600.3	824.2	1,481.8	1,079.1	1,382.2	12,027.1	1,253.2
% change on previous year	N/A	N/A	34.8	6.0	N/A	–48.5	79.8	–17.9	28.1	46.7	–89.6

Sources: EIU, *International Tourism Reports No. 1, 1995*; *Tourism Statistics of China, 1994.*

Notes: * China International Travel Service

** China Travel Service

*** China You Travel Service

N/A Not Available

APPENDIX 9–3
Number of Star-rated Hotels: 1994

LOCALITY	5-STAR	4-STAR	3-STAR	2-STAR	1-STAR	TOTAL
Beijing	12	21	31	76	41	181
Tianjing	1	3	8	13	3	28
Hebei	0	0	13	27	1	41
Shanxi	0	0	5	13	4	22
Inner Mongolia	0	0	4	5	11	20
Liaoning	1	2	15	29	16	63
Jilin	0	0	11	17	14	42
Heilongjiang	0	0	9	16	14	39
Shanghai	7	11	35	37	12	102
Jiangsu	1	5	42	41	1	90
Zhejiang	0	1	27	7	1	36
Anhui	0	0	4	36	8	48
Fujian	0	4	25	25	3	57
Jiangxi	0	0	4	20	4	28
Shandong	0	6	27	23	5	61
Henan	0	0	7	11	1	19
Hubei	0	1	18	30	4	53
Hunan	0	1	5	20	11	37
Guangdong	10	19	94	156	24	303
Guangxi	1	3	16	14	5	39
Hainan	0	3	13	10	6	32
Sichuan	0	5	11	15	10	41
Guizhou	0	0	2	8	5	15
Yunnan	0	4	3	25	13	45
Tibet	0	0	3	3	4	10
Shaanxi	2	6	11	5	1	25
Gansu	0	0	5	19	2	26
Qinghai	0	0	1	6	2	9
Ningxia	0	0	1	6	0	7
Xinjiang	0	1	2	24	10	37
TOTAL	**35**	**96**	**452**	**737**	**236**	**1,556**

Source: *Tourism Statistics of China, 1994.*

APPENDIX 9–4
Number of Hotels by Economic Type and Capacity: 1994

Locality	Total	State-owned	Collective	Private	Others	More than 500	300–499	200–299	100–199	Less than 99
Beijing	249	135	37	0	77	25	37	30	51	106
Tianjin	39	21	4	0	14	1	2	6	12	18
Hebei	63	60	2	0	1	0	6	10	26	21
Shanxi	40	38	1	0	1	0	3	4	15	18
Inner Mongolia	43	36	3	0	4	0	0	3	12	28
Liaoning	90	54	5	0	31	0	5	10	30	45
Jilin	51	47	1	0	3	0	2	3	15	31
Heilongjiang	58	52	2	0	4	0	2	4	19	33
Shanghai	111	78	3	0	30	15	16	25	38	17
Jiangsu	106	82	9	0	15	1	9	11	40	45
Zhejiang	117	77	16	0	24	3	5	13	46	50
Anhui	83	72	5	0	6	0	1	6	32	44
Fujian	105	67	4	1	33	0	6	18	35	46
Jiangxi	49	41	3	0	5	0	0	11	21	17
Shandong	142	110	15	0	17	1	3	11	37	90
Henan	30	24	3	0	3	0	0	3	11	16
Hubei	120	105	5	0	10	0	2	19	41	58
Hunan	72	59	0	0	13	0	2	11	26	33
Guangdong	838	489	128	12	209	15	45	69	213	496
Guangxi	75	49	3	0	23	1	12	15	23	24

APPENDIX 9–4 (cont'd)

Locality	Total	State-owned	Collective	Private	Others	More than 500	300-499	200-299	100-199	Less than 99
Hainan	108	51	24	2	31	0	3	11	35	59
Sichuan	111	94	4	0	13	1	10	21	49	30
Guizhou	26	23	0	0	3	0	1	3	11	11
Yunnan	88	60	24	0	4	0	5	5	31	47
Tibet	22	14	7	0	1	0	1	0	3	18
Shaanxi	27	10	0	0	17	3	8	5	6	5
Gansu	32	31	1	0	0	1	4	0	12	15
Qinghai	9	9	0	0	0	0	2	1	1	5
Ningxia	15	14	1	0	0	0	0	0	7	8
Xinjiang	76	67	6	0	3	0	3	7	26	40
TOTAL	**2,995**	**2,069**	**316**	**15**	**595**	**67**	**195**	**335**	**924**	**1,474**

Source: China National Tourism Administration, *Tourism Statistics of China, 1994*.

APPENDIX 9–5
Number of Hotels, Rooms and Occupancy Rates: 1994

Locality	Number of Hotels	Number of Rooms	Room Occupancy (%)
Beijing	249	52,533	71.31
Tianjin	39	5,395	63.67
Hebei	63	9,429	51.49
Shanxi	40	4,992	57.09
Inner Mongolia	43	3,189	58.03
Liaoning	90	10,299	64.19
Jilin	51	5,356	58.58
Heilongjiang	58	6,380	58.49
Shanghai	111	27,859	70.89
Jiangsu	106	14,129	63.66
Zhejiang	117	15,792	66.78
Anhui	83	8,990	52.80
Fujian	105	13,110	58.44
Jiangxi	49	6,687	59.83
Shandong	142	14,118	56.50
Henan	30	2,979	62.00
Hubei	120	13,841	60.29
Hunan	72	9,049	63.29
Guangdong	838	103,578	63.48
Guangxi	75	12,872	48.07
Hainan	108	11,294	57.06
Sichuan	111	17,185	55.81
Guizhou	26	3,146	63.03
Yunnan	88	9,156	62.72
Tibet	22	1,679	39.14
Shaanxi	27	7,411	50.65
Gansu	32	4,539	58.82
Qinghai	9	1,451	52.17
Ningxia	15	1,627	50.99
Xinjiang	76	8,215	57.44
TOTAL	**2,995**	**406,280**	**62.17**

Source: China National Tourism Administration, *Tourism Statistics of China, 1994.*

APPENDIX 9–6
Tourist Arrivals: 1978 to August 1995

Year	Arrivals ('000)	% Change	Tourism Receipts (US$ m)	% Change
1978	1,809	–	263	–
1979	4,204	132.4	449	70.9
1980	5,702	35.6	617	37.3
1981	7,767	36.2	785	27.3
1982	7,924	2.0	843	7.4
1983	9,477	19.6	941	11.6
1984	12,852	35.6	1,131	20.2
1985	17,833	38.8	1,250	10.5
1986	22,819	28.0	1,530	22.5
1987	26,902	17.9	1,862	21.6
1988	31,695	17.8	2,247	20.7
1989	24,501	–22.7	1,860	–17.2
1990	27,462	12.1	2,218	19.2
1991	33,350	21.4	2,845	28.3
1992	38,115	9.0	3,947	38.7
1993	41,527	9.0	4,683	18.7
1994	43,685	5.2	7,322	56.4
1995[a]	30,266	–	5,262	–

a From January to August.

Sources: *Market Focus, China*, Singapore Tourist Promotion Board, 1994; *Travel China*, Vol. 7, No. 22, 1995.

APPENDIX 9–7
Top Tourism Generating Countries to China: 1994

Number	Country	Arrivals ('000)	% change over 1993
1	Japan	1,141.2	25.1
2	U.S.A.	469.9	17.5
3	Russia	399.8	*
4	Korea	340.3	79.2
5	Mongolia	301.2	30.7
6	Singapore	231.9	15.4
7	Malaysia	208.7	23.9
8	Philippines	184.9	26.0
9	U.K.	167.0	8.5
10	Thailand	163.7	7.5

APPENDIX 9–7 (cont'd)

Number	Country	Arrivals ('000)	% change over 1993
11	Germany	148.8	7.2
12	Indonesia	120.4	9.0
13	Canada	113.2	7.7
14	France	111.8	–2.7
15	Australia	109.5	10.3
16	Kazakhstan	106.3	*
17	D.P.R.K.	57.0	–21.9
18	Italy	55.5	13.8
19	India	35.6	11.0
20	Kyrgyzstan	31.6	*
21	Sweden	30.4	30.0
22	Netherlands	30.1	22.2
23	Switzerland	26.1	7.1
24	Pakistan	24.2	–3.6
25	New Zealand	20.4	7.7
26	Finland	20.3	8.9

* Russia, Kazakhstan and Kyrgyzstan were calculated under the same heading of "Former Soviet Union" in the previous year's statistics; comparison not applicable when they became separate entities.

Source: *Tourism Statistics of China*, China National Tourism Administration, 1994.

APPENDIX 9–8
Foreign Visitor Arrivals in Key Cities: 1989 to 1993
(in '000)

City	1989	1990	1991	1992	1993
Beijing	460.2	637.5	913.9	1,204.6	1,450.4
Chengdu	32.4	44.2	53.3	63.9	65.8
Chongqing	20.5	18.7	26.8	46.9	52.1
Dalian	27.5	35.8	52.1	67.6	78.0
Guangzhou	264.9	324.5	444.6	517.6	460.9
Guilin	131.8	138.4	199.2	264.9	279.3
Hangzhou	66.1	86.6	136.8	183.8	199.8
Harbin	8.8	39.0	39.0	65.2	58.8
Kunming	40.1	49.8	57.5	107.1	167.8

APPENDIX 9–8 (cont'd)

City	1989	1990	1991	1992	1993
Nanjing	54.4	72.9	96.8	110.8	127.7
Shanghai	397.7	460.6	612.7	781.3	852.8
Shenyang	17.1	26.3	29.6	41.5	55.7
Shenzhen	49.1	93.2	108.4	169.8	203.2
Suzhou	59.9	80.7	116.3	146.8	184.5
Tianjin	27.0	35.5	38.4	55.3	73.0
Urumqi	22.2	32.6	42.8	65.4	60.5
Wuxi	33.1	38.5	57.0	74.3	87.7
Xiamen	32.5	41.7	66.8	83.7	108.9
Xian	137.9	154.0	237.8	336.3	363.7
Zhuhai	7.1	10.8	24.1	43.5	51.4

Source: *International Tourism Reports No. 1*, EIU, 1995.

APPENDIX 9–9
Foreign Visitor Arrivals In Provinces: 1994

Provinces	Arrivals	Tourism Receipts (US$ '000)
Guangdong	2,013,370	6,103.6
Beijing	2,009,000	2,029.7
Shanghai	850,000	1,321.8
Fujian	447,420	844.5
Jiangsu	221,770	702.2
Zhejiang	180,550	612.7
Liaoning	166,430	230.9
Yunnan	124,400	522.1
Guangxi	120,030	438.1
Shaanxi	113,000	438.6
Shandong	112,300	349.4
Tianjin	105,290	167.9

Source: *Tourism Statistics of China*, China National Tourism Administration, 1994.

APPENDIX 9–10
General Information on Investment in Jiangsu

TYPES OF DIRECT INVESTMENT

Sino-Foreign Joint Ventures

In accordance with the Law of Sino-foreign Joint Venture Enterprises, all joint ventures approved and registered in China are deemed as independent Chinese legal entities protected by Chinese law. The percentage of foreign investment in authorised capital shall not be less than 25%. All parties can invest either with currency or with buildings, equipment, technology, materials, intellectual property or rights using the place and shall not take back their investment during the cooperation period. The profit of the company shall be shared by the parties according to their proportion of investment.

Sino-Foreign Contractual Joint Ventures

In accordance with the Law of Sino-foreign Contractual Joint Venture Enterprises, such companies are organised based on the contracts signed by the partners. The Chinese partner shall provide right of land use, natural resources, labour or present building and equipment, etc. while the foreign party shall provide the capital, technology, equipment or materials needed. The form of investment and profit-sharing are to be agreed in the contract.

Wholly Foreign-owned Enterprises

In accordance with the relevant Chinese laws, such enterprises shall be wholly owned by foreign investors and be approved and registered in China as independent legal entities. All foreign investment, profit and other legal rights shall be protected by Chinese laws.

LAND USE RIGHT

In accordance with the Regulations of P.R. China on Transmitting Right of Using Land published by the State Council on 26 May 1990, the right of using land may be transmitted for real estate or industrial development or other economic activities, under agreed place, period, usage and other conditions. The Administrative Committee of STNTVZ will provide users with the right of using the land after the payment of users. The longest period of land use is 70 years for residence, 50 years for industry and 40 years for commerce, tourism and recreation. After expiration, users may apply to renew the right to use the land.

INVESTMENT PROTECTION

All approved and registered foreign investing enterprises in STNTVZ are Chinese legal entities protected by Chinese laws as follows:

(i) right of owning and using property of the enterprises;
(ii) right of independently operating and managing the enterprises;
(iii) right of employing, dismissing and deciding salary of personnel of the enterprises;
(iv) right of profit sharing and capital sharing after expiration or termination of the enterprises;
(v) all patents and trade marks of foreign-owned enterprises are protected by the *Patent Law* and *Trademark Law*;
(vi) foreign-owned enterprises may submit any dispute to arbitration or Chinese court;
(vii) the nation shall not nationalise and draft the foreign-owned enterprises, with the exception of special circumstances, and such drafting shall be done legally and the enterprises shall be compensated;
(viii) other legal rights according to relevant Chinese laws.

PREFERENTIAL POLICIES

As a national vacation zone, the STNTVZ enjoys eight preferential policies given by the State Council:

(i) All foreign-owned enterprises in the zone are allowed a reduced income tax rate of 24% and those involved in manufacturing and committed to doing business with an operating period of over ten years will be exempt from income tax for two years from the initial profitable year. Taxes from the third to the fifth years will be reduced by 50%.

(ii) Foreign-owned enterprises importing their own building materials, equipment and office facilities within the total investment volume, are exempted from customs duties and the consolidated tax. This includes household goods, vehicles for personal use within a reasonable amount for overseas businessmen and professionals on long-term assignments to the zone. Raw material, spare parts, components, fittings, accessories and packing stuff indispensable to the manufacture of export tourist goods will be submitted to customs as bonded freight.

(iii) Machinery, equipment and other building material needed for infrastructure in the zone can be imported free from duty and product (value added) taxes.

(iv) Special duty-free shops can operate in the zone.

(v) Joint ventures providing automobile services can be established using China-made automobiles. Additional charges for purchasing domestically made spare parts and automobiles and special consumption taxes will be remitted for an approved quantity of vehicles.

(vi) The zone allows the establishment of Category A travel agencies run by Sino-foreign joint ventures handling international tourist business.

(vii) Land for construction will be handled in accordance with the Provisional Regulations of P.R. China on Transferring Right of Using Land, Decree No. 55, 1990 State Council. Revenues from leasing land, on the date of the zone's approval for development, should be spent for infrastructure construction within five years.

(viii) Foreign exchange earnings generated by the tourist industry of the zone can be wholly retained for five years from the date of its approval of the project for further development.

In addition to these, the local government also grants favourable policies to enterprises in the STNTVZ.

(i) Investors in the zone shall enjoy the lowest land leasing prices regulated by the state. Projects that maximise the utilisation of resources, tourism and recreation, infrastructure, tourist commodity manufacture and exclusive investment with a total investment of over US$10 million shall have the land price reduced further by 10% and, if the fee is paid at one time, the price will be further reduced by 5%. Urban land use tax is exempt.

(ii) For foreign-owned enterprises building houses, the part retained by the local government in property tax shall be wholly returned to the enterprises within five years from the month the houses are completed.

(iii) An income tax rate of 24% shall be imposed on foreign-owned enterprises in the zone, and the income tax shall be exempt in the first two years and reduced by 50% in the next three years. For infrastructure projects, income tax shall be exempt in the first five years and reduced by 50% in the next five years. Fifty percent of the income tax imposed shall be returned within ten years.

(iv) For foreign-owned enterprises in the zone, the imposition of education added tax and urban construction maintenance tax shall be postponed. Fixed assets investment adjustment tax and local income tax shall be exempt.

(v) When the profit of foreign investors is remitted abroad, income tax of that part of profit shall be exempt. If the profit is re-invested in the zone with an operational period of not less than five years, 40% of the imposed income tax of that part of the profit shall be returned within five years. If the reinvested enterprises manufacture exported products, or have advanced technology, the imposed tax of the reinvested profit shall be wholly returned. If the monthly income of any foreign employees is less than RMB 4,000, personal income tax is exempt.

(vi) Domestic enterprises may invest and establish projects in the zone and operate independently. Such enterprises enjoy the same preferential policies as those for foreign-owned enterprises.

(vii) The vacation zone may employ any qualified personnel freely.

Source: Suzhou Taihu National Tourism Vacation Zone Development Group Co.

REFERENCES

China National Tourism Administration, *Tourism Statistics of China*, 1994.

The Economist Intelligence Unit, *EIU International Tourism Reports*, No. 1, 1995.

Joe Studwell, *Unlocking China: A Key to Investment Regions*, The Economist Intelligence Unit Limited, 1993.

"Key Industries Excel", *Shanghai Star*, 8 December 1995.

Lew, Alan A. and Lawrence Yu, *Tourism in China*, Westview Press, 1995.

Shanghai Jin Jiang (Group) Holding Co., *Culture and Recreation*, 17 December 1995.

Shanghai Municipal Tourism Administration, *Welcome to China, Shanghai,* Vol. 5, Issue No. 5, 1995.

Shanghai Tourism Today, Shanghai Tourism Bureau, 1995.

Travel China, Vol. 7, No. 19, 1995.

Chapter 10

Town and Village Enterprises in Jiangsu

BY
CHIAN Thian Shian
Philip LAM
LIM Soon Tong
ZHANG Xiliang

INTRODUCTION

THERE ARE SEVERAL main types of enterprises through which business activities are conducted in China. These enterprises include the following:

(i) ***State-owned Enterprises:*** These are firms owned by the state and controlled by the central government. Thus, they are known as state-owned enterprises (SOEs).
(ii) ***Private Enterprises:*** These are private enterprises known as individual businesses or private businesses. After 1993, the latter were legally referred to as privately-owned enterprises. The difference between these two forms of enterprise is that the former has seven or fewer employees (Chan, 1995).
(iii) ***Town and Village Enterprises:*** Town and village enterprises (TVEs) are broadly defined. The activities they are involved in are diverse and they have operated in many dif-

* The authors are extremely grateful for the extended interview with Mr. Li Fu Sheng, Local Party Secretary and Director of Wujiang Municipal State Tax Bureau, Jiangsu province, who provided immeasurable information and knowledge on this topic.

ferent forms throughout their evolving history. Generally, TVEs are privately- or collectively-owned (non-state-owned) enterprises involved in non-agricultural work (Zweig, 1992). They are registered with the Agricultural, Industrial and Commercial Corporation (AICC) which is discussed in more detail below. There are four categories of TVEs, namely township, village, cooperative and individual (Wickramanayake *et al.*, 1995; China TVEs, 1994). These are differentiated solely by the kind of ownership. For example, as the name implies, a "township" is owned by a municipal authority while a "village" is owned by a village community.

TVEs have emerged as a significant and growing industrial force in China's economy. They now account for almost one-third of China's industrial output and nearly one-half of its total industrial employment.

In 1993, there were over 24 million TVEs in China. However, the majority of them are small, family-run service businesses. In recent years, there has been an increasing number of export-oriented and joint venture TVEs which are significantly impacting China's production and export levels. TVEs provide opportunities to foreign investors wishing to venture into China, especially through the process of joint ventures. The popularity of partnership in joint venture TVEs among foreign investors is apparent from the US$5.85 billion that they attracted in foreign capital in 1991.

DISTINCTION BETWEEN TVEs AND OTHER ENTERPRISES

Distinction Between TVEs and SOEs

According to the World Bank, China's SOEs in 1991 produced almost RMB 83 billion worth of industrial output. Over 300 of these enterprises had revenue exceeding US$100 million. SOEs are the centrepiece of the Chinese state economic planning system and they account for over one-half of the country's industrial output (MacMurray and Woetzel, 1994). Unfortunately, a substantial number of the SOEs are inefficient and they require state subsidies. SOE subsidies amounted to 14% of government revenue in 1992.

There are distinct differences between SOEs and TVEs. The range of different types of TVEs precludes the possibility of making generalisations which are correct for each and every TVE. Moreover, there is insufficient academic research into TVEs to conclusively identify their distinguishing characteristics. Nonetheless, the differences noted in Table 10–1 can generally be observed in most TVEs.

In terms of the key differences between TVEs and SOEs, the former exist outside of the planned economy. Unlike SOEs, they are not owned by the state but, instead, by the town or village, partners, individuals or families. Although SOEs implement management responsibility systems (discussed in more detail below) in a manner similar to TVEs, the systems practised by TVEs are much more flexible and they have greater variety. This primarily is because TVEs are controlled to a lesser extent by the central government. Thus, the management systems used by them are generally more efficient than the ones used by SOEs.

TVEs are financed by funds accumulated through internal profits from agriculture, personal savings, investments from domestic or overseas partners and some bank loans. SOEs, on the other hand, are financed mainly by government funds and bank loans allocated within the central economic plan.

Most TVEs still produce simple products through means of low technology and equipment, and their quality control systems cannot compete with those of SOEs. The latter use higher technology, employ more modern equipment and use more powerful machinery. Unlike SOEs, which have stable supplies of raw materials, energy and other resources for production, TVEs must search the market place to find materials for their operations, and they sometimes face difficult conditions due to the lack of resources. TVEs generally produce to meet market demand. Their pricing policy is also more flexible than that of SOEs. In fact, SOEs production and pricing policies are not market oriented; instead, they are set by the central government.

TVEs and Private Enterprises

In 1993, there were 24.5 million TVEs in China. Out of this total, 0.43 million were township and 1.2 million were village enterprises. The majority of TVEs were individual and they accounted for over 88% of the national total. In the fourth category of cooperative TVEs, there were approximately one million.

TABLE 10–1
A Comparison of TVEs and SOEs

	TVEs	SOEs
Ownership	- Individually or privately (town or village or partner) owned. - Exist "outside" the planned economy.	- Owned by state and controlled by the central government.
Labour Management/ Reward	- Flexible, demand driven and can source for labour from the open market. - Rewards generally tied to enterprise performance and individual output.	- Bureaucratic. - Practise "life long employment". - Welfare-orientated (welfare schemes include employees' family).
Financing	- Collective or private funds derived from internal profits from agriculture, personal savings etc.	- Government funds and bank loans within the central economic plan.
Product and Technology	- Low-end products in general. - Use of equipment with lower technological level. - Limited quality control systems.	- Sophisticated end products. - More up-to-date equipment, production and quality control systems. - Use of equipment with higher technology.
Source of Supply	- Depends on open market. - Supply constraint due to size.	- Stable supply of raw materials and energy.
Market Orientation	- Driven by market forces with prices based on market demand.	- Government policy driven with price mostly set by the central government.
Management	- Identified after discussing with AICCs and replaceable. - Flexible and operating under AICCs. - Market driven.	- State appointed and entrenched. - Less flexible and little autonomy. - Government policy driven.
Culture	- Profit oriented. - Pragmatic. - Aligns quickly with market forces.	- Motivation for higher output/performance lacking. - Conservative in approach. - Resistant to change.

Turning to the size of the workforce, townships were the largest employers with an average of 66 employees per enterprise. Cooperative TVEs had an average of nine employees while individual TVEs had two or three employees and this could include the owner.

On the revenue side, township enterprises were the most productive. They accounted for sales of RMB 31,505 per employee. This was followed by village TVEs with RMB 28,500 per employee which is 9% lower. The figure for cooperative TVEs was RMB 21,102 per employee while individual TVEs ranked fourth with RMB 16,955 per employee. The latter figure was only 54 and 59% of the figures for township and village enterprises, respectively.

TABLE 10–2
A Breakdown of China's TVEs: 1993

	Town	Village	Cooperative	Individual	Total
No. of enterprises	433,809	1,251,425	1,038,528	21,805,510	24,529,272
No. of employees	28,808,032	28,869,267	9,137,095	56,638,688	123,453,082
Sales revenue (RMB '000)	907,601,770	822,786,190	192,812,680	960,330,660	2,883,531,300
No. of employees per enterprise	66.4	23.1	8.8	2.6	–
Sales revenue per employee (RMB)	31,505	28,500	21,102	16,955	–

Source: 1993 statistics complied from *Annual Yearbook of China's TVEs, 1994.*

A distinction should be drawn between cooperative and individual TVEs, and private enterprises known as individual and private businesses. Neither the individual nor private businesses are regulated by the AICCs.

Before 1978, individual businesses were officially condemned and they had to undergo reformation. For instance, those considered capitalistic in nature had to undergo a process of "self-confession" and "self-criticism." It was only in 1978, at the Third Plenary Session of the Eleventh Central Committee, that Mr. Deng Xiaoping's rural reform programme was formalised. It was at the Thirteenth Congress of the Chinese Communist Party in 1987 that the state recognised the role of the private sector. Even then, this role was to be in the context of a "market economy with socialist characteristics". In that year, enterprises with eight or more employees, and which were not TVEs, were legally defined as private businesses.

In 1992, there were 15 million individual businesses and 139 thousand private businesses. The former comprised one to two employees while the latter averaged 16 employees. In terms of sales revenue, individual businesses contributed RMB 90,720 per employee which outperformed townships by 287%. Private businesses generated sales revenue per employee of RMB 49,008 which was 155% more than that of townships.

TABLE 10–3
China's Private Enterprises: 1992

	Individual	Private	Total
No. of enterprises	15,339,000	139,000	15,478,000
No. of employees	24,677,000	2,318,000	26,995,000
Sales revenue (RMB '000)	2,238,700,000	113,600,000	2,352,300,000
No. of employee per enterprise	1.6	16.7	N/A
Sales revenue per employee (RMB)	90,720	49,008	N/A

Source: Complied from *Journal of Enterprising Culture,* Vol. 3., No. 3, September 1995.

Although TVEs are still generally less efficient than private enterprises, any entrepreneur who wishes to venture into China must not ignore the importance of the AICC. It can be very helpful, especially in assisting with information gathering and looking for a partner. Currently, TVEs are very popular as partners in foreign joint ventures. For example, as of April 1992, over 1,000 joint ventures out of the 2,500 joint ventures in Jiangsu province were with TVEs. In some cities, like Nantong, nearly 80% of all the new joint ventures formed were with TVEs (Jiangsu Municipal Government, 1994).

HISTORY OF TVEs IN CHINA

The growth of China's TVEs date from the late 1970s. It was after Chairman Mao's death that China's central government began to initiate economic reforms. These included the following changes:

(i) expanding the role of prices and market allocation in the economy;
(ii) reducing barriers to international trade and investment;
(iii) transferring authority from central planners to enterprise managers, and provincial and municipal governments; and
(iv) creating a system of dual pricing, that is, planned pricing as well as market pricing for industrial goods.

At that time, the central government did not have a clear vision of what the reformed economy should be, nor a clear plan for reforming the economy. Its actions were incomplete and tentative. For example, industrial reform focused on gradually relaxing controls over SOEs. The "open door" strategy (part of the four modernisations) which sought to reduce barriers to international trade and investment, concentrated on expanding trade and investment activities in a few special zones along China's south-west coast.

Nonetheless, growth was rapid, particularly in terms of industrial expansion. However, joint ventures, foreign-owned firms and private industry contributed only one-sixth of the incremental output increases from 1980 to 1992. China's southern coastal provinces' contribution to China's total industrial output grew to 36% in 1992. This was only modestly above their 30% contribution in 1978 and still below their 36.6% contribution in 1952.

What is noteworthy is that in the course of reform, the central government encouraged local governments to venture into new, non-state industries. The objective behind this strategy was to provide jobs for the teeming number of workers in rural areas. The additional loans and tax incentives provided by the central government enabled the number of these enterprises, and the types of goods that they produced, to increase sharply. From 1983 to 1988, the number of TVEs and their employees tripled. Generally, TVE expansion was especially strong in Jiangsu and Zhejiang, as well as in the suburbs of major cities.

JIANGSU TVEs

History

Jiangsu's TVEs differ from other provincial TVEs because the former mainly originated from the development of village cooperatives. Before 1949, the textile related cottage industry, as well as other traditional cottage activities, existed in many villages. However, after 1949 (the emergence of the People's Republic of China), these business activities were only partly retained to meet farming and social needs. In 1958, there was an outburst of activities and campaigns to industrialise the co-operatives pursuant to the government's call. For example, the slogan, "The people's cooperatives need to operate industry" encouraged the cooperatives to develop an industrial base. In that year, the number of industrialised cooperatives grew to 39,000 with a workforce of over one million. Jiangsu's TVEs' total production output then reached RMB 1.48 billion and it constituted 17% of Jiangsu's total output.

In the 1960s, Jiangsu TVEs faced a period of setbacks from "leftist" disruption as well as from a series of natural disasters which were spread over a period of three years. These events resulted in a weakening of farming activities which adversely affected industrialisation. By the end of 1962, the number of industrialised cooperatives fell to only 1,673 and the value of production output dropped to a mere RMB 66 million. Subsequently, output recovered to RMB 3.17 billion in 1965.

In August 1970, the government encouraged the cooperatives to manufacture farm machinery and to establish other farm support industries. This revived the industrialisation efforts of the cooperatives. Coupled with abundant labour, production output rose to RMB 22.7 billion, twice the value in 1970. It was also after the disruptive incident of the "Gang of Four" that "leftist" ideology was finally set aside and the co-operatives' performance began to accelerate. Thus, by the end of 1978, there were over 55 thousand cooperatives which employed a workforce of over 2.5 million and they had an annual production output of RMB 62.56 billion. The industrialised cooperatives had become a major economic force in Jiangsu.

Pursuant to the government's move towards a socialist market economy, the cooperatives were exposed to market demand, albeit imperfectly. In 1980, the output of industrialised cooperatives had reached RMB 107.7 billion. The government continued to emphasise the importance of industrialised cooperatives from 1983 to 1985. By 1989, the combined production output of all TVEs had reached RMB 1,291.74 billion. This was 43.41% of Jiangsu's total production output. Moreover, the number of TVEs with an output of more than RMB 5 million each reached 3,413.

In fact, the TVEs' rapid growth came as a surprise to the Chinese government. Mr. Deng Xiaoping said in a meeting with foreign visitors on 12 June 1987 that "the greatest achievement which we did not expect is the TVEs' growth" (Zweig, 1992).

Current Position

Table 10–4 summarises some comparative data pertaining to the four classes of TVEs in Jiangsu province for 1993. In 1993, Jiangsu had a total of 984,882 TVEs. Of these, 3.6% were township and 7.8% village TVEs. Individual TVEs accounted for 86% of the total. Although township TVEs were small in number, they accounted for 43% of the total number of employees employed by TVEs in the province. They also contributed to one-half of the province's total sales revenue generated by TVEs. Turning to the number of employees per enterprise, township TVEs employed 114 on average while village TVEs had only 39 employees on average. Considering productivity, an average employee in a township TVE generated an annual sales revenue of RMB 48,143 followed closely by village TVEs at RMB 43,137. Lagging behind were individual TVEs with an average sales revenue of RMB 14,449 per employee.

TABLE 10–4
TVEs in Jiangsu Province: 1993

	Town	Village	Cooperative	Individual	Total
No. of enterprises	35,921	77,018	24,963	846,980	984,882
No. of employees	4,119,675	3,014,658	170,351	2,169,558	9,474,242
Sales revenue (RMB '000)	198,332,880	130,043,520	3,446,710	31,347,120	363,170,230
No. of employee per enterprise	114.7	39.1	6.8	2.5	–
Sales revenue per employee (RMB)	48,143	43,137	20,233	14,449	–

Source: 1993 statistics complied from *Annual Yearbook of China's TVEs, 1994.*

In comparing Jiangsu's TVE figures with the national average, there is a sharp contrast in both the number of employees as well as the sales revenue among the four categories of TVEs. For instance, Jiangsu's township TVEs employed 114 persons on average while at the national level, this figure is only 66. In terms of sales revenue, Jiangsu's TVEs played a significant role. The town and village categories together accounted for over 90% of the province's total TVE sales. At the national level, individual TVEs were very significant as they contributed over 33% of the total sales revenue. A comparative summary of this data among the four categories is presented in Table 10–5.

TABLE 10–5
Comparison Between Jiangsu TVEs and the National TVEs: 1993

		Town	Village	Cooperative	Individual	Total
Sales Revenue	Jiangsu	54.6%	35.8%	1.0%	8.6%	100%
	China	31.5%	28.5%	6.7%	33.3%	100%
Sales Revenue per employee (RMB)	Jiangsu	48,143	43,137	20,233	14,449	N/A
	China	31,505	28,500	21,102	16,955	N/A
No. of Employees per enterprise	Jiangsu	114.7	39.1	6.8	2.5	N/A
	China	66.4	23.1	8.8	2.6	N/A

N/A - not applicable
Source: Complied from *Annual Yearbook of China's TVEs 1994.*

Jiangsu's TVEs contributed 12.6% to China's total sales revenue. However, at the TVE level, Jiangsu's townships accounted for 21.8% of the national township TVE sales revenue. Furthermore, Jiangsu's village TVEs contributed 15.8% to the national village total sales revenue. Interestingly, 8.2% of China's township TVEs and 6.1% of its village TVEs were located in the Jiangsu province. However, Jiangsu's individual TVEs comprised only 3.9% of the national total. Overall, Jiangsu is the home of 4% of the nation's TVEs. The peculiarity of Jiangsu's TVEs is the prominent influence that the township's administration has in running its township enterprises. Townships alone contributed over one-half of the province's TVEs sales revenue.

Industry Profile of Jiangsu TVEs

In all four categories of Jiangsu's TVEs, the industry segment stands out prominently as shown in Table 10–6. In the township category, 82% were in the industry segment and only 8% were in wholesale and retail-

TABLE 10–6
Profile of Jiangsu Township and Village Enterprises: 1993

	Agriculture	Industry	Construction	Transport	Wholesale and Retail	Restaurants	Services	Others	Total
Township:									
No. of Enterprises	288	29,439	1,493	1,003	2,811	450	312	125	35,921
No. of Employees	9,215	3,377,853	618,731	62,228	32,900	6,390	9,749	2,609	4,119,675
Sales Revenue ('000)	153,550	180,892,570	10,178,360	708,860	5,715,270	191,540	277,540	215,190	198,332,880
Village:									
No. of Enterprises	340	69,659	1,207	1,193	3,149	938	440	92	77,018
No. of Employees	6,472	2,867,478	74,304	25,797	26,371	7,303	4,926	2,007	3,014,658
Sales Revenue ('000)	171,150	126,369,350	1,008,450	396,160	1,691,650	193,300	103,370	110,090	130,043,520

Source: 1993 statistics from *Annual Yearbook of China's TVEs, 1994*.

ing. Although construction accounted for only 4% of the number of enterprises, it employed 15% of all employees. In the village category, over 90% were concentrated in the industry segment. This segment also employed 95% of the total employees in the village category.

Similar patterns can be observed for cooperative TVEs where the heavy concentration was also in the industry segment (see Table 10–7) which accounted for 78% of all enterprises and 76% of all employees. Nearly 8% of these enterprises were in construction which employed 15% of all employees.

However, there is a different pattern for individual TVEs. Only 50% of these enterprises were in industry, 17% were in transportation, while another 16% were in the wholesale and retailing segment.

In comparing the four categories of TVEs, it can be observed in Panel A from Table 10–8 that in the construction segment, townships, employed 414 workers on average whereas villages employed only 61 on average. More significantly, in the wholesale and retail segment, the average sales revenue per employee for townships was RMB 173,716 as compared to RMB 64,148 for villages, and only RMB 10,518 for cooperative TVEs (see Panel B in Table 10–8). But in the transportation segment, cooperatives came out on top with RMB 26,833 per employee as compared to RMB 11,391 for township TVE's and 15,357 for village TVEs.

There is also a vast difference for the service segment where townships had 31 employees per enterprise, on average, and the villages had only 11 on average. The sales revenue generated per employee also differs widely for the service segment. It ranges from RMB 28,468 for townships to around RMB 8,720 for both cooperative and individual TVEs.

Trends in Jiangsu TVEs

The growth rates of Jiangsu's township and village enterprises have been very moderate (see Table 10–9). One possible explanation for this trend is that entrepreneurs are now turning to private enterprises instead of setting up TVEs. For example, the former grew from 40,000 enterprises in 1988 to 139,000 in 1992. Nevertheless, considering the total sales revenue generated, TVEs were experiencing accelerated growth in these years, as much as 157% in 1993. Focusing on the sales revenue contributed per employee, the increase was from RMB 14,138 to RMB 46,026,

TABLE 10–7
Profile of Jiangsu Cooperative and Individual Enterprises: 1993

	Agriculture	Industry	Construction	Transport	Wholesale and Retail	Restaurants	Services	Others	Total
Cooperative:									
No. of Enterprises	N/A	19,55	2,009	1,237	1,240	335	392	196	24,963
No. of Employees	N/A	130,05	25,057	4,399	6,487	1,389	2,261	701	170,351
Sales Revenue ('000)	N/A	2,936,42	268,800	118,040	68,230	24,030	19,730	11,460	3,446,710
Individual:									
No. of Enterprises	N/A	423,81	58,198	146,230	136,414	29,535	35,980	16,811	846,980
No. of Employees	N/A	1,253,15	278,887	234,153	235,149	69,110	63,027	36,077	2,169,558
Sales Revenue ('000)	N/A	20,644,19	1,807,140	2,724,710	4,414,350	935,730	550,130	270,870	31,347,120

Source: 1993 statistics from *Annual Yearbook of China's TVEs, 1994.*

TABLE 10–8
Comparison of the Four Categories of Jiangsu TVEs: 1993

Panel A: Average Number of Employees Per Enterprise

TVEs	Agriculture	Industry	Construction	Transport	Wholesale and Retail	Restaurants	Services	Others
Township	32.0	114.7	414.4	62.0	11.7	14.2	31.2	20.9
Village	19.0	41.1	61.5	21.6	8.4	7.8	11.2	21.8
Cooperative	N/A	6.6	12.5	3.5	5.2	4.1	5.8	3.6
Individual	N/A	2.9	4.8	1.6	1.7	2.3	1.7	2.1

Source: 1993 statistics from *Annual Yearbook of China's TVEs, 1994.*

Panel B: Average Sales Revenue Per Employee (RMB)

TVEs	Agriculture	Industry	Construction	Transport	Wholesale and Retail	Restaurants	Services	Others
Township	16,663	53,552	16,450	11,391	173,716	29,975	28,468	82,480
Village	26,444	44,070	13,572	15,357	64,148	26,468	20,984	54,853
Cooperative	N/A	22,578	10,727	26,833	10,518	17,300	8,726	16,348
Individual	N/A	16,474	6,480	11,636	18,772	13,540	8,728	7,508

Source: 1993 statistics from *Annual Yearbook of China's TVEs, 1994.*

which is a three-fold increase. One possible explanation is the authorities' tighter tax collection measures which were intended to weed out bogus TVEs.

TABLE 10–9
Jiangsu Township and Village Enterprises Distribution in Industry Sector

	1985	1990	1991	1992	1993	1994
No. of TVEs	98,567	113,159	105,231	116,314	112,939	111,782
(i) township	33,541	35,018	33,754	38,927	35,921	36,153
(ii) village	65,026	78,141	71,477	77,387	77,018	75,629
Distributed in						
Agriculture	2,365	878	820	1,894	628	570
Industry	81,560	99,883	93,903	93,937	99,098	98,916
Construction	3,087	2,933	2,561	3,982	2,700	2,407
Transportation	3,826	2,670	2,238	2,929	2,196	1,744
Commercial	7,729	6,795	5,709	13,572	8,317	8,145
No. of employees ('000)	6,270.9	6,729.3	6,841.6	7,302.5	7,134.4	6,883.9
(i) township	3,634.2	3,816.9	3,960.9	4,346.1	4,119.7	3,976.2
(ii) village	2,636.7	2,912.4	2,880.7	2,956.4	3,014.7	2,907.7
Distributed in						
Agriculture	66.2	23.5	19.4	35.6	15.7	15.6
Industry	5,116.6	5,881.2	6,040.3	6,094.3	6,245.3	6,030.1
Construction	830.0	632.0	593.6	883.1	693.0	672.8
Transportation	162.4	114.7	124.0	117.9	88.0	75.2
Commercial	95.7	77.9	64.3	171.6	92.4	90.2
Sales revenue (RMB billion)	35.21	95.14	121.13	209.29	328.37	385.32
(i) township	21.73	58.28	74.50	129.58	198.33	224.13
(ii) village	13.48	36.86	46.63	79.71	130.04	161.19
Distributed in						
Agriculture	0.22	0.19	0.21	0.52	0.32	0.66
Industry	31.03	87.70	113.96	187.17	307.26	378.38
Construction	2.40	4.29	4.61	11.84	11.19	2.13
Transportation	0.58	0.86	0.83	1.37	1.10	0.25
Commercial	0.98	2.10	1.52	8.39	8.50	3.90

* Commercial includes wholesale, retail, restaurants and services.

Source: 1994 statistics from *Jiangsu Yearbook, 1995*.

STRUCTURE AND OPERATIONS OF TVEs

An important milestone in the development of TVEs in Jiangsu province has been the establishment of the AICCs. The following sections discuss their influence and relationship to the development of TVEs.

The Role of AICCs

In the early 1980s, the central government exerted increased control over the development of TVEs in the countryside. Setting up AICCs was part of this effort. An AICC is similar to a holding company. Its main functions are corporate administration and asset management of the TVEs within its purview. Each town and each larger village have their own AICCs. The general manager of the AICCs is designated by the town or village council. Normally the post is occupied by the deputy secretary of the Communist Party branch committee in that town or village. Thus, the communist party has some control over TVEs. An AICC employs workers (apart from the general manager) to carry out its functions. A typical AICC consists of one corporate office which deals with administrative affairs, and four companies which handle agriculture, industry, trading businesses and subsidiary activities, respectively.

An AICC, therefore, is a township collective economic entity within the social structure of the town. Its functions include resource development, enterprise set up, asset management, production service and coordination. This is in line with the town party branch committee and town council guidelines. Hence, an AICC is directly under the leadership of the communist party. The AICC must report to the town party and town council, and must obtain approval on important matters such as economic development strategy, business planning, project development, technology introduction and transfer, and personnel policy.

Under an AICC's management system, the decision-making process of a TVE involves first, a bottom-up procedure, and then a top-down procedure (see Figure 10–1). For example, if a TVE wishes to start a new business, it first submits a proposal to the AICC's corporate office and then the AICC reports and discusses the proposal with the town party committee. If the proposal is approved by the Party, then the AICC gives approval to the TVE which then starts the business. This system, by the way, also enhances the AICC's support of subsequent action taken by a TVE.

TVE Financing

Over the years, TVE financing has come from different sources. In the early stages, especially before AICCs were established, TVEs financed their operations mainly via retained earnings from agricultural production. After agricultural reforms emerged in the countryside, farmers became more productive and agriculture production became much more profitable because the land was returned to the farmers (Yang *et al.*, 1995). Retained earnings from agriculture in each town provided sufficient funds to finance the operations of TVEs, but not expansion.

FIGURE 10–1
Relationship of AICCs with TVEs and Party Branch

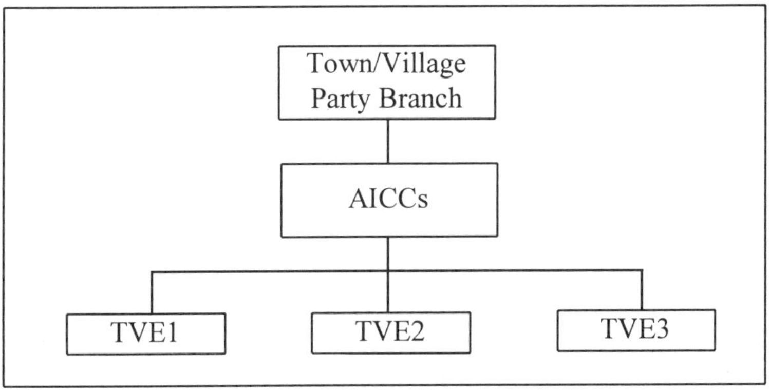

Another source of financing came from personal funds. Individuals or families invested their savings into profitable TVEs and received returns in the form of interest. With the establishment of AICCs, TVEs could apply for funds for new projects or to expand production. These loans have now become the main source of funds for most TVEs.

The village cooperative economic fund management service station is the department which handles funds management. The station is directly under the control of the AICCs in each town. It is a self-accumulation, self-management, self-service cooperative organisation within the town. Its main functions are fund raising, fund management, fund use and loan services. By controlling the financing process, AICCs control and coordinate project development and production scale, and they also guide the direction of future TVE developments.

Before the 1980s, it was very difficult for TVEs to get bank loans since they existed outside of the centrally planned economy. That is, they were not provided for financially in the national economic plan or budget. Now, as part of the support from government at all levels, TVEs can apply for loans from government-owned banks.

Currently, another popular form of financing is through joint ventures with foreign or domestic partners. This opportunity has come about partly because of the Chinese government's tighter financing policy in the last several years to curb inflation.

TVE Labour Management

The successful implementation of a "management responsibility" system has played an important role in the development of TVEs in Jiangsu province. Under this system, managers are given the authority and financial incentive to increase production. Managers are generally required to meet fixed profit levels which are then turned over to the local government. Profits above the target level are divided among the general manager and the employees of the TVE according to a set formula. This can add significantly to salary levels which may be as high as RMB 1,000 per month. In some localities, managers who fail to meet their assigned targets are replaced (Chan, 1995).

There is some variety in the management responsibility system in the southern part of Jiangsu. One popular system is the "Assets Appreciation Evaluation with Fixed Production Elements". This was first tried out in Tongluo Town, Wujiang. Based on the fixed assets, working capital and manpower of a TVE, AICCs set profit and other targets as well as allocate profits according to government policy. This system has accelerated the progress of the enterprise and increased its profit margin. Currently, there are about 500 TVEs in Wujiang that have adopted this system (Shen, 1995).

Apart from this system, there are other types of management responsibility systems such as the cooperative shares system, the leasing responsibility system, the joint state-private operations system and the mortgage contract with risks system. The various types of systems can be adapted to the different levels of TVEs production abilities, to stimulate their efficiency and progress.

In the implementation of a management responsibility system, the balance between responsibility, authority and benefits is highly emphasised. For example, a general manager of a TVE charged with achieving the target set by the AICC, has the authority to decide company strategy, project development, business scope, pricing policy for products, internal duties and the responsibilities system, the combination of production elements, labour management and personnel policy. Clearly, this type of structure is an impetus to successful TVE operations.

Appropriation of Earnings

Like SOEs, TVEs also pay a turnover tax and a business tax to the state according to state tax policy. In addition, TVEs have to contribute some portion of their earnings to the AICCs. This contribution is usually made on the basis of asset usage and/or the allocation of administration fees by the AICCs. The AICCs will generally reinvest these funds into the businesses of the TVEs under their control. It should be noted that the funds from one TVE need not be reinvested into the business of that TVE. In fact, these funds are often reinvested in the businesses of TVEs which are not doing as well. As a return on investment, TVEs pay interest to individual investors.

Since the town/village council represents the people within the town/village, TVEs have to contribute some portion of their earnings to the town/village council. The town/village council then uses these funds to develop infrastructure, education, agriculture and public facilities to benefit the people under its jurisdiction.

TVEs can retain about one-half of their net earnings to build up capital reserve. This provides an increased asset base for further development. According to the contract between TVEs and their employees under the management responsibility system, TVEs may pay the employees a bonus on the basis of their performance.

TVE SUCCESS FACTORS

Favourable Macroeconomic Policies

A milestone in China's economic reform was the Third Plenum of the Communist Party's 11th Central Committee in December 1978. There, Deng Xiaoping's rural reform programme was formalised. This was also a turning point for TVEs in China.

The government's residence registration system served to restrict rural labour from moving into urban centres. This meant that there was a pool of labour (albeit generally unskilled) in rural areas. This also meant that if sufficient jobs were not created, then there would be unemployment. Indeed, the central party committee and state council attached great importance to the development of TVEs and pointed out that this type of development was the only way for farmer's incomes to increase and to have prosperity in the countryside. Thus, the government encouraged the creation of TVEs and they bore the brunt of the burden of job creation. Starting in 1981, the government granted a three year tax holiday to all new rural enterprises.

Over time, economic reform and the open door policy have removed inhibitions about profit-oriented business activities and have enabled TVEs to take advantage of opportunities to make profits. In 1984, the state council formalised the political and legal status of TVEs. This gave TVEs the legal "personality" needed to get bank loans. Correspondingly, bank credit to TVEs was made more readily available.

Provincial party committees and the Jiangsu government have held provincial working conferences on TVEs annually since 1985. These are held to solve major issues in TVE development, to adopt measures to promote TVE growth, and to protect TVEs' legal rights and interests. The Provincial People's Congress passed the first set of regulations for the management of TVEs in Jiangsu.

Market Driven Strategies

TVEs are among the most market-oriented enterprises in China. They have continuously developed markets and gradually adopted market-oriented business practices. TVEs' funds, raw materials, energy and products were not provided for under the centrally planned economy. They did their best to tap the market. The 14th Communist Party Central Conference supported new efforts to develop a socialist market economy, that is, a market economy with socialist characteristics. This provided new opportunities for TVEs to develop. TVEs were the pioneers of the socialist market economy and subsequent market economic reform promoted the TVEs' growth and development which, in turn, further accelerated the growth of the socialist market economy. In their *de facto* operations, TVEs are far more market driven than SOEs in almost all key aspects.

As discussed earlier, TVEs had to compete with SOEs for inputs, labour and technology. In reality, TVEs faced the "hard" budget constraints whereas SOEs faced the "soft" ones. This was because the central government was ready to assist SOEs financially and materially if they exceeded their budgeted requirements. Actually, Beijing had no choice since the failure of SOEs potentially leads to massive unemployment, a heightening of social tension and chaos, a situation that Beijing will not tolerate at any cost (Yang *et al.,* 1995). But this was not the case with TVEs which, apart from certain macroeconomic policies, were generally left to survive on their own merit.

TVEs make use of incentive based pay schemes to compensate their directors, workers and sales people. Because TVEs were outside the centrally planned economy, they were not provided with any assured market for the goods which they produced. Thus, TVEs had to motivate their employees and marketing people to produce their products competitively and to sell them in the open market.

TVEs have wide discretion in the pay schemes of their directors. The fundamental similarity in these pay schemes is that the directors earn more if the TVEs generate more profits. Generally, pay schemes are decided by the directors. These directors usually pay workers, who carry out easily identifiable pieces of work, a fixed amount for each piece of work. An example is silk embroidery where payment is made for each piece of completed work. Where integrated production processes prevent this pay scheme from being implemented, a fixed-cum-variable pay scheme is often adopted. Pay schemes for sales people usually consist of three components: fixed wages, commission and other benefits, with the commission component constituting the most important part of their pay.

Emphasis on Changes and Perfecting the Operating Mechanism

Based on the practice of contractual management responsibility systems, TVEs in Jiangsu spearheaded a set of flexible management responsibility systems and created a flexible mechanism. In recent years, equity cooperative systems were promoted in TVEs. This enhanced TVEs' management systems.

One key feature of TVEs' commitment to change is their readiness to replace their directors. The TVE director is a key person who has wide discretion and the power to run a TVE as he sees fit. Thus, the director's entrepreneurial and management skills are often critical to the success of the TVE. The director also has the responsibility to meet the objectives which the AICC mandated when they appointed him the director of the TVE. If the director cannot meet these objectives, then he is replaced. Indeed, there are TVEs which have changed their directors more than ten times in a period of several years.

Improvements in Expertise and Technology

In the course of their development, TVEs gradually overcame the worst aspects of some of their weaknesses such as low technological equipment and poor quality control. They attached importance to capital acquisition, adopted new technology, new equipment, expedited the technical renovation of key enterprises and trained their employees accordingly. Over the years, the province implemented 1,750 items of the Spark Programme (*xinghuo jihua*) and this provided models for the development of TVE technology programmes. The Spark Programme was launched by the State Science and Technology Commission in 1985 to promote the transfer and diffusion of more advanced technological and managerial expertise from China's research institutes and SOEs to TVEs.

Apart from the government supported transfer of expertise and technology, TVEs have taken the initiative to develop their own expertise and technology. TVEs made arrangements with both SOEs and the research institutes for the transfer of expertise and technology. These arrangements have ranged from borrowing certain personnel from the SOEs or research institutes to the delivery of the TVEs' goods in exchange. SOEs and research institutes do not operate on market principles and usually they make no effort to charge anything close to the market rate for the expertise and technology transfer. Furthermore, TVEs often engage SOEs and research institute employees on a part-time basis. Again, incentive based pay schemes are often used. In some cases, TVEs have even "poached" employees who ultimately become full time employees. As their expertise and technology improved, some TVEs have begun to turn to joint ventures with foreign parties to further improve their expertise and technology.

Broad Vision, Targeting at Overseas Ventures and Markets

In recent years, TVEs have expanded their markets internationally. Foreign funds and technology have been attracted in the process. Since 1987, the growth rate of export goods has been higher than TVEs' gross production growth rate. Export income accounted for up to 20% of total income. At the same time, they ventured into overseas markets. By the end of 1992, 65 TVEs had set up overseas branches (*Jiangsu TVE Yearbook*, 1993).

The Future of TVEs' Success Factors

TVEs grew tremendously during the mid-1980s. This was during a time of relatively easy availability of inputs and markets awaiting the supply of goods. At present, it is no longer so easy to get inputs such as loans. This is because of the government's anti-inflationary policy and the greater intensity of competition for capital. Furthermore, there is also greater competition for existing markets.

Expertise and technology transfers are no longer well below market prices. This is because SOEs and research institutes are both facing market forces and they have begun to impose market prices for such transfers. Intellectual property laws have not only been passed, but they are likely to be enforced in the future as China prepares to join the World Trade Organisation.

With regard to the residence registration regulations, these have already been enforced in a rather lax manner for many years. The right to reside is strictly regulated by the local authority. These regulations may well be repealed in the future. In any case, there now is a large population of young peasants who have left their hometowns to look for work. The mobility of these peasants means that TVEs will have to pay the full market rate to retain these workers.

Apart from the above, the Chinese government's decision to reduce the tariff which was imposed upon imported goods will expose Chinese enterprises to much keener competition from imported goods. As of 1 April 1996, the existing 43% tariff will be reduced by one-half. Of course, the very same enterprises will also be able to buy imported inputs at lower prices. Exactly how the strategic competitive balance will change for Chinese enterprises is uncertain.

Thus, even though TVEs have been successful so far, the factors which have enabled them to succeed need not necessarily enable them to continue to do so. Indeed, the success factors may not continue to hold in the future and, hence, TVEs may face a very challenging business environment.

BUSINESS OPPORTUNITIES

For business entrepreneurs planning to venture into Jiangsu, there are abundant opportunities. The most popular areas for investment are the silk, textiles and food processing industries.

Silk

Jiangsu and its southern neighbour, Zejiang province, are the two principal producers of silk in China. In 1993, TVEs in these two provinces together produced 60% of the raw silk and 70% of the silk products produced by the country's TVEs. Table 10–10 illustrates Jiangsu's production in silk and cotton relative to other prominent centres in China.

Jiangsu also has a renowned silk embroidery research institute in Suzhou. The double-sided embroidery technique is a secret of the institute. The institute also trains local citizens in embroidery. It usually takes a person up to five years to master these skills.

The cities of Wujiang, Hangzhou, Suzhou and Huzhou are known as China's four silk capitals. We had a chance to visit Wujiang which is south of Suzhou and west of Shanghai. The city has a 1,085-year history and was designated a city in 1992. It has a population of 772,000 and it has 23 towns within its jurisdiction. In 1993, the gross national product of the city exceeded RMB 6 billion and its annual export of silk was one-sixth of national output. Industry output comprised 95.4% of the city's total output. Silk alone contributed 47% to this total output.

Apart from silk, the city has light industries manufacturing food products and building materials. In addition, there are arts and handicraft industries. Wujiang is a convenient one-stop silk processing centre. It caters for the whole process, from planting mulberry trees to raising silkworms and, further, to printing and manufacturing garments.

Nearby Shengze town is famous for its many silk TVEs, especially on the western side of the town which is known as The East Silk Market. It is the place where merchants meet to trade in silk. The population of the town is about 110,000.

Located within Shengze is the Jiangsu Yingxiang Group. It is a township TVE and it is reputed to be one of the top ten township TVEs in the country. The group was founded in 1992 and before that it was known as the Wujiang Shengze General Mill for Dyeing and Printing. In 1994, this group had a total workforce of over 3,000. It had fixed assets of over RMB 1 billion and annual sales of RMB 2 billion. Its net income was over RMB 100 million. Apart from silk production, the group also has within its portfolio hotels (e.g., Feiying Hotel, Yingxiang Hotel and

Shenying Hotel), restaurants and property developments (e.g., Yingxiang Villa and the Bank Building).

For businesses planning to venture into Jiangsu province, silk (and its related products) is definitely an investment possibility. There appear to be abundant opportunities in the manufacture of raw silk and artificial silk. In addition, there is a well trained embroidery labour force. Jiangsu also has reasonably good telecommunications and transportation services. The 318 National Highway runs parallel to the Taipu river from the east to the west and the Grand Canal runs from north to south parallel to the 205 Provincial Highway.

TABLE 10–10
Silk and Textile Production by Province: 1993

Province	Textile ('000,000 metres)		Dyed Textile ('000,000 metres)	Silk (tonnes)	
	Total	Cotton		Raw	Products
Jiangsu	1,842.35 (2)[a]	1,165.51 (2)	2,093.03 (2)	12,788 (2)	57,040 (1)
Zhejiang	1,426.45 (4)	381.95	3,914.44 (1)	28,103 (1)	56,223 (2)
Shandong	1,518.66 (3)	1,464.31 (1)	493.34 (3)	1,373	6,845
Hubei	513.19	482.73 (4)	46.48	102	2,199
Guangdong	2,015.48 (1)	498.06 (3)	–	2,235	516
National Total[b]	10,641.83	5,151.51	7,614.20	69,285	160,939

[a] Figures in brackets are the national ranking in quantity.
[b] The "National Total" refers to the quantity as produced by TVEs only.
Source: 1993 statistics from *Annual Yearbook of China's TVEs, 1994.*

Other Opportunities

Apart from silk, there are opportunities in the apparel, plastic products, food processing and beverages industries for entrepreneurs to explore. In the case of leather products, it is Shanghai's TVEs that take the lead and not Jiangsu (see Table 10–11). This is mentioned here because of the close proximity of the two locations.

Plastic products are another investment possibility worth exploring. Jiangsu province ranked fourth and its neighbour, Zhejiang, followed just behind in fifth place in terms of tonnage (see Table 10–12).

Food processing also has potential in Jiangsu which ranked number one for rice as well as wheat products (see Table 10–13). In addition, there are beverage products such as soft-drinks. This industry is particularly relevant in view of its proximity to Shanghai and its strategic position in the Yangtze river basin. (Yang *et al.*, 1995).

TABLE 10–11
Apparel Products Production by Province: 1993

Province	Apparels			
	Clothing ('000,000 pieces)	Leather Shoes ('000,000 pairs)	Textile Shoes ('000,000 pairs)	Leather Products ('000,000 pieces)
Shanghai	206.25	217.36[a] (3)	15.07	606.67 (1)
Jiangsu	367.94 (5)	55.91	32.84	3.85
Zhejiang	693.63 (3)	167.55 (4)	137.91 (2)	0.02
Fujian	696.28 (2)	222.64 (2)	116.32 (4)	4.71
Henan	202.70	61.98 (5)	205.01 (1)	434.76 (2)
Guangdong	1,416.64 (1)	263.02 (1)	93.95 (5)	–
National Total[b]	5,808.20	1,213.96	976.60	1,345.87

[a] Figures in brackets are the national ranking in quantity.
[b] The "National Total" refers to the quantity as produced by TVEs only.
Source: 1993 statistics from *Annual Yearbook of China's TVEs, 1994.*

TABLE 10–12
Plastic Products Production by Province: 1993

Province	Plastic Products (tonnes)		
	Total	Materials for bags and clothing	Materials for shoe products
Hebei	817,333[a] (1)	1,682	65,622 (2)
Jiangsu	555,837 (4)	50,149 (2)	2,589
Zhejiang	533,102 (5)	426,482 (1)	106,620 (1)
Shangdong	581,026 (3)	7,830	3,850
Guangdong	750,000 (2)	–	–
National Total[b]	4,716,953	495,541	245,996

[a] Figures in brackets are the national ranking in tonnage.
[b] The "National Total" refers to the quantity as produced by TVEs only.
Source: 1993 statistics from *Annual Yearbook of China's TVEs, 1994.*

TABLE 10–13
Food Processing and Canned Food Production by Province: 1993

Province	Food Processing (tonnes)			Canned Food (tonnes)		
	Total	Rice Products	Wheat Products	Total	Fruit Products	Vegetable Products
Liaoning	11,216 (2)[a]	4,788 (2)	116	37,079	22,434	3,537
Jiangsu	25,819 (1)	6,805 (1)	13,286 (1)	31,711	3,131	14,266 (4)
Zhejiang	278	193	24	207,885 (3)	75,981 (4)	117,523 (1)
Shangdong	1,317	24	827 (3)	265,307 (1)	232,617 (1)	10,790 (7)
Henan	3,011 (4)	141	1,519 (2)	247,657 (2)	168,204 (2)	12,339 (5)
National Total[b]	62,555	23,415	20,087	1,621,115	932,224	326,185

[a] Figures in brackets are the national ranking in quantity.
[b] The "National Total" refers to the quantity as produced by TVEs only.
Source: 1993 statistics from *Annual Yearbook of China's TVEs, 1994*.

CONCLUSION

The differences between TVEs and SOEs can be summarised as follows:

(I) SOEs are owned and controlled by the state and they are within the centrally planned economy while TVEs are not;
(ii) SOEs practise the "iron rice-bowl" philosophy and they provide generous benefits to their employees whereas TVEs tie their employees' pay to productivity;
(iii) SOEs can resort to the centrally planned economy for budgets to cater for their financing and supplies of raw materials whereas TVEs have to find their own financing as well as supplies of raw materials, albeit sometimes with the help of the AICCs;
(iv) SOEs' management follow government guidelines and procedures while the TVEs' management have wide discretionary power concerning how TVEs should be run; and
(v) most SOEs are not market-oriented whereas TVEs have been market-oriented for many decades.

The AICCs play a significant role in the development of TVEs. For example, each town and village has its own AICC which handles the TVEs' corporate administration and asset management. The deputy secretary of the Communist Party branch committee of the town/village in question is usually appointed as the general manager of the AICC. Thus, the TVEs, through the AICCs, are under the Communist Party's control. Indeed, the AICCs must get the town/village Communist Party's approval for certain key decisions. However, once approval is obtained, the general manager of the TVE has wide latitude in day-to-day operations.

Even before 1949, cooperatives existed in China. They were involved in cottage industries. After 1949, the cooperatives were encouraged to develop an industrial base and the number of cooperatives grew significantly. In the early 1960s, the TVEs' growth was stunted by leftist elements and natural disasters. From 1965 onwards, the TVEs grew steadily. From 1985 onwards, with various favourable macroeconomic policies, TVEs grew even more dramatically until they now account for almost one-third of China's industrial output and nearly one-half of its total industrial employment.

There are a number of factors which account for the success of TVEs. Some of the more salient ones include the following:

(i) favourable macroeconomic policies;
(ii) adoption of market driven strategies in sourcing for supplies of raw materials, labour and financing, and in compensating their management and employees;
(iii) flexibility and readiness to improve, including a change in general managers when they were not successful;
(iv) improving their expertise and technology by turning to SOEs, research institutes and foreign joint venture partners; and
(v) venturing into overseas markets.

In the future, TVEs will face numerous challenges as the supply of raw materials, labour and financing becomes more scarce, the cost of expertise and technology becomes more expensive, competition for markets becomes more fierce and the reduction of tariffs on imported goods becomes more widespread. Although these challenges cast some uncertainty over TVEs, there is ground for being optimistic that TVEs will survive as viable entities for doing business in China. But not all TVEs will survive the challenges ahead. A foreign partner who proposes to enter into a joint venture with a TVE should appreciate the fundamental differences between TVEs and other enterprises, the success factors and the threats to its continued success. It must be in this context that the multitude of business opportunities available need to be considered.

REFERENCES

Annual Yearbook of China TVEs, China Agriculture Publishing Press, 1994.

Chan Sandy S., "The Development of China's Private Entrepreneurship", *Journal of Enterprising Culture*, Vol. 3, No. 3, September 1995.

Gao Yinuo, "The Second Upsurge of TVEs", *Jingji Ribao (Economic Daily)*, Beijing, 13 June 1993.

Jiangsu Statistics Yearbook, Jiangsu Municipal Government, 1994.

Jiangsu Statistics Yearbook, Jiangsu Municipal Government, 1995.

Jiangsu TVE Yearbook, Nanjing University Press, 1993.

MacMurray Trevor and Jonathan Woetzel, "The Challenge Facing China's State-Owned Enterprises", *McKinsey Quarterly*, Spring 1994.

Shen Rongfa, *Reform, Opening and Wujiang Practice*, Nanjing University Press, 1995.

Vong John, Ma Rong and Yang Mu, *China's Rural Entrepreneurers: Ten Case Studies*, Times Academic Press, 1995.

Wickramanayake Ebel, Chen Yafang and Wen Ming, "Resurrection of the Private Micro-Enterprises in China: Experience in Urban and Rural Areas", *Journal of Enterprising Culture,* Vol. 3, No. 3, September 1995.

Yang Mu, John J. Williams and Cao Yong, "Resurrecting Shanghai for the 21st Century: The Shift in China's Regional Economic Strategies", *China Business Review*, December 1995.

Zweig David, "Reaping Rural Rewards", *China Business Forum,* 1992.

FIRM ANALYSES

Chapter 11

Shanghai Baoshan Iron and Steel General Works

BY
ANG Chwee Peng
CHAN Khai Heen
CHONG Aik Chien
Gary HEW Keong Chan

INTRODUCTION

THE STATE-OWNED Enterprises (SOEs) are the pillars of China's economy. Besides accounting for approximately 48% of the 1994 GDP (*The Economist*, 10 June 1995), the taxes and profits from SOEs also represent an important revenue contribution to the Chinese fiscal system. In addition, SOEs employ about 42% of the total Chinese labour force and produce about 60% of the total industrial output in China (*Lianhe Zaobao*, 5 September 1994).

Following China's economic reform from a planned economy to a market economy, many SOEs now are facing losses and are relying heavily on government subsidies in order to survive. Some of the problems faced by SOEs are:

(i) inability to adapt to a competitive environment;
(ii) definition of ownership is not clear;
(iii) market mechanism is not fully developed;
(iv) low efficiency;
(v) high social responsibility; and
(vi) poor management practices.

One of the largest Chinese SOEs, the Baoshan Iron and Steel General Works,[1] was started in the late 1970s at the beginning of China's economic reform. This project was strongly criticised at that time by both the Chinese and foreign observers because of its high implementation cost. *The Financial Times* (3 November 1981) described Baosteel as a "monument to inefficiency". In spite of its initial difficulties, Baosteel subsequently performed so well that it was ranked as one of the top three performing state-owned enterprises in China in October 1995 by the Chinese Ministry of Finance (*Lianhe Zaobao*, 23 October 1995).

Although the Chinese government has achieved good results in its economic reform since 1979, most of the large Chinese SOEs are still facing many difficulties during the transition from the central planning system to the market economy system (Yang *et. al.,* 1995). An exception to this pattern is Baosteel. The authors interviewed some of Baosteel's senior staff to explore the reasons for its success.

This chapter describes the evolution of SOEs from a centrally planned system to a market economy as well as the challenges they faced during the transition. The Baosteel project was initiated immediately after the reform in 1979 and so this chapter provides an overview of the operating environment of the corporation when it first started. The performance of Baosteel is assessed using the McKinsey 7-S framework. The chapter then describes the changing business environment in China as it affects Baosteel and other SOEs of similar size, and suggests ways for Baosteel to address these issues. Hopefully, this chapter will provide readers with a useful insight into how other less successful SOEs in China could be rejuvenated by adopting the practices found at Baosteel. Implicitly, this knowledge can be rolled forward into business and consultancy opportunities in China.

CHINESE STATE-OWNED ENTERPRISES AND ECONOMIC REFORM

The Operating Environment of SOEs Prior to Reform in 1979

Prior to economic reform, the SOEs were accustomed to operating under a centrally planned economic system where raw materials, resources and

---

[1] This company is frequently referred to as Baosteel and this designation is used throughout the chapter.

outputs were determined by the central government planning office. The main task of SOEs was to fulfil production targets set by government authority; of course, management had very little liberty in decision making. As a result, most SOEs are extremely risk averse, inflexible and generally inefficient.

The typical characteristics of SOEs operating prior to reform are described below.

(i) ***Subject to Two Systems of Leadership:*** The SOEs were subjected to two types of leadership control, the "line control" from the industrial ministry of the central government and the "block control" from the local governmental institution in which they were operating. For example, Baosteel was subject to line control from the Ministry of Metallurgy and block, or administrative, control from the Shanghai municipal government. Investment and working capital were mostly financed by grants from government loans via the banking system according to government plans. The SOEs returned all of their profits, if any, to the state. The government, in turn, covered all losses incurred by these enterprises. This caused uncertainty over who was responsible for enterprise goals which contributed to low levels of efficiency and lack of accountability.

(ii) ***No Recognition of the Principle of Demand and Supply:*** Due to the nature of the centrally planned economic system, managerial decisions were basically administrative reactions to instructions from the state planning authority, without any consideration of market factors. The SOEs were subjected to strict production plans and they were supplied with most of their material inputs by the central government As a result, there was very little long-term strategic planning in response to market changes.

(iii) ***No Management Accountability:*** The SOEs had little operational or functional autonomy. Business concepts, such as profits, prices and taxes, were used merely for accounting purposes and they had no effect on the operation of the enterprise. The main goal of SOE managers was to fulfil production targets and not to maximise profits. As a result, there was no incentive for the managers to improve efficiency or to enhance productivity to attain higher profitability.

(iv) ***State Pricing:*** Product prices were determined by the central pricing authorities and government agencies controlled the distribution of products from the producers to the users. These prices did not reflect the costs of production or the supply/demand balance of the market. This resulted in the stockpiling of unneeded goods or chronic shortages.

(v) ***No Power to Allocate Income Based on Performance or Job Quality:*** The wages of SOE employees were basically standardised based on the national wage scale, with some adaptation according to region and profession. Compensation was set with no reference to the employees' performance or enterprise productivity. The wages were low and remained unchanged for long periods of time. There was no distinction made between good and bad performance. The wage gap between the highest and the lowest paid worker was narrow, in the region of three to one. Therefore, employees had little incentive to upgrade and strive for better results.

On the other hand, there is no "labour market" in China *per se*. University graduates (or any school drop-outs) are assigned jobs by the relevant state agency to work in SOEs, and it is often difficult for SOEs to reject any new employees. Moreover, employee dismissals are against communist ideology. As such, SOEs have little control over the size and composition of their workforce.

The Operating Environment of SOEs After Reform in 1979

In order to improve economic efficiency, the Chinese government decided to transform its economy from a planned economy to a market economy beginning 1979. As part of the economic reform, the industrial reform started off with the principle of profit retention, which allowed all enterprises to retain their profits and to pay bonuses. The profit retention system developed into "self-responsibility and autonomy" for profits and losses, which provided enterprises with greater autonomy and accountability. It was hoped that the responsibility system would provide enterprises with an incentive to improve performance.

Prior to economic reform, prices were controlled by the state, but as economic reform progressed, state authorities gradually liberalised control over the prices of industrial products. The key feature of reform was decentralising control and promoting management autonomy and responsibility. Since 1992, the government has begun to provide a uniform legal framework for various forms of shareholding companies, and the introduction of company law for limited companies. The purpose of these legal changes was to overcome the problem of excessive government intervention in the operations of SOEs by separating management from ownership. The effectiveness of this measure has yet to be seen. Some of the highlights of the economic reform are described below.

(i) ***Gradual Reduction of the Content and the Scope of State Planning:*** The SOEs became empowered to make decisions based on market factors. By 1984, only 30 to 40% of the industrial production was attributable to central planning.

(ii) ***Implementation of a Contractual Responsibility System:*** From 1985 to 1991, thc government introduced the "contract responsibility system" into SOEs. Performance targets, output quotas to the state and financial obligations to the government were specified and mutually agreed upon in advance between the SOEs and the government. Excess profits generated by these enterprises, after meeting the minimum level of contribution to the government, could be used freely by management under the concept of self-management. SOEs were free to decide on production, prices, sales, purchase of raw materials and so forth but they were not given autonomy over decisions relating to investments, exports, imports and dismissal of workers; these matters were still managed by the relevant government authorities.

(iii) ***Establishment of a Market-driven Pricing Mechanism:*** The number of goods with prices controlled by the state has been diminishing as more prices are set through market forces. SOEs are now able to set the prices of their output based on production costs and demand/supply conditions. The resulting performance of the SOEs in terms of profit or loss now gives a more accurate reflection of their economic viability.

(iv) ***Greater Autonomy:*** In the process of market reform, enterprises were given greater autonomy and accountability. Under The Regulations on Transforming the Management Mechanisms of State-Owned Industrial Enterprises promulgated by the state council in July 1992, a set of 14 rights were given to the SOEs (MacMurray, 1994). With this legislation the SOEs have the right to the following:

    (a) Make decisions on production and management (including the right to adjust the scale of production and management).
    (b) Determine the prices of products and services.
    (c) Sell products.

(d) Purchase materials.
(e) Import and export.
(f) Make decisions on investment.
(g) Use retained earnings.
(h) Sell fixed assets.
(i) Form tie-ups, acquisitions and mergers.
(j) Employ workers.
(k) Manage personnel.
(l) Allocate wages and bonuses.
(m) Establish internal organisations.
(n) Refuse funds, materials, and service allocations by government agencies.

All of these rights are fundamental and natural in most countries in the world. However, only a relatively small number of SOEs in China have been given all of the 14 rights. For most SOEs, decisions on investment, exports and imports, and the dismissal of workers are still controlled by government agencies.

CURRENT CHALLENGES FACED BY STATE-OWNED ENTERPRISES

Notwithstanding the real progress of China's industrial reforms to date, the SOEs are still facing many problems. The more important ones are mentioned below.

(i) ***Inability to Adapt to Competitive Environment:*** After many years of operating under central planning, many SOEs are accustomed to state subsidies and low productivity. They are unable to catch up with the pace of economic reform where obstacles to inter-provincial trade disappear and import restrictions and foreign investment barriers collapse. Most SOEs find it difficult to adapt to this new competitive environment.
(ii) ***Unclear Definition of Ownership:*** Under the communist ideology, SOEs are owned by the people (represented by the state council in the central government). Although all SOEs are owned by the state at the central level, in practice, most of the state-owned enterprises are controlled by the respective ministry as well as the local gov-

ernment. Even if SOEs' control rights (and income) have been delegated to municipal or other sub-central governments, the state (central government) retains the ultimate right over SOEs' assets. The general lines of authority over property rights between levels of government and management remains vague and the SOEs' managers have not been given sufficient market based governance, autonomy and risk-reward incentive structures in managing the enterprises.

(iii) ***Market System Not Fully Developed:*** Although a market driven economy has been implemented, the interaction among the various factor markets (for example, inputs such as capital, labour and technology) is still not perfect. This is due to imperfect information flows and government control (for example, tight monetary policy and a standardised wage system). As a result, resources are not efficiently allocated to meet the market driven output level.

(iv) ***Low Efficiency:*** Many SOEs still continue to exhibit poor performance. Although measures of SOE losses are highly imprecise because, technically, firms have a tax incentive to under report profits, it is estimated that the unprofitable SOEs under the budget[2] have increased from 26.4% of all SOEs in 1992, to 30.3% in 1993 and to 41.4% in 1994 (Broadman, 1995). Besides poor management, old production facilities, lack of capital for improvement and competition from foreign investment operating in China, a significant portion of SOE losses have been due to policy factors such as government controlled sales prices set at below levels, below cost, for example.

(v) ***Heavy Social Responsibility:*** In addition to concentrating on the production and distribution of their output, SOEs are also burdened with the heavy responsibility of providing employees with social services. These services include housing, education, hospitals, social security (pensions and unemployment, accident and health insurance), food services and retail outlets. Besides these subsidies to their employees, SOEs are also expected to provide financial support for public services. This heavy social responsibility has left

---

2 SOEs "under the budget" refers to SOEs that have been treated as independent accounting units and have received capital or financial subsidies from the central government, regardless of whether a sub-central government entity maintains operational control of the enterprise.

many SOEs with very limited resources for growth and improvement opportunities.

(vi) ***Lack of Capital:*** A shortage of capital, especially working capital, is one of the biggest obstacles facing the SOEs. The lack of capital in SOEs is mainly due to the credit squeeze caused by the tight monetary policy of the Chinese government to fight domestic inflation. In addition, the inability of SOEs to produce products that are wanted in the market and the poor distribution of products in China which increases inventory levels, results in a wastage of resources. In a recent survey undertaken by the *Chinese Daily's Business Week*, it was found that 44% of the enterprises in China view shortage of working capital as their most serious problem. Shortage of capital has restricted the further growth of many SOEs.

BACKGROUND AND DEVELOPMENT OF BAOSTEEL

When China first started its economic reform in 1978, the government decided to build a modern steel mill comparable to those found in developed countries to serve as a benchmark for its industrial development. The Baosteel project began on 23 December 1978 along the mouth of the Yangtze river, about 26 kilometres from the centre of Shanghai.

The project was implemented in phases. Phase one of the project (costing RMB 12.8 billion)[3] was completed and put into operation on 15 September 1985[4] with an annual production capacity of 3.2 million tonnes of crude steel. Unlike other steel mills in China, Baosteel was modelled after Japanese plants in terms of technology and plant facilities. The plant has state-of-the-art automated and computer controlled equipment. Baosteel received modern management know-how through a technology transfer agreement with an established Japanese steel producer. From the beginning, Baosteel adopted the management system of Japan's Shin Nippon Steel Mill, especially in organisational structure,

---

3 The entire fund for Phase one was financed by the central government either directly or through the China Construction Bank and the China Industrial and Commercial Bank.

4 Phase one was confined to the blooming mill while the hot rolling and cold rolling mills were constructed in Phase two. This was done to enable the company to meet the demand from other Chinese steel plants and to start earning profits as quickly as possible.

production management, human resource management and quality control management. Baosteel also sent about 700 of its engineers and operators for training in Japan. In addition, Japanese experts came to Baosteel to assist in the plant construction and manpower training.[5] Unlike other steel plants in China, the manpower of the plant was kept to the minimum, closer to that of the developed countries.

Phase two of the project (costing RMB 17.2 billion) was partially funded from Baosteel's earnings. This phase was completed in June 1991 with new facilities such as the cold strip rolling mill, the hot strip rolling mill and a continuous slab caster. The annual capacity was increased to 7.3 million tonnes of crude steel that were processed into hot rolled strips, cold rolled strips and seamless tubes.

Phase three of the project (which began in December 1993 and is estimated to cost RMB 62.4 billion) will increase the annual capacity to 13 million tonnes when it is completed in 1999. This phase is being internally funded completely from retained earnings. About 88% of the equipment in this phase is either being constructed in-plant or purchased locally.

With regard to its future prospects, Baosteel's potential is attractive considering the following factors:

(a) it has modern and large-scale equipment with relatively high energy efficiency and high productivity;
(b) its strategic coastal location facilitates the import of high quality iron ore from overseas; and
(c) it has achieved productivity of 600 tonnes of steel output per employee and it is expecting to reach a target of 900 tonnes per employee by the completion of the third phase.

Performance of Baosteel

Table 11–1 gives an overview of Baosteel's performance during the period from 1987 to 1993. During this period, Baosteel reduced the number of direct employees from 38,000 in 1987 to just 26,000. The annual steel production output was increased from 3.2 million tonnes in 1987 to 7.2 million tonnes in 1993. In 1994, Baosteel employed 17,955 employees and achieved a turnover of RMB 21.67 billion (excluding value-

5 It was revealed during interviews that this arrangement will help to foster an environment suited to the Japanese management concepts which Baosteel adopted.

added tax). At the end of 1995, the number of direct employees was just over 13,000 while annual production increased to 8.5 million tonnes.

TABLE 11–1
Baosteel's Performance: 1987 to 1993

	1993	1992	1991	1990	1989	1988	1987
No. of Employees[a]	26.00	28.00	31.00	32.00	33.50	35.00	38.00
Steel Output[b]	7.20	6.70	4.70	3.80	3.60	3.50	3.20
Output/ Employee[c]	0.27	0.23	0.15	0.11	0.10	0.10	0.08
Sales Revenue[d]	15.80	11.90	8.40	6.70	3.90	2.90	2.50
Profit Tax[e]	4.50	2.70	2.30	1.50	0.91	0.46	0.27
Depreciation[f]	2.80	1.50	0.69	0.63	0.54	0.39	0.17

a: number of direct employees in thousands.
b: steel production output in millions of tonnes.
c: steel output in million of tonnes per employee.
d: sales revenue in billion RMB.
e: profit taxes remitted to the central government in billion RMB.
f: depreciation provision, including major maintenance cost, in billion RMB.
Source: Li Zhang Xieng and Fan Zo Wen, *Introduction to Baosteel's Modern Management System,* People's University of China Press, 1993.

Analysis of Baosteel: The Success Factors

Traditional strategy theories provide a framework for reviewing the success factors of an enterprise. One of them is the McKinsey 7-S framework which states that the competitive advantage of a firm arises from creating a proper fit among key organisational characteristics. These characteristics are structure, strategy, systems, style, skill, staff and superordinate goals (Waterman *et al.,* 1980). Therefore, excellent enterprises design these factors into their organisations in accordance with their strategies. The 7-S framework can be viewed as a way to implement and create traditional competitive advantages. The traditional approach to strategy stresses the "creation of advantages". D'Aveni (1994) summarises the traditional sources of competitive advantages into four arenas, namely cost and quality, timing and know-how, strongholds and deep pockets. This framework together with McKinsey's 7-S framework are used to analyse the success factors of Baosteel and to explain

Baosteel's success as compared to other SOEs in China.

The first source of advantage deals with cost and quality. Baosteel has created this source of advantage in competing with domestic steel makers as well as foreign steel producers. In competing with the former, Baosteel's ability to achieve better quality production has ensured its leadership among the domestic suppliers. To compete with imported steel, Baosteel has built efficient operations via the technology received from Japan and Germany. This has enabled it to adopt a low pricing strategy.

The second source of advantage is timing and technological knowledge. This is largely based on the unique assets held by a firm. For the domestic market, technology imported from Japan and Germany is a source of advantage to Baosteel. Because it is the first Chinese steel mill to install foreign technology, Baosteel has gained a timing advantage as "first mover".

The third source of advantage concerns strongholds. Firms can create a competitive advantage by raising barriers to entry so as to exclude new entrants, or to limit its buyers and suppliers from entering the industry through vertical integration. Six entry barriers identified by Porter (1980) are: economies of scale, product differentiation, capital requirements, switching costs, access to distribution channels and cost disadvantage (other than scale). Economies of scale and capital requirement are general protections to all steel mills from new entrants. By forming joint ventures with a car manufacturing company and an Australian ore mining company, Baosteel has limited buyers and suppliers from entering the industry. The fact that Baosteel has set up 11 sales branches and 22 retail offices throughout China suggests that Baosteel has established a stronghold over its distribution channels.

The final source of advantage is deep pockets. Companies that have substantial financial and managerial resources will usually outlast smaller firms in competition. Although Baosteel is not the largest steel mill in China, it has established a deep pocket advantage through 17 years of successful operations. Baosteel is able to finance 100% of its Phase three expansion with retained earnings. In addition, it has access to borrowing capital because of an excellent credit rating.

McKinsey's 7-S Framework

As mentioned earlier, Waterman *et al.* (1980) in their adapted 7-S framework assert that organisational effectiveness stems from the interaction of seven factors: structure, strategy, systems, style, skill, staff and superordinate goals (see Figure 11–1). There is no hierarchy among these seven factors; all seven factors must be simultaneously combined and balanced. In other words, the seven factors must match for an organisation to succeed. Moreover, the interaction of these seven factors determines the core competency that can be acquired by an organisation and this serves as the basis of strategy formulation. These seven basis of factors are described and related to the experience of Baosteel below.

FIGURE 11–1
The 7-S Framework

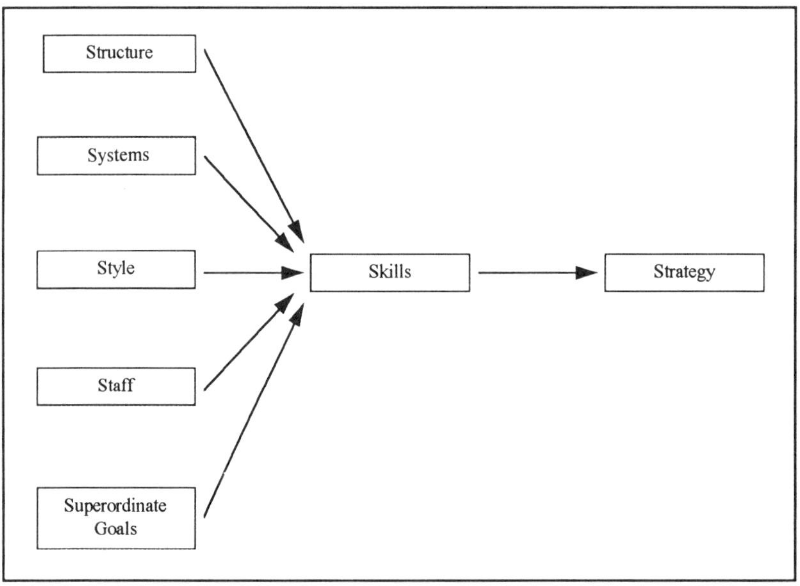

Source: Waterman *et. al*, 1980.

(i) ***Structure:*** There are three major elements which are important when establishing a firm's structure, namely formation of formal internal reporting relationships among sub-groups of people, the grouping of workers into business units to form the whole organisation, and ensuring their communication and coordination effectiveness. A well-designed organisation structure facilitates the effective allocation of tasks among members and, therefore, it is a crucial dimension for a firm to be successful.

Baosteel has adopted a modern organisation structure from the Japanese. It is a hybrid form which includes two main aspects. One deals with its core businesses of iron making and steel smelting. These activities are highly centralised and they are coordinated and controlled by top management. This structure ensures quick action in coordinating large numbers of people.

The other aspect deals with non-core business activities, such as by-product production, external dealings, logistical support and employee welfare. These activities are largely decentralised to the authority of middle and lower management. In adopting this structure for non-core business activities, Baosteel has actually transferred some of its support departments into independent subsidiaries. At the same time, it has outsourced many activities and the decentralised structure has enabled the firm to be flexible in coordinating these alliances. Besides the formal structure, employees of Baosteel have formed informal groups to improve efficiency in areas such as quality control.

(ii) ***Systems:*** Systems include all of the formal and informal procedures within the firm that allow it to function on a day-to-day basis. These systems include staff evaluation, accounting, training, quality control, material acquisition and inventory control. Clearly, system improvements lead to better organisation effectiveness.

During the various phases of development, Baosteel has not only imported sophisticated hardware from Japan and Germany for the production of iron and steel products, but it has also incorporated the Japanese management and process control software systems. To achieve high quality in steel fabrication, computer systems are used to monitor and dynamically control the various processes. It has also adopted the ISO 9000 Quality Management System (certified by BSI) to strengthen its process quality control and to enhance the quality examination of products and processes. Computer integrated manufacturing software was adopted in 1995 for high speed analysis and integration of data and information coming from different channels so as to have all important decisions made on a scientific basis.

The company also has a system in place for sales and production planning, and research and development planning that allows for a long range, holistic approach to planning and the execution of projects. Manpower development is linked to strategic human resource planning for subsequent phases of expansion. To encourage innovation and teamwork, the company also has incentive systems in place for rewarding individuals as well as teams for innovative and continuous improvement ideas. This incentive system has assisted the company in successfully implementing the Japanese quality control circle (QCC) concept.

(iii) ***Style:*** The management style of top managers is an important element in an excellent enterprise. The way in which managers behave in the decision making process will affect the performance of the entire organisation.

Baosteel is China's largest investment since economic reforms commenced and it is utilising the latest equipment, imported technology and modern facilities. Moreover, from the beginning, it has embarked on a contemporary style of people-centred and autonomous management.

The people-centred system is manifested in the lower management layer of the organisation that is built around five distinct sections. The central component of this system is the front-line supervisory section. It receives production plans from the planning section (setting production schedules and targets) while receiving support from the maintenance section (performing total productive maintenance to the plant facilities and equipment) and the control section (standardising work procedures and documentation). Reporting to the supervisory section are teams of self-managed, operating level staff members.

Staff members organise themselves into small groups to propose new solutions on quality/process improvements and cost reduction for study in the typical QCC fashion using the plan-do-check-action (PDCA) problem solving approach. In recent years, 13,485 small groups have been established and 15,273 issues have been selected for study (*Baosteel Annual Report, 1994*). In this type of autonomous management environment, moral encouragement is emphasised first and material awards are ranked second. Successful groups are rewarded and recognised at different levels (corporate, industry, national) depending on their level of contribution.

(iv) ***Staff:*** People in the organisation are an important factor for organisational success. Waterman *et al.* (1982) argue that having, or developing, good people is critically important to organisational effectiveness.

Baosteel strives to develop working teams that are highly disciplined and skilled in order to achieve the company's goals. It has established a Management Research Training Centre, a Continuous Engineering Education Centre and a Senior Technician Training Centre to provide cadre training, worker training, ideological and political education, special technology education, and business and management education. Employees are also sent for overseas attachments and training to learn new skills and technology. The training commitment is evident in training expenses incurred that were equivalent to 1.5% of the annual payroll in 1993.

Baosteel has also reformed the traditional wage and reward system. Job evaluations are conducted to establish the salary scale for each different job position. The criteria used include the technical content, job complexity, responsibilities and accountability of the job. Besides the various types of allowances and increments based on the years of service contribution, an employee with higher technical skills and qualifications is also rewarded under the skill based compensation system.

The skill based compensation system has encouraged employees to constantly upgrade themselves through the various continuing education programmes offered by the company. The annual promotional examination provides a career advancement path for the employees. In 1994, 4,329 employees attended various cadre post training and continuous engineering education, while 20,458 employees completed on-the-job advanced technical training and post transfer training (*Baosteel Annual Report, 1994*). Baosteel only recruits workers that have a high school education at a minimum. This restriction coupled with continuous training and education means that the employees can undertake job enlargement, and this feature has contributed to the successful manpower reduction programme over the years.

Unlike other Chinese steel plants, Baosteel scored above average in all eight aspects of the employee psychological survey carried out in 1991 (*Baosteel Economy and Management*, 1994). The survey dimensions included job satisfaction, motivation, welfare, health, teamwork and communication. This outcome demonstrates the high employee morale at Baosteel.

(v) ***Superordinate Goals (Shared Values):*** Superordinate goals are guiding concepts, or a set of values and aspirations, shared by each member of an organisation. They are often indicative of the future direction that top management wishes to infuse throughout the organisation. Superordinate goals are the driving force pulling the whole organisation together to achieve a set target.

Baosteel established a set of company objectives that has been sloganised as the "three highs and five bests". The former include building the highest quality products, achieving the highest efficiency and striving for the highest effectiveness while the later include developing the best teams, adopting the best methodology, utilising the best technology, employing the best management practices and making the best product.

These goals are market, people and competition oriented and they reflect the company's aspiration to achieve world-class standards. It is a far cry from the old communistic ideology that characterised the typical SOEs in the past. These goals are widely adopted in long-term management planning and they are perpetuated in the daily practices of the employees. They have influenced capital expenditures, research and development activities, and the daily production continuous improvement activities or QCC. Finally, they have forged a company culture that harnesses the best results from employees, management and technology.

(vi) ***Skills:*** Skills are the things that make up a firm's core competency. In an intense competitive environment, a constant acquisition of new skills will enable the continuous success of a firm.

Baosteel's strong commitment and high investment in training and education described above have continuously upgraded the skills of the employees to keep pace with technological change in steel production. The scientific and technical development plan ensures continuous improvement in the production process and the development of new products in line with the product quality differentiation strategy. Also, Baosteel must have the competence to meet the localisation plan for designing and making new equipment/tools to complete its phase three plant expansion. Baosteel has spent US$89 million to acquire the management software skill upgrading programme from Japan. This package allows Baosteel employees to visit the Nippon Steel plant in Japan for a transfer of skills.

(vii) ***Strategy:*** There are many views on what constitutes strategy. Mintzberg (1978) has defined strategy as a pattern in a stream of decisions or actions. This view of strategy is more than what a firm intends or plan to do; it also includes what a firm actually does. Thus, strategy can be intended or emergent. Obviously, the way an organisation plans its actions and the way it actually performs are critical factors in determining how effectively a firm is operating.

The main manufacturing strategy of Baosteel is overall product differentiation in producing high quality steel products using high quality raw materials, and modern, high technology and efficient production methods. This ensures that its products have an edge over domestic competitors. Also, Baosteel exported 0.975 million tonnes, or 15% of its total production in 1994, equivalent to one-third of China's total exports of steel products. This serves to benchmark and measure its product quality against world standards. Quality of service is also not neglected. In its commitment to provide quality products to customers, Baosteel never delays any compensation for objections on quality. Baosteel has also passed the ISO 9001 assessment by BSI, testimony to its process quality standard.

Baosteel has implemented the "long- and medium-term schedule for scientific and technical development" to identify and work on important research and development issues that require breakthroughs. Positive results from this programme include process improvements such as the reduction in the rejection rate for hot rolled sheets from 0.97 to 0.09% and from 0.09 to 0.054% for cold rolled sheets (*Baosteel Annual Report, 1994*).

Non-core activities such as transportation, power generation, staff welfare services, staff housing, medical and cafeteria services have traditionally imposed a high burden on social and welfare expenses (as much as 6% of the overall cost structure) on the Chinese SOEs (MacMurray, 1994). To better focus on improving the productivity of its core business in steel making, Baosteel has undertaken a strategy of aggressively outsourcing these non-core activities to the local government or other companies. The "spin-off" companies have the autonomy to operate these services professionally. Under the contractual terms of Baosteel, these service providers are paid fixed fees to manage these services and to assume full accountability for their own profit and loss. In doing this, Baosteel can maintain better control over its own social and welfare costs while effectively downsizing the workforce.

FUTURE CHALLENGES

The Chinese economy is in a period of rapid transition. Internally, the industrial reform emphasises competition among local and foreign companies. China is further opening up its economy by reducing import tariffs and making it easier for foreign produced goods to be sold in the domestic market in order to become a member of the World Trade Organisation (WTO). The two future challenges faced by Baosteel concern mini-mills and the WTO.

Threats from the Mini-Mills

Recent news indicates that the Chinese government is welcoming foreign investment in mini-mills. The future influx of these mini-mills may pose a serious challenge to Baosteel. As demonstrated in both the European and U.S. steel markets, mini-mills have successfully captured a significant market share from the traditional integrated mills (like Baosteel). They have also been shown to be more profitable through higher efficiencies, higher productivity and lower manufacturing costs.

It is argued that the three key success factors of these mini-mills are: management style and strategies, economic and financial factors, and technology related factors (Hischhon, 1982). Baosteel's success as an integrated mill in China is the result of similar factors: adoption of the latest technologies (continuous casting similar to mini-mills and dynamic computer process control) from Japan and Germany, adoption of a scientific management style and market-oriented strategies, and the ability to continuously improve productivity. Baosteel's key success factors (and government assistance) could well be the shield against an initial onslaught of the mini-mills.

The steel industry in China, as in many other parts of the world, may develop into three complementary major segments in the future: integrated mills, mini-mills and alloy/specialty mills. Many integrated mills in China that have not been technically and managerially retooled like Baosteel will surely face financial difficulties with their market share subject to erosion by the mini-mills. Baosteel may be a significant case example for other Chinese SOE integrated mills to emulate, and be prepared to complement, with the coming of mini-mills.

Entry into the World Trade Organisation (WTO)

China is currently seeking entry into the WTO. Some of the conditions which it must satisfy to be accepted as a member of the WTO include reducing tariffs and removing quotas on imports. China will certainly have to relax import controls on iron and steel products as part of the concessions to be made for admission to the WTO. With the removal of these import controls, high quality iron and steel products of the types produced by Baosteel can then be imported freely with little or no tariff. This will pose a direct threat to Baosteel because its customers will then have the choice of buying imported iron and steel products at competitive prices and this will erode the profit margin currently enjoyed by Baosteel from its domestic customers.

Since 90% of Baosteel's output is sold in the domestic market where it now enjoys protection from imports, the liberalisation of import controls will certainly hurt the profitability of Baosteel as it will then have to compete with imports from efficient foreign iron and steel producers. This will affect Baosteel's "entrenched" position in the domestic market.

Baosteel's Future Strategies

To counter the future challenges of the mini-mills incursion into the Chinese market and the opening up of the Chinese market to the world, Baosteel must respond appropriately to ensure that its success can be sustained. Baosteel must benchmark the quality of its steel products and its productivity of steel making to meet world standards. To achieve world-class quality in its products, Baosteel must sustain its research and development programme and build a learning organisation whereby new technologies can be learned and applied to improve its steel processing capabilities. Joint ventures with world-class organisations could help to hasten the pace of technology assimilation. Baosteel must continuously develop its core competency (skill) in steel making. This would reduce the threat of losing domestic market share to better quality foreign steel.

As an integrated steel mill, economy of scale is an inherent advantage (or disadvantage) that Baosteel must continuously exploit. Baosteel must continuously operate its furnace and rolling mills at optimum capacity. This will require Baosteel to have control over the supply of raw materials and the demand for its finished products. To achieve this position, it would be advantageous for Baosteel to backward integrate with raw material suppliers and forward integrate with customers.

To maintain profitability, Baosteel must lower its overall business cost. The three critical cost drivers affecting Baosteel are: transportation cost, purchasing and selling (trading) cost, and financing cost. Baosteel must focus attention on these three cost drivers and build up its capabilities in managing these components of the business. Baosteel's future strategy must include the transfer of these capabilities into its core competencies.

By adopting the appropriate strategy, Baosteel will be able to maintain a competitive advantage as an integrated mill to complement the arrival of the mini-mills and alloy/specialty mills. Baosteel will also be able to compete successfully with foreign competitors, with its world-class quality products and cost competitiveness. Baosteel's factors of success, evaluated against the 7-S framework (described earlier in this chapter), are important ingredients in developing its core competencies (skills) to support its future strategies.

REFERENCES

Baoshan Iron and Steel General Works, *Annual Report,* 1994.

Baoshan Iron and Steel General Works, *Baoshan Economy and Management Journal*, 1994.

Broadman, H.G., *Meeting the Challenge of Chinese Enterprise Reform*, World Bank Report, 1995.

Chen Min, "The Evolving Environment of the Chinese State Enterprises", *Asian Management System – Chinese, Japanese and Korean Styles of Business*, Thunderbird/Routledge Series in International Management, 1995.

Chen Min, "Reforming Managerial Mechanisms of Chinese State Enterprises", *Asian Management System – Chinese, Japanese and Korean Styles of Business*, Thunderbird/Routledge Series in International Management, 1995.

D'Aveni Richard A., *Hyper-Competition*, The Free Press, New York, 1994.

Editorial, *Lianhe Zaobao*, 5 September 1994.

Editorial, *Lianhe Zaobao*, 23 October 1995.

Editorial, *The Financial Times*, 3 November 1981.

Hischhon, Joel S, *Continuing Success for U.S. Mini-Mills*, in Proceedings of Metal Bulletin's, Second International Mini-Mills Conference, 1982.

Li Zhang Xieng and Fan Zo Wen, *Introduction to Baosteel's Modern Management System*, People's University of China Press, 1993.

MacMurray, Trevor and Jonathan Woetzel, "The Challenge Facing China's State-owned Enterprises", *The McKinsey Quarterly* No. 2 , 1994.

Mintzberg Henry, "Patterns in Strategy Formation", *Management Science,* No. 24, 1978.

Porter Michael, *Competitive Strategy*, The Free Press, New York, 1980.

"Shrinking the Chinese State", *The Economist*, 10 June 1995.

"The Private Life of a Chinese", *The Economist*, 16 September 1995.

Waterman R.H. Jr., "The Seven Elements of Strategic Fit", *The Journal of Business Strategy*, No. 3, Winter 1982.

Waterman R.H, T. Peter and J. Phillips, "Structure Is Not Organisation", *Business Horizons*, June 1980.

Wu, Pei Liang and Xue Xin Ming, *The Organisation Structure of Baosteel*, People University of China Press, 1993.

Yang Mu, John J. Williams and Cao Yong, "Resurrecting Shanghai for the 21st Century: The Shift in China's Regional Economic Strategies", *China Business Review*, December 1995, pp. 11–29.

Zhang Jun Jie, Lu Sheng Zong and Xu Jin Liang, *Behavioural Science and the Management of Baosteel*, Shanghai Scientific Publisher, 1991.

Zhang Jun Jie and Tan Dao Ming, *The Front-line Management of Baosteel*, People's University of China Press, 1993.

Chapter 12

Analyses of Two Joint Ventures*

BY
Tina TAN Kim Choo
YEE Poh Cheng
Husin TJANDRA
WONG Chee Cheong

INTRODUCTION

CHINA'S BOOMING ECONOMY has attracted many foreign investors. Numerous companies have rushed into the Chinese market to tap the many available opportunities. There are several modes of business entry into the Chinese market and one of them is joint venture (JV). So far, an estimated 200,000 JVs have been established in China. Shanghai and Nanjing are two of the attractive places in China for foreign investors. These cities provide good infrastructural support and skilled workers.

From the perspective of a foreign investor, the benefits of JVs in China include access to China's huge market, availability of local contacts, cheap labour and tax incentives. For the Chinese partner, the acquisition of new technologies and management practices, access to additional capital, and expansion of domestic market share are key motivational factors. As advised by the foreign investment department of

* Our sincere appreciation is extended to Dr. Low Kee Yang; thanks also to the managers from Huafei, Mr. Li Jinlong, Ms. Li Xiaojiao and the managers from SBOC, Ms. Fong and Mr. Xie Baoqin; thanks also go to Ms. Mao Qin and Mr. Fang Seowwen from the Enterprises with Foreign Investment Management Department of Nanjing Municipal Economic Commission.

Nanjing Economic Development Board, potential investors interested in JVs in China should be aware of the critical issues which are discussed below.

Choice of Location

Location can be assessed by considering several factors. The first is the availability of infrastructural support. This determines the availability and the accessibility of basic utilities such as electricity, water, sewerage and transportation which the business needs to operate smoothly. Second, is a good understanding of the legislative structure. A foreign investor should have adequate knowledge of the legal framework of China and, in particular, the country's JV laws. This would enable an understanding of the Chinese partner in terms of capital and technology required, profit sharing, freedom of import and export and foreign exchange. In addition, there is a need to be aware of the latest developments in JV policies. Finally, an investor should have a good understanding of the people and the culture of the host country in which they plan to invest.

Partner Selection

The Chinese market is an emerging and dynamic economy. It may be difficult for foreigners to gain access to the local distribution channels and business practices. Entering into a JV with a local partner may facilitate entry into the Chinese market. It also shortens the time taken for entry. A successful JV provides for the complementary contribution of resources by the major parties involved. These contributions are valued by the parties. For example, the selected local partner should be sincere, have adequate capacity and possess a good network of contacts with the relevant approving authorities and government entities.

Contracts

Most JVs fail because of unrealistic expectations. The contract becomes the most important document in the event of conflict between the partners. Problems inevitably arise when the JV contract does not specify the character of the business, the goals of each party, the resources to be contributed by each of the partners, their rights, responsibilities or obligations, their share of profits and mode of distribution, ways of resolving disputes, or other key aspects of the venture. Thus, the contract should be specific, realistic and have resolution mechanisms so that any disputes can be better managed. The negotiation phase is one of the most important phases in a JV. It is crucial that both parties spend enough time to gain a full understanding of the needs and the level of sincerity of their potential partners.

Tolerance Over Differences

Major differences with respect to decision making, management processes, management style, and corporate culture between the foreign investor and the local partner, can lead to serious conflicts which, in turn, can contribute to the failure of JVs. For example, foreign investors may strive to impose their management processes, such as planning and budgeting practices, on the JV affiliate. Cross cultural understanding is necessary before significant changes can be made.

Two Case Studies

With the above factors as a frame of reference, this chapter studies two successful joint ventures; one is Huafei in Nanjing while the other is Shanghai British Oxygen Company (SBOC) in Shanghai. The objective is to learn about the critical success factors as well as the problems faced by the JVs. Huafei is a JV between Philips Electronics N.V., Huadong Electronic Tube Factory and Jiangsu Investment Co. Huafei was established in 1988 in Nanjing to manufacture television (TV) tubes. Philips' interests in this JV included access to the huge Chinese domestic market and low labour costs. Huadong's interest, on the other hand, was to tap Philips' technological know-how and management practices. Jiangsu Investment is a venture capitalist company. At the inception of the JV, it was thought that the combination of Philips' brand name in the international market and Huadong's brand name in the domestic market would provide better confidence in the venture. The parties projected a payback period of five years.

SBOC is a JV between Wusong Chemical and the British Oxygen Company (BOC), a multinational company based in the U.K. SBOC was established in Shanghai in 1988. It manufactures industrial gases which are needed by 95% of industries in Shanghai. While BOC's main interest was to enter into the newly industrialised Shanghai market, Wusong's interest lay in the technology transfer and the capital from BOC. The investors targeted a payback period of eight years.

HUAFEI

Huafei Color Display Systems Company Limited (Huafei) manufactures flat screen (FS) TV colour picture tubes. Since its establishment, Huafei has been the largest JV in Jiangsu province and is one of the largest projects between the Chinese electronic industry and business interests from western Europe. Its shareholders are Huadong Electronic Tube Factory from China, Philips Electronics N.V. from the Netherlands and Jiangsu Investment Company from China; their shareholdings are 45, 30 and 25%, respectively. Philips, at present, is involved in some 16 JVs in China and intends to increase this number to 25 within the next few years.

The JV has a total investment of US$180 million and a registered capital of US$63 million. The contract was signed on 10 November 1987, and the JV is to last for a period of 25 years. The company was established on 30 April 1988, and production started on 10 November 1990. The plant and office building occupy areas of 201,000 square metres and 51,000 square metres, respectively.

Huafei currently records an annual output of 1.6 million sets of colour display systems and has a 10% market share in China. It was ranked 12th in the listing of the Top 500 Industry Enterprises in 1995 by the electronic and communications equipment manufacturing industry.

Huafei has performed well and has attained its payback within the targeted five-year time frame. In 1995, Huafei achieved 22% growth in output, 23% growth in net profit and 8% growth in turnover. The JV has been profitable since it started and is now planning a second phase of expansion in which the total investment will be increased to US$300 million. After the expansion, Philips will have a shareholding stake of 55%, Huadong Electronic Tube Factory 27% and Jiangsu Investment Company 18%. The JV will continue to enjoy tax rebates and the preferential treatment for the coastal region.

Analysis of Huafei

(i) ***Structure:*** Huafei is organised into seven departments: technology and quality; production plant; engineering plant; material management; marketing and sales; finance and accounting; and human resources. See Figure 12–1.

FIGURE 12–1
Organisational Chart of Huafei

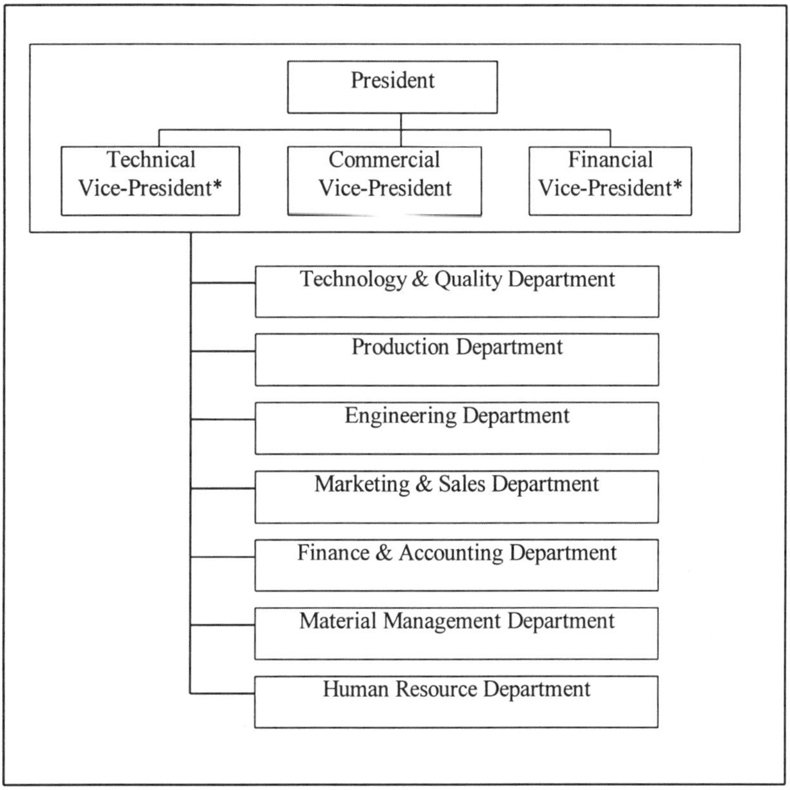

* position held by expatriate

The management level comprises the President, the Technical Vice-President (TVP), the Commercial Vice-President (CVP) and the Financial Vice-President (FVP). Each department is headed by a general manager (GM). There are three expatriates in Huafei. They are the FVP from Philips Taiwan (HQ for component division) and the TVP and his assistant from Philips Electronics N.V. They were appointed based on their managerial competence and industry experience. The local president reports to the board of directors made up of both foreigners and locals appointed according to the equity shareholding of the JV parties. As the board meetings are held twice a year, only strategic issues and critical conflicts are resolved at this level. Other operational matters are handled by the respective departmental general managers. This management structure has facilitated the fair sharing of management responsibilities. Both foreign and local parties are represented through appointments to crucial managerial positions and are given the required level of authority.

(ii) ***Skills:*** Of the staff in Huafei, 79% have received secondary school education, 20% university education and 1% postgraduate education. The staff are relatively young; 78% are below 30 years old, 17% are 30 to 40 years old and 5% are above 40 years old. The average age of the staff is 25 years. Compared to industry standards, Huafei's staff are considerably younger and more highly skilled. This has enabled Huafei to expand faster.

(iii) ***System:*** Huafei believes in quality assurance and is practising the ISO 9002 standard to achieve international quality recognition. Philips uses its own quality standard called KEMA which is more stringent. Both standards focus on continual improvement in the product and the production process, and they have helped to lay a solid foundation for Huafei's quality management. As examples of progressive management, employees are encouraged to give suggestions to improve the production process, and only those who make repeated mistakes are penalised.

Over the years, Huafei has received several awards, the latest being the "Quality Satisfaction Product" award issued in 1995 by the National Customers' Committee. (The TV tubes carry the brand "Huafei" instead of "Philips" since the latter owns less than 50% of the stake). These awards have further boosted the reputation of the company and, in turn, reinforced the employee's loyalty to Huafei.

(iv) ***Strategy:*** The competitiveness of Huafei can be assessed by using Michael Porter's five-forces model. Huafei's strategy can be explained by its response to each of these forces.

(a) ***New Entrants*:** The entry barriers to the TV colour tube manufacturing business in China include the huge capital required for investing in factory and equipment, the shortage of skilled labour and brand establishment. Huafei expects at least three new companies to enter the TV colour tube manufacturing business in China within the next two years. They will compete with the seven existing companies. In response to this new competition, Huafei will adopt both a market penetration strategy for its existing products and a product development strategy for its current market. In other words, it will continue to improve the quality of existing products as well as develop a new product series in the phase two expansion. Product selection has been based on the market demand forecast provided by the government to all the TV colour tube manufacturers.

(b) ***Bargaining Power of Suppliers:*** Huafei purchases input materials mainly from Philips since there is a lack of supply in the market for materials of the required quality. However, Huafei is aware of the disadvantage of having a single supplier, namely the lack of bargaining power. As such, they also have sourced some of their input material from countries such as Japan and other local companies. For instance, their glass supply is sourced from another Philips JV in Jiangyi that manufactures glass. Basic supplies, such as electricity and water, are offered at a low price by the government as part of their incentive to encourage JVs.

(c) ***Bargaining Power of Customers:*** The key customers of Huafei include Changhong, Panda and Suzhou-Philips. The largest client, Panda, purchases 30% of its TV colour tubes from Huafei. However, there is low bargaining power for Huafei because the customers can easily switch to other vendors for their supplies. In order to retain these customers, Huafei strives to increase product quality and provides attentive post-sales service support.

    Huafei exports 25% of its output, mainly to Philips in Hong Kong, Japan, India and Singapore. It also exports to European countries such as France and Italy. The export earnings have enabled Huafei to maintain a stable foreign currency balance.

(d) ***Industry Rivalry:*** Although Huafei is the only TV colour tube manufacturer in Nanjing, its market share in China is only 10%. Several major competitors from other parts of China can be identified. They include Xianyang in Shanxi, Lotus in Shanghai, Matsushita in Beijing, and Toshiba in Xian and Shanghai. Xianyang is the biggest competitor, producing about five million TV tubes per year. Despite the lower total volume of units produced, Huafei scored higher for productivity. Its value added per employee is RMB 800,000 per year, far exceeding the RMB 10,000 per year for Xianyang.

Among Huafei and its competitors, there is minimal differentiation in product features as the specifications of TV colour tubes are standardised. Prices also differ very little since each one is willing to collaborate on price. Thus, the only ways to compete are through quality, service and promotion. Huafei emphasises quality and strives to be better than the Japanese. It is also aggressive in promotion strategy which includes comprehensive pre-sales talks to customers.

(e) ***Threat from Substitutes:*** Huafei has considered the threat posed by substitutes. Liquid crystal display (LCD) technology also could provide a substitute for TV colour tubes, but not in the next ten to 15 years. This is because the picture quality of LCD is still far inferior to that of TV tubes. Moreover, the production cost of LCD is higher.

(v) ***Style:*** Huafei's culture is an integration of western management with the Chinese business model. Full awareness of the Chinese situation, streamlined administration and high efficiency are always kept in mind whenever the management of Huafei formulates and reviews their managerial and organisational rules. These factors have facilitated a standardised working method, characterising the Huafei culture.

(vi) ***Staff:*** There are 1,800 employees in Huafei. Of these, about 100 are from Huadong while the remainder were recruited from the market. The staff turnover rate is 5% for the management level and 8% for the operator level. Several measures were adopted to inculcate loyalty among employees, including the human resource system.

Every Huafei employee receives a basic salary and a bonus based on performance and the company's profit. At retirement, employees also receive a pension as in a state-owned enterprise (SOE). As an incentive, the company provides housing for employees who have performed well. Being a JV, Huafei has substantial flexibility in managing its funds, especially in the employee remuneration package. This has enabled it to compete for better employees.

Also, Huafei has implemented a provident fund scheme, somewhat similar to Singapore's Central Provident Fund (CPF), where the company contributes 10% of the employee's salary while the employee contributes 5% into a common fund account. The employee is allowed to withdraw from the fund after five years of employment. Employees are informed of their balance every month.

There is no reinvestment out of these savings and the interest rate follows the bank rate.

For training purposes, employees are sent for courses based on their work requirements and their potential. English-language courses and a wide range of technical and management courses are offered. Unlike a state-owned enterprise, Huafei has combined recruitment with training so as to provide systematic career development for employees. This includes sending them for training overseas to places such as western Europe, Hong Kong and Singapore. The Nanjing University is also a popular training place for Huafei's employees.

(vii) ***Shared Values:*** Huafei's vision is to be a leading enterprise within China in terms of technology, management and skill. It believes that future prospects lie in close cooperation between Chinese and foreign business interests despite differences in cultural backgrounds and nationalities.

Critical Success Factors

Having discussed some of the significant characteristics of Huafei, attention is focused below on major success factors.

(i) ***Selection of Product:*** According to the Chinese government's 20-year plan for the electronic industry announced in 1980, output was to be increased from US$5 billion to US$40 billion by the year 2000, assuming a yearly growth rate of approximately 11%. In particular, the "big four things" (i.e., washing machines, colour TVs, radio cassette recorders and refrigerators) were the top priorities for the years 1986 to 1995. In reality, growth was substantially higher and TV production was approximately 22% per year during the period 1981 to 1985. Realising the good prospects in the TV tube industry, Philips responded to this opportunity by entering into the JV with Huadong.

(ii) ***Selection of Location and Partner:*** Initially, Philips saw potential in the China TV market and wanted to invest in the Yangtze river delta which is known for its fast growing economy and concentration of high-tech industries. Nanjing was chosen by Philips because of its closeness to potential customers and support industry and, also, because of its proximity to Shanghai. Furthermore, the universities there produce many graduates with expertise in the electronic and electrical fields. Low labour cost was not the major reason for Philips entering into the JV; instead, the company was interested in expanding operations to improve its Asia-Pacific support.

Huadong, in Nanjing, was the only electrical manufacturing firm in Jiangsu province which was considered to be high-tech by the Chinese. It was recommended by a Philips consultant who was attached to Huadong for a period of time. Huadong had been established for around 50 years and had some experience in TV tube manufacturing. It was thought that this would greatly help Philips to deal with the unfamiliarity of the Chinese TV tube manufacturing industry as well as the various approvals required by the relevant authorities on investment matters. Consequently, Huadong was engaged as the JV partner.

(iii) ***Trust and Commitment:*** The JV has turned out well because it was built on trust and commitment. Both the Chinese and the foreign parties cooperated sincerely and leveraged on each other's strengths so as to synergise their needs. The essential contribution of Philips consisted of capital, advanced technology, technical training and management development. Philips introduced to Huafei the whole technology package of the production line which manufactures colour picture tubes and their deflection units. On the other hand, Huadong contributed a knowledge of China's environment, the distribution network of TV makers in Nanjing, Shanghai, Wuxi, Yangzhou, Suzhou and Chengdu and, finally, contacts with the government and legal entities. Mutual trust and commitment was further manifested in the competence-based appointment of managerial posts and their enthusiasm in the phase two expansion.

(iv) ***Influential Local Partner:*** The local president has been highly commended for his contribution to the success of Huafei. As described by the FVP, it is not an easy task to run a business in China. One has to go through many complicated legal procedures with the state commissions and councils. It is through the local president's *guanxi*, and his tactfulness in dealing with the government authorities, that Huafei has managed to deal with critical matters within shorter time frames, such as getting approval to acquire land for the factory and to purchase equipment.

(v) ***Good Human Resource Management:*** Despite the tight supply of skilled workers in the market, Huafei has successfully recruited about 1,700 employees from the market and is able to maintain its employee turnover rate at less than 10%. This is directly attributable to Huafei's comprehensive, but flexible, human resource package which includes:

(a) a performance-based salary structure (basic salary plus bonus);
(b) performance-based staff benefits, such as housing;
(c) welfare schemes, for example a CPF-style savings and pension; and
(d) training programmes and career development.

Problems Encountered

The running of Huafei has not been a totally smooth process. The following issues still need to be addressed.

(i) ***Insufficient Investment Capital:*** In view of the competition in the TV tube manufacturing industry, it is essential for Huafei to expand quickly in order to maintain a leading position. The phase two expansion is one of the expansion initiatives. Since there has not been enough capital generated from past earnings to fund this expansion, Philips will be contributing the required additional funds. This will redistribute shareholder's equity such that Philips secures the majority stake. There is concern that Huadong might lose its controlling power with the dilution of shares. We believe that the Chinese partners were agreeable to this change of power because higher priority was given to the expansion and because they trust Philips' sincerity.

(ii) ***Slow Localisation:*** The difficulty in sourcing input materials from local suppliers that meet standards is the main reason for slow localisation. Philips has been, and still is, the main supplier of Huafei. Thus, there is little bargaining power for Huafei in terms of lead time and volume in parts ordering.

(iii) ***Change of Customer Taste:*** Dynamic changes in customer taste and technology advancement are regular phenomena in the TV industry. The demand for TV sets has experienced a recent change because of customer preference for larger TVs, namely the 21-inch to 29-inch sets. This signals a need for Huafei to re-assess its production plan and consider manufacturing 29-inch TV tubes. Otherwise,

Huafei may face an over-supply of the smaller-sized TV tubes while missing the market window for 29-inch TV sets.

Recommendations

(i) ***Guaranteed Loan from Philips:*** In the long run, the additional capital required for expansion can be provided by accumulating retained earnings. But in the short term, two alternative solutions are to issue bonds or to have Huafei borrow from Philips and use its share as collateral. Both would avoid the dilution of Huadong's stake. As for Philips, it can still earn interest from the loan and, at the same time, underscore its commitment to Huadong.

(ii) ***Technical Assistance to Local Suppliers:*** Although Huafei has begun sourcing some input materials from other countries, such as Japan, this will increase flexibility only in order volume and lead time, but it will not lower the cost. One way to increase localisation is by working closely with potential suppliers to assist them in minimising the quality problems of input materials. This is a win-win solution. Alternatively, Huafei could decide to integrate vertically, but this would require a major restructuring of its business model.

(iii) ***Fast Response to Market Demands:*** To respond to customers' changing tastes in a more timely manner, Huafei could conduct more regular market surveys or research. However, market research can be expensive. Once the demand is known, appropriate action can be planned immediately to seize a greater share of the market.

SHANGHAI BOC (SBOC)

Established in February 1988, SBOC is a JV between Wusong Chemical and BOC. Located in Shanghai, the company is one of 15 joint ventures of the expansion of BOC in China. Its core business is the manufacturing of industrial gases, mainly oxygen, nitrogen, argon and helium.

Currently, SBOC produces 80 tonnes of liquefied industrial gases and 78,000 units of bottled industrial gases per day. SBOC's local market share for liquefied and bottled industrial gases is 60% and 30%, respectively. The net profit and turnover growth for 1995 were 5 and 8.4%, respectively.

Analysis of SBOC

(i) ***Structure:*** Given an equal shareholding between Wusong and BOC, strategic directions for SBOC are steered by a board of directors which meets monthly. This board consists of four representatives from Wusong and four representatives from BOC. The arrangement is advantageous because there is an equal representation from the two companies. But when corporate interests differ, decision making may not be so efficient and compromises may be required.

Operationally, SBOC is headed by the chairman, a local manager transferred from Wusong Chemical, and two general managers, one a local transferred from Wusong, and the other an expatriate sent by BOC. In charge of the production, marketing, finance, development, personnel and chief engineering departments are local managers transferred from Wusong. The organisation chart of the company (see Figure 12–2) outlines the clear definition of the functions of each department.

(ii) ***Skills:*** SBOC is committed to upgrading the skills of its employees. Managers are sent to the BOC Gases College, a training centre set up by BOC for business and English-language training. The courses include sales and marketing, economics, accounting, human resource management, management theory, production management and BOC corporate culture.

The company is also committed to seeking good employees. Amongst the criteria for recruitment is the ability to speak English. As such, candidates are recruited by many other companies. Highly competitive salaries and employee welfare packages are crucial for recruiting and retaining staff. SBOC is well aware of this fact.

(iii) ***System:*** SBOC has imbibed the "BOC way" of managing the corporation. The company has adopted BOC's system for the training and development of its staff. (Wang, 1995). The training programmes held by SBOC are regularly reviewed. BOC also transferred to the locals the technology for the production of local gases. In fact, about 70% of the bottled gases are produced using the technology introduced by BOC.

The SBOC JV has been so highly regarded that its management has been invited to help in JVs in other provinces, especially in the transfer of management practices and technology.

(iv) ***Strategy:*** It is useful to analyse the competitive forces facing SBOC and the strategies that the company has adopted to achieve better market performance.

FIGURE 12–2
Organisation Chart of SBOC

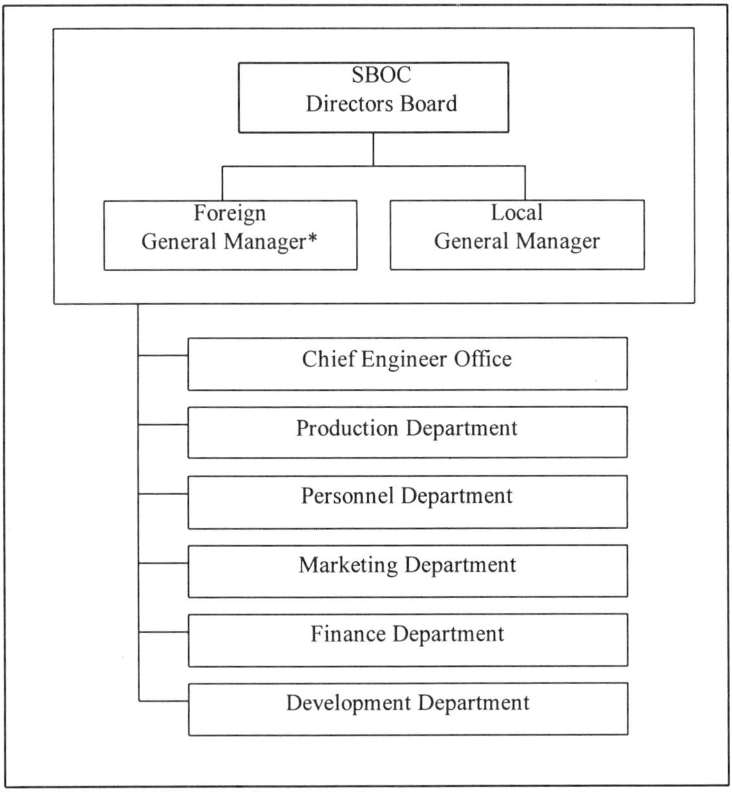

* position held by expatriate

(a) ***Threat of New Entrants:*** Entry barriers for industrial gas manufacturing are high, mainly because the business is capital intensive. The initial investments in equipment, plant and machinery are substantial. Since the establishment of SBOC, there have been at least two new entrants in Shanghai province. One is a JV between a local party and the French Liquidified

Gas Company while the other is a JV between Baoshan and Blackers.

Faced with the need to protect its market share, SBOC has differentiated its product line from these direct competitors by providing better quality products and higher after sales service. Effort has also been put into market research for new products to meet customers' demands. This increased emphasis has led to the establishment of a marketing department in the company.

(b) ***Bargaining Power of Suppliers:*** As agreed by contract, the Wusong factory supplies raw gases to SBOC. Hence, the company has little bargaining power over the supplier. In addition, the JV contract specifies that Wusong may increase the price for raw gases if inflation drives up the price of electricity prices.

(c) ***Bargaining Power of Customers:*** The company currently has about 3,000 customers, mainly from the electronic, glass manufacturing, medical and steel industries. Most of the regular clientele have chosen to conduct their business with SBOC because of the company's good reputation.

(d) ***Industry Rivalry:*** Since there are about six key competitors, a herd effect is also common among the competitors when launching new products. But SBOC was the earliest and is the most established business in the industry.

In terms of pricing strategy, SBOC offers its gases at prices that are higher than average. This is partly because of the higher cost of raw gases from the Wusong factory. However, with the higher price comes better quality products and services. There is a strong emphasis on attending to the service requests from clients as quickly as possible.

The company is also very aggressive in marketing efforts. For example, the company proactively pre-installs gas processors at clients' bases free-of-charge. Hence, clients feel obligated to purchase gas from SBOC.

(e) ***Threat From Substitutes:*** Industrial gases are required by 95% of all industries in Shanghai. Hence, there are good prospects for continued high demand. Currently, there are no substitutes for industrial gases.

(v) ***Style:*** The management style in Wusong has been top-down and autocratic. After establishing the JV, management was encouraged by BOC to adopt a more participative approach.

The general manager also believes in further career development for employees. Although the company has lost a few employees, it still believes in creating opportunities for staff at lower levels to progress up the corporate ladder.

(vi) ***Staff:*** SBOC has 310 employees, most of whom were transferred from Wusong. On average, they are paid about 50% more than their counterparts at Wusong. Based on salary alone, the average pay package at SBOC is slightly lower than the average for other joint ventures in the industry. However, the company scores higher than the average when employee benefits, such as housing, medical and pension benefits, are factored into the remuneration package. The reason why SBOC is unable to give employees a higher pay package is employees from both Wusong and SBOC share the same canteen, factory and administration blocks and, therefore, salary comparisons are likely to be made. In such circumstances, it would be difficult to raise the salary levels at SBOC without similarly raising the salary levels at Wusong.

Annual staff turnover is 8%, which is about the industry average. The mobility of new university graduates employed by the company is not as high as that of experienced staff because good jobs in China are difficult to find. Typically, the probation period for new employees is three months.

(vii) ***Shared Values:*** SBOC embraces the philosophy that the "customer is king", and this is communicated to all staff. The company always emphasises quality service to clients. It hopes that this client-oriented approach will help it to become the leading manufacturer of industrial gases within the Yangtze river delta.

The general manager noted that the company's vision is to be the pioneer of new gas technologies. As such, the company strives to keep abreast of technology and hopes to be the first mover in new gas products. This would enhance SBOC's reputation for high quality and for being a user of advanced technology.

Critical Success Factors

(i) ***Partner Selection:*** BOC chose Wusong as the JV partner mainly because the chemical factory had been established for more than 50 years. Over this period it developed a good reputation, a comprehensive range of plant, equipment and machinery, as well as a highly skilled workforce. The ability to use existing facilities brought about large savings in terms of time and money. In fact, SBOC was able to start production immediately after signing the JV contract. BOC was interested in Wusong's existing facilities and the 3,000-client distribution network. This allowed BOC to gain access to China's local market in the shortest possible time. On the other hand, Wusong was interested in the additional capital and technology, as well as the management practices contributed by their foreign partner.

(ii) ***Planning for Future Growth:*** The expected payback period for this JV was eight years. However, after operating for eight years, the foreign investor has not recovered the initial investment. But BOC is not alarmed by this as the priority is market access and expansion. Moreover, Shanghai is a highly industrialised province where the industrial gas business is very lucrative and most of the manufacturing industries require industrial gas supply.

The collected revenue was used to pay back the investment. One half of it has been used to reinvest in research and development, including the production of helium and carbon dioxide. Funds were also required to import new equipment. SBOC has had to raise an additional US$30 million through bank loans. This large amount of capital was needed partly to build gas processors at the customer sites as part of SBOC's marketing strategy to make their customers feel obligated to use their gas. Each gas processor costs US$4 million. Currently, four such gas processors have been built. BOC also has entered into JVs with small and medium enterprises in other parts of China. These JVs will not compete with other BOC JVs in China as they are mainly dealing with lower end production.

(iii) ***Learning From the Foreign Partner:*** The success of this JV is largely attributable to the willingness of the Chinese to adopt new concepts and practices. For example, the Chinese learned the concept of a market economy. This has inculcated in them a sense of urgency to produce high quality gas in the right quantity so as to optimise inventory. Workers have become more market oriented and they are aware of the importance of quality.

As another example, the Chinese have learned the value of productivity. Unlike Wusong, SBOC employees are all contract workers and are required to maintain a certain level of productivity.

Contracts of employees who do not meet performance standards are not renewed. SBOC's staff strength has been reduced by 100 workers since the formation of the JV. The organisation structure also has been streamlined by eliminating unnecessary managerial assistants.

Lastly, the Chinese have learned how to make decisions based on consensus and consultation. More management personnel now are involved in the discussion of an issue before a decision is made, unlike previously when only the directors made decisions and gave instructions.

Problems Encountered

(i) ***Insufficient Investment Capital:*** As part of its expansion and cost reduction plan, SBOC's management is actively considering buying the raw gas factory from Wusong. Negotiations have taken place at the board level. However, it is not likely that Wusong will allow a majority stake by BOC of the U.K. Basically, the gas industry is too lucrative to allow foreign investors to have control. Besides, the government is also limiting the amount of funds available for small and medium industries. Thus, SBOC may not have sufficient capital to meet expansion needs.

There is an increasing possibility that BOC may establish a wholly-owned subsidiary in China without any Chinese partner. BOC has already formed its first wholly owned subsidiary in Wuhan. However, there are considerably fewer incentives for forming wholly owned subsidiaries as government policy discourages these because they do not benefit the Chinese as much as a JV.

(ii) ***Forex Imbalance:*** SBOC's foreign currency balance is very low at the moment. The initial foreign investment capital in U.S. dollars is diminishing steadily. The main reason is the low volume of exports. This was aggravated by an incident a few years ago when an export shipment of helium gas exploded in transit. Currently, the only way of obtaining more foreign currency is to exchange the RMB. Fortunately, the exchange rate is controlled by the central government and the JV is able to obtain RMB at a reasonable fixed rate with the government banks. Fluctuations, therefore, are contained. Other alternatives, such as trading bonds, options or futures, are considered to be too risky and complicated to be managed by SBOC. Getting additional loans is becoming more difficult as banks are more strict with loans which require tedious declarations. Nevertheless, SBOC is planning to balance its foreign currency reserves within the next five years.

(iii) ***Sourcing and Retaining Staff:*** SBOC's salary scale and range is slightly below the MNC market rate and the staff turnover rate of 7% is around the industry average. Management understands that raising salaries is crucial to retaining good people because of the competition from larger MNCs. However, implementation will be difficult.

(iv) ***Delay in Decision Making:*** One of the key reasons for delays in decision making is the bureaucratic U.K. style of management. For example, on one occasion the approval from the BOC U.K. to purchase the new facilities from BOC's own facility supplier was delayed for three months, by which time the price of the gas had dropped 40%. This upset the Chinese partner. Another cause of slow decision making is the different holiday structure adopted by the foreign partner. The U.K. has a relatively long holiday structure and this can delay company operations.

(v) ***Cross-cultural Differences:*** SBOC has experienced management by two different expatriates so far. The previous expatriate knew Mandarin and could adapt to Chinese culture easily. Most importantly, he could communicate directly with his subordinates. The current foreign general manager cannot speak Mandarin and has difficulty interacting directly with workers. He has to depend on translation but, fortunately, some SBOC employees are conversant in English.

There are also differences in spending priorities between foreign and local management. For instance, the British are more concerned with company image and find it necessary to improve the reception area. The Chinese, in contrast, are more concerned with meeting the operational budget. Foreigners also are more willing to invest in staff training. For instance, BOC China has built a training centre for management. Finally, the British tend to be more risk averse as compared to the other investors such as the Americans.

Recommendations

(i) ***Issue Bonds:*** SBOC should consider various ways of raising funds in the international, and local, debt and equity markets. Issuing bonds or warrants could be on the agenda. Since raising debt is, in general, more costly, SBOC should consider going public and listing on the Shanghai Stock Exchange.

(ii) ***Manage Foreign Exchange:*** SBOC must look into ways of increasing its export market share to solve the problem of foreign exchange imbalance. The new product must target both international and local markets so as to contribute to the forex earnings. Besides this, trading in derivative products, such as options and futures, should be considered as part of the risk and investment in management skills.

(iii) ***Improve Salary Scheme:*** To compete with the MNCs on salary offerings, SBOC can introduce a variable component into its current salary scheme. This can be in many forms including incentives for punctuality and bonus schemes.

(iv) ***Develop Staff Loyalty:*** Besides the salary scale and range, SBOC should consider improving welfare benefits, the reward system and the working environment to increase morale and job satisfaction as part of the strategy for retaining employees. A frequent review of reasons for employee terminations would be useful for identifying the weak areas in SBOC human resource management.

(v) ***More Authority to Foreign Manager:*** To avoid unnecessary delays in crucial decision-making, the foreign general manager should have the requisite authority. Management also should consider reducing areas which need policy consent from the parent companies.

(vi) ***Adapt to Cross-cultural Differences:*** To minimise cross-cultural differences, social activities such as parties, dinners and outings can be organised to help the foreign general manager as well as the local Chinese to appreciate each other's respective cultural backgrounds better.

SUMMARY

The two case studies examined here are successful JVs. The objective was to analyse the success factors in each case including their experiences and motivations in forming the JVs. There are five factors that appear to have contributed to the success of the two JVs.

(i) ***Partner Selection:*** Each JV was able to leverage the local partner's experience in the Chinese market. Before the JVs, Wusong and

Huadong already had well-established customer bases. In particular, Wusong had built a network of pipes to transfer gas from the factory to the clients. Huadong also had an existing distribution channel for colour TV tubes.

(ii) ***Additional Capital From the Foreign Company:*** The foreign companies were able to provide additional capital for the JVs. For both JVs, the increase in funds was used to build new factories as well as to upgrade the existing equipment to exploit newer technologies.

(iii) ***Modern Management Practices:*** The foreign companies were able to bring modern management practices to the JVs. Philips helped Huafei become more quality conscious. Quality assurance methods, such as ISO 9002 and KEMA, were taught in the JV. On the other hand, SBOC advocated participatory management and reward systems for their employees. This helped to generate more ideas, and increased the level of commitment to management decisions.

(iv) ***Technology Transfer:*** The local companies were able to learn more advanced technologies from the foreign counterparts. This enabled the Chinese companies to increase their product lines, production capacity, as well as productivity, thereby increasing their overall market share.

(v) ***Choice of Location:*** Choice of location was a crucial factor to the JVs' success. Nanjing provided a continual supply of good labour that was necessary for Huafei's expansion plans. It also allowed the JV to be closer to their potential customers as well as supporting industries. For SBOC, Shanghai provided a large market size for industrial gases because it is one of the most industrialised cities in China.

REFERENCES

Bath Vivienne, *Asia Business Law Review*, Singapore, 1994.

Campbell Nigel, *A Strategic Guide to Equity Joint Ventures in China*, Pergamon Press, London, 1989.

De Brujin Erik J. and Xianfeng Jia, "Managing Sino-Western Joint Ventures: Product Selection Strategy", *Management International Review*, Vol. 330, New York, 1993.

Ministry of Foreign Trade and Economic Cooperation, *Summary of China's Foreign Investment Policy*, 1992.

Roehrig Michael Franz, *Foreign Joint Ventures in Contemporary China*, St. Martin's Press, New York, 1994.

Rugman A. M. and Hodgetts R. M., *International Business: A Strategic Management Approach*, McGraw Hill Series, London, 1995.

Vernon-Wortzel H. and, L. H. Wortzel, *Global Strategic Management: The Essentials*, 2nd Edition, John Wiley and Sons, London, 1991.

Wang Tom, "Experiencing Human Resources Management in China", *China Business Review,* World Scientific Publishing, Singapore, 1995.

Chapter 13

Panda Electronics Group

BY
Jonathan NG
CHEONG Hock Yan
Josephine TEONG

INTRODUCTION

THE AGGRESSIVE AND sweeping economic reform policies of China have put many of its 100,000 state-owned enterprises (SOEs) (which collectively employ more than 100 million workers and contribute almost one-half of China's industrial production) under immense competitive pressure. They must make a quick transition from a relatively protected position to one which has to compete locally and internationally.

In the past decade, the government has introduced a number of measures to change the operating environment of SOEs. These have included the development of a market system in China, the separate ownership and management of SOEs and a greater decentralisation of decision making authority to the enterprise level. To cope with the competition, many SOEs are "forced" to consider market-oriented organisational restructuring, explore creative financial sourcing, revamp existing labour practices, exploit business partnerships and technology sharing opportunities with other established MNCs, and institutionalise modern operational and management practices to meet the challenge of the market place. The Nanjing Panda Electronics

Group typifies this entrepreneurial spirit which is emerging in many market-oriented SOEs in China.

Founded in 1936, and with a current employee base of 10,000, the Panda Electronics Group is one of the largest electronics SOEs in China. Its main products consist of short wave communication systems, satellite communication systems, mobile communications systems, televisions (TVs), VCRs, radios, recorders, component audio products and household electrical appliances. According to official sources, 90% of the group's revenue is derived from the sales of consumer electronics products. It is currently the market leader in the domestic TV market with an 18% market share. It is also one of 20 SOEs approved by the central government for a debut public listing on the Hong Kong Stock Exchange by the end of 1996. It will be the first Chinese consumer electronics company to be listed overseas.

Similar to many other SOEs, Panda is currently seeking potential business partnership opportunities with foreign companies to expand its market share and to tap the growing domestic market for consumer electronics. This chapter offers an understanding of the success factors underlying Panda's operations. This knowledge is important to potential business interests that are contemplating the China market. Moreover, specific opportunities which are available in the electronics industry, including possible joint venturing with Panda, are discussed.

PANDA – WHAT SETS IT APART AND WHY

Besides being the largest and most established electronics SOE in China, Panda has an impressive record in the local electronics industry. Three factors are prominent: financial performance; market leadership; and product and service quality. These factors are discussed in more detail below.

Impressive Financial Performance

Panda takes pride in its strong financial performance (see Table 13–1) which has averaged around 30% sales growth annually in the past five years. Total sales revenue has grown 84 times from RMB 50.17 million in 1974 to RMB 4,220 million in 1994. Profit has increased 42 times from RMB 11.33 million to RMB 470 million in 1994 and average profit growth is 34.4% annually. There has been a substantial increase in fixed capital assets, from RMB 47 million to RMB 364 million in 1994.

TABLE 13–1
Panda's Financial Performance: 1979–94
(RMB millions)

	1979	1986	1991	1994
Revenue	50.2	404	1,810	4,220
Profit	13.3	59.6	134	470
Profit margin	22.5%	14.8%	7.4%	11.1%

Source: Panda Electronics Group Report.

Over the past ten years, Panda's production has switched from military products to consumer products, with the ratio of military products to consumer products decreasing from 9:1 in 1974 to 1:9 in 1994. In 1994, 2.2 million sets of "black and white" Panda television sets, 1.8 million colour sets and more than two million sets of audio products have been produced. Panda television sets have captured about 18% of the China television market share while audio products accounted for 8% of China's output in 1991. According to official sources, Panda's revenue in 1995 is expected to be over RMB 5 billion (*Asian Wall Street Journal*, 31 October 1995). This makes Panda's sales performance comparable to other established SOEs, such as the joint venture Nanjing Automobile Company.

The impressive 30% increase in annual sales turnover over the past few years is indicative of the growing affluence of Chinese consumers who now have higher disposable income as a result of economic prosperity in the country. The latter is evidenced by the 30% increase in gross output in the electronics industry in recent years (UNIDO, 1992). According to estimates, the buying power of Chinese households owning colour TVs has jumped as much as 20 to 40% from 1992 to 1994 (*Asian Business*, September 1994). With thc improvement in infrastructure, power supplies and increased urbanisation, the demand for electrical appliances is expected to grow even faster than in previous years and, similarly, the demand for better quality products and services is also expected to increase.

Current Market Leadership and Reputation for Product and Service Quality

With an 18% market share, Panda is currently the market leader in the TV business, with three other domestic companies (Jin Xing Co. of Shanghai, Chang Hong Co. of Szechuan and Kang Jia, a joint venture) trailing behind with a 15% market share each. The remaining market share is captured by some ten other foreign brands. What makes Panda stand out among its competitors is the well-acknowledged quality image associated with the Panda brand name.

The company is best known in China for its impeccable achievements in product innovation and product quality awards. Its products have won multiple international, national and provincial level quality awards. In 1994, Panda was ranked 62nd among China's top 500 enterprises and, at the same time, it won the highest accolades and received the "Golden Horse Award" in China's enterprise management awards, the "Golden Bridge Award" in China's electronics industry enterprise management awards, and "China's highest quality award", among others. This already commendable achievement was capped with the recent award of the ISO 9000 certification in late 1995. For these reasons, Panda remains a well-established brand name among commercial and residential customers. According to Mr. Kong, Vice-Director of the group, the Panda brand name is valued in excess of RMB 1 billion.

EVALUATION OF PANDA'S BUSINESS STRATEGY AND FUTURE OPTIONS

Given its impressive financial performance, and the favourable business assets described above, it is prudent to ask about Panda's business strategy and its effectiveness in the face of increased competition from rivals in the electronics market. For the purpose of evaluating the business strategy of Panda, the "four arenas analysis" framework developed by D'Aveni (1994) is used. Besides helping managers to assess the competition and market conditions, the framework has been recognised for its ability to provide managers with a simple model for understanding and predicting competitors' moves. In addition, the model identifies how the competition will be challenged in the four different arenas of cost and quality, timing and know-how, stronghold and deep pockets.

The cost and quality advantage occurs when a special advantage (in terms of higher sales volume or higher profit margins) is gained by adopting either a low cost product, a product differentiator or a focused strategy in the marketing of products or services. The timing and know-how advantage occurs when a firm possesses assets and knowledge which are of value to the market. The stronghold advantage occurs when a firm is able to restrict (directly or indirectly) the number of competitors, and when it can influence the pace and mode of competition in the market. Finally, the deep pocket advantage occurs when a firm has resources that can outlast rivals in very competitive marketing.

As suggested by D'Aveni (1994), and echoed by leading authorities on strategic business planning (Hamel and Prahalad, 1994), today's business battlefield has changed significantly over the years in terms of the pace and mode of competition. Firms that adopt cost leadership or a product differentiation strategy, find themselves confronting business rivals with more advanced technology, a shorter product life and shorter design cycles. But by careful timing and the faster delivery of more innovative products and services to the market, rival firms have been able to subtly erode the competitive advantage of established firms which have enjoyed a competitive advantage in the cost and quality arena.

The conventional wisdom in establishing the stronghold advantage (through higher barriers to entries, economies of scale, product differentiation, higher switching cost for buyers and so forth) has been increasingly susceptible to technological breakthroughs, which allows smaller rival firms to compete aggressively against established corporate giants. By aligning itself with other firms and, hence, developing a deep pocket advantage through the synergy of combination, the smaller firm is then better positioned to take on more powerful rivals. Despite impressive financial performance, current market leadership and an established reputation for quality products and services, Panda finds that it is under similar pressures to outwit and outmanoeuvre rivals in the four arenas so as to protect its competitive advantage and disrupt those of competitors.

Cost and Quality Advantage Analysis

As popularised by Michael Porter in the 1980s, companies that are trying to create a competitive advantage in the market place will normally adopt one of the three generic strategies of cost leadership, product differentiation or focus. While the cost leadership strategy involves offering a mass marketed, low priced and low quality product, the differentiation strategy involves offering a high quality product at a premium-price. This is contrasted with the focus strategy which targets a premium priced product for a smaller niche market. However, as advocated by D'Aveni (1994), the competitive advantage offered by these business strategies is easily eroded through the moves and counter moves of competitors in the market place.

(i) ***Panda's Current Cost and Quality Strategy:*** As noted earlier, Panda has always positioned itself as the manufacturer of premier quality products and services. Its product differentiation strategy has made the Panda brand a household name for quality products and services despite relatively higher prices. Panda perceives that it has a national obligation to be innovative and to create the best. Management and employees are proud of its distinctive achievement in product quality. To ensure that the superior quality and reliability required by customers are met, Panda believes that quality requirements should be incorporated into the design of the product. To this end, staff and financial resources have been committed to the Reliability Test Centre at its corporate headquarters in Nanjing to perform a continuous evaluation of the quality and reliability of products.

    During the BSM site visit to Panda, the extent of management commitment to quality improvement witnessed was surprising. Besides a visual display of efficiency targets and rejection rates, the factory defective rate on the production floor measured 1,000 parts per million. Field returns were 1% of production. Although modest by international standards, this achievement is impressive by Chinese manufacturing standards.

(ii) ***The Cost and Quality Disposition of Competitors:*** In the period before China institutionalised its economic reforms (prior to 1978), Panda enjoyed the sanctuary of a largely protected state-owned enterprise where competitive business strategies were virtually non-existent. However, competition intensified over the years as several major domestic rivals, such as Jin Xing (from Shanghai), Chang Hong (from Szechuan) and Kang Jia (a joint venture), began fighting for a larger portion of the local market share. These three firms command 45% of the market in equal shares as compared to

Panda's 18%. Foreign brands, such as Sony, National and Toshiba share the remaining market.

From a previous stronghold in consumer electronics, Panda is under increased pressure to sustain the current 18% market share leadership. In the past decade, Panda positioned products successfully against local TV manufacturers by differentiating its products and service and charging premium prices for their superior quality. According to sales staff in several retail stores in Shanghai and Shengzhe, Panda's products are priced about 15% higher than the competition for a similar range of colour television sets. Consumers thus seem willing to pay the price differential for Panda's superior quality and service. Owning a Panda television set is very much a status symbol for residential and commercial customers, including hotels and restaurants.

However, with the influx of foreign brands entering the lucrative consumer market (such as Sony, Panasonic and National), Panda is in an unattractive position since local consumers are exposed to higher quality and more advanced technology, currently not offered by Panda's premium prices. In relative terms the situation faced by Panda is exemplified in Figure 13–1. The price differential is much smaller between Panda and the foreign brands than is the perceived quality differential.

Thus, the competition has become more intense as foreign brand manufacturers position their products within the reach of the now affluent commercial and residential Chinese consumers. The established foreign brands carry with them certain status symbols and the perception of better technology. For instance, the Jinling Hotel, a five-star hotel in Nanjing, has decided to change the Panda TVs in their hotel rooms to a foreign brand so as to maintain its image as a premier international hotel in the region.

With the rapidly increasing consumer demand for electronics products, the TV industry as a whole has enjoyed good sales performance. With a 30% annual sales growth over the past decade, Panda had prided itself for achieving a much better sales performance than its local rivals. However, the increased demand for cathode ray tubes (CRT) by local and foreign competitors has not been sufficiently balanced in the short term. This in turn has affected Panda because it is still dependent on local and foreign suppliers for the CRTs. As a result, Panda has to contend with the higher material costs of imported CRTs due to local supply constraints. The effect (as acknowledged by Mr. Kong, Vice-Director of Panda) has been a corresponding reduction in its profit margin from a healthy 22.5% in 1979 to about 7% in 1994.

FIGURE 13–1
Cost and Quality Advantage Analysis

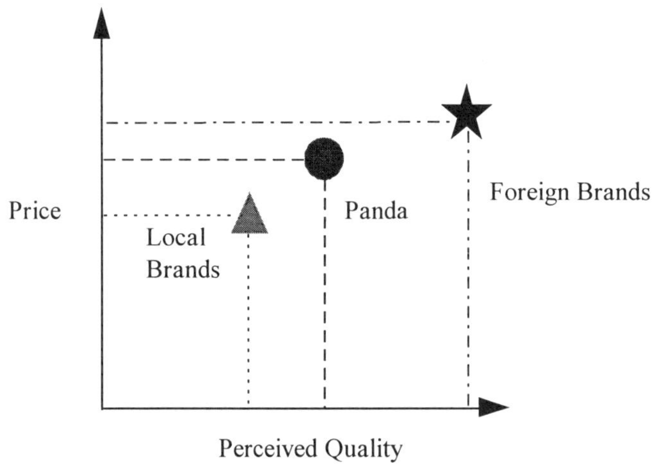

(iii) ***Redefining Product Quality for Competitive Advantage:*** The painful lessons learned from the declining profit margins has made Panda recognise the need to continuously reposition itself and to shift business strategy *vis-à-vis* local and foreign competitors. While it is not Panda's corporate philosophy to engage in extended price wars with competitors, the company does have several options available which can help to regain lost ground and take the competitive advantage away from rivals. Foremost on the agenda is for Panda to redefine perceived quality. Instead of pursuing a common ratio of price to value ("you get what you pay for" in their current business strategy), Panda needs to emerge as an innovative firm which provides better value to the customer ("you get more than what you pay for").

In terms of the price and perceived quality dimensions, this means shifting Panda's position to the right in Figure 13–2 to match the quality of foreign brands. Clearly, this calls for a continuous and revolutionary improvement in the quality of its products and service. It demands a redefinition of product quality and involves outwitting the competitors with smaller, but effective, moves and countermoves.

FIGURE 13–2
Cost and Quality Advantage Analysis

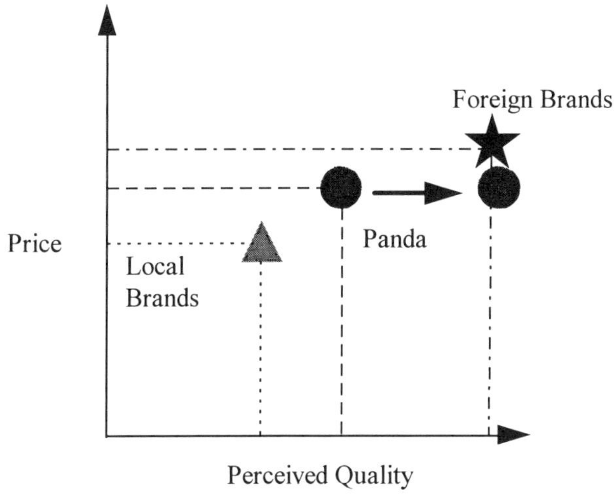

To achieve this goal, Panda will need to expand the capability of its research and development arm, and quickly learn and adopt modern production management techniques which are lacking at the moment. There is also a need to continue benchmarking against international production and quality standards. To outperform the competition, Panda needs to challenge rivals in the different market segments by tailoring products to match the aspirations and values of customers in terms of features, budget and performance.

For example, Panda could position its products to attract working class families by catering to their growing affluent lifestyles. But this requires more expertise in consumer marketing, creative advertising and innovative product design to meet the budget and buying power of a growing number of small family units. Moreover, it must create a reputation as a firm which better understands the needs of consumers and that has the industrial foresight to envisage unarticulated needs.

As a newcomer to competitive mass consumer marketing, this means that Panda requires the experience of potential business partners who are themselves reputed for their marketing efficiency and effectiveness. To extend its quality image, Panda must continue to exploit well-established distribution channels and service centres to make its service a key component of overall quality. This means retraining and retooling people at these different distribution channels and service centres as well as implementing incentives to motivate distributors to be more responsive to customers.

(iv) ***Managing Cost Structure and Business Risks:*** On the other side of the business equation, Panda needs to reduce its existing cost structure to compete against foreign competitors. According to estimates given by Mr. Kong, the cathode ray tubes are about 70% of the total component costs for a TV. Other component costs are shown in Table 13–2.

TABLE 13–2
Product Cost Breakdown

Product Components:	
CRT	42%
Other purchased components	18%
Total Component Cost	60%
Labour:	
Direct	15%
Indirect	5%
Total Labour Cost	20%
Overheads	20%
Total Cost	100%

According to UNIDO (1992) statistics, the unit cost of material for Chinese manufacturers is significantly higher (about 20%) than the material cost of international manufacturers. This is attributed to a larger share of imports in material inputs, higher foreign exchange rates paid by importers of components and a tight world market for these components. Similar to other SOEs, Panda is also burdened with the social costs of providing medical care, housing, retirement insurance and social facilities for its 10,000 employees. MacMurray and Woetzel (1994) estimated that social costs are approximately 6% of the total costs, or 40% of wages. With these high social costs, Panda needs to take deliberate cost control measures.

(v) ***Being Open to Modern Management and Marketing Practices:*** Panda's management has acknowledged, despite a long corporate history, that it is a novice in managing and marketing products and services. According to Mr. Kong, the company has only undertaken more regular and aggressive media advertising only in recent years. With the entry of many foreign companies into the consumer electronic market, each fighting for a bigger share of the market, Panda recognises the need to be flexible in moving towards modern, but proven, marketing strategies in order to maintain market share and to penetrate the international market.

Mr. Kong also disclosed that the impetus for a recent organisational restructuring (from a centralised to a more decentralised, but lean, matrix structure) was the sluggish response of the distribution channels to consumers' needs and service expectations. In terms of personnel policy changes, Panda is one of the few SOEs which has implemented some form of performance-based incentive or employee share scheme. In April 1992, employees were given a predefined percentage share of the company's profit based on their level of appointment and length of service.

Timing and Know-how Advantage Analysis

As advocated by D'Aveni (1994), the possession and utilisation of unique assets or knowledge which are of value to the customers enables a firm to gain a competitive advantage over rivals. However, the creation of these assets or knowledge can be eroded easily by rivals through the imitation of products over time. Hence, to enjoy the benefits of "abnormal profits" associated with the timing and know-how advantage, Panda must be willing to be the first to develop assets or knowledge that no one else has, and to force competitors into entirely new markets within short time intervals.

(i) ***Panda's Current Timing and Know-how Strategy:*** To exploit its timing and know-how advantage in the domestic market, Panda has committed significant resources and effort to technology and upgrading, respectively. For Panda, commitment to technology leadership and new product development is a major growth engine. With some 3,500 technically trained employees, Panda is able and willing to invest in technological know-how. It believes that continual improvement and expansion, driven by leading edge technologies applied to product design and manufacturing processes, allow core competencies to be developed.

Towards this end, Panda has established product research centres of excellence all over China. It is also investing in flexible manufacturing and automated mass production techniques. Moreover, the company has established international cooperation with technology transfer partners, alliances with renowned Chinese universities for joint research programmes and technology transfers with other Chinese enterprises in the same industry to promote growth opportunities. While committed to technological improvement, it is also necessary for Panda to look at the development of its core competency in the TV business.

(ii) ***Building and Protecting Core Competency:*** The design and production of cathode ray tubes constitute a critical knowledge area in the television business. The absence of specific knowledge in this area limits the firm's ability to improve picture resolution, display quality and design. Despite being the largest and oldest electronic SOE in China, Panda does not possess the required technical knowledge for CRT production.

Currently, Panda's CRT requirements are sourced from local and overseas firms, with one-third supplied by Hua Fei (a joint venture CRT maker also based in Nanjing), one-third supplied by other Chinese sources and the remaining one-third from abroad. Given excess worldwide demand, Panda is especially vulnerable since 80% of its revenue is derived from television sales, and material costs are more than 40% of total product cost. Compared with more established rivals, Panda is disadvantaged because of lack of access to leading edge technology, or to developments such as large screen or flat screen technologies which have been widely adopted by Japanese manufacturers.

Panda, therefore, needs to consider building up its core competencies in CRT production and TV technology over the long run. This can be achieved through joint ventures with established CRT producers or foreign manufacturers. Alternatively, Panda could align itself strategically with other established CRT producers to ensure that materials and cost are kept within a reasonable range so as not to lose a competitive advantage in this dimension. In the latter case, it would need to protect its business interests through enforcing contractual obligations with strategic partners.

(iii) ***Exploiting the First Mover Advantage:*** Besides developing and protecting the core competencies in CRT production and related TV technology, Panda needs to develop the ability to respond quickly to consumers' needs. Being the current market leader, a first mover advantage can be exploited by offering newer models and better technology more quickly in carefully selected market segments. However, to effect this strategy, Panda needs to develop strong market penetration skills to match the competition in order to maintain its market leadership position. Similarly, Panda must match rival TV technology with a more innovative and flexible product development capability in order to customise its products for the segmented market and, yet, launch them into the local market economically.

Stronghold Advantage Analysis

Firms which are in a position to restrict the number of competitors in the market are said to enjoy a stronghold competitive advantage over their rivals. However, as noted by D'Aveni (1994), stronghold advantage, if not protected, can also be eroded over time. It is evident from Panda's declining market share that the company has a limited hold over rivals. The challenge is coming from the influx of foreign brands that have entered the domestic market in recent years. These new entrants to the domestic TV market have brought with them newer technological features and they have raised consumers' expectations and awareness by shifting the structure of the existing market.

While high capital requirements for development, combined with stringent quality tests, may deter some firms from entering the business, other firms have been able to align themselves with international players, such as Sony, National and Philips, to compete locally. With China's imminent entry into the World Trade Organisation (WTO) and its planned reduction of tariffs from the current average of 35.9 to 13%, including the abolishment of all import quotas, licensing and other non-tariff import control mechanisms by the year 2000 (*Business Times*, 20 December 1995), Panda will face additional pressures.

(i) ***Panda's Current Stronghold Strategy:*** Over the years, Panda has been exploiting the advantage of its established market infrastructure against rival companies. The Panda Electronics Group has established some 153 branches in 20 provinces and cities all over China. It currently has more than 400 service centres across the country. Its distribution networks and number of service centres are currently the largest in China, making its products easily accessible to local consumers in major provincial cities. With a vertically integrated distribution model and the stringent selection of suppliers (due to a relatively stronger bargaining position in the consumer electronics market), Panda has been able to successfully integrate backwards and forwards into product development, manufacturing, and the distribution of products and services (*Asian Wall Street Journal*, 31 October 1995). In this way, it effectively controls the major consumer chain from the design room to the production floor, and to the retail outlets.

This structure has created huge barriers for new entrants to the lucrative electronics market, and it has limited the expansionist ambitions of smaller rival companies. However, with the growing competition from other local producers (such as Jin Xing in Shanghai and Chang Hong in Szechuan) and the emergence of many foreign brand companies in the local market, Panda is finding it difficult to rest merely on the strength of its distribution networks and service centres. It needs to strengthen the stronghold advantage of its current domestic distribution channels further.

(ii) ***Strengthening the Distribution Network:*** To maintain a strong hold over the domestic market and to increase barriers for potential new entrants, Panda must exploit its well-established distribution channels and service centres that are presently set up across China. This means extending the coverage of distribution channels in new geographic market segments and making service teams technically more efficient, and professionally more responsive to customers' needs. Continuous.skill training and education programmes for its technical and marketing channels must be planned and developed if the company aims to recapture the market share lost to local and foreign competitors. More importantly, Panda's management must instil in employees and support staff the same corporate desire and strategic intent, to be better than foreign competitors in understanding and serving the needs of customers.

(iii) ***Exploiting "Home Court" Advantage:*** In the face of the current competitive environment, Panda must exploit the "home court" and customer loyalty advantage that has been established over the years in the domestic market. Being the largest and most established electronics SOE in the production, marketing and servicing of television sets in China, Panda can tap on customer familiarity and loyalty to its advantage. There is a need for Panda to reinforce its corporate image as the producer which will create more value for its brand of quality electronics products *vis-à-vis* local and foreign brands.

To achieve this, the company must be prepared to engage the assistance and expertise of established marketers to develop specially tailored marketing plans aimed at displacing the "foreign is better" perception among potential commercial and residential customers, and provide loyal customers with the required assurance in better value quality products and service. In addition, Panda could consider aligning itself with the government in order to promote and build consumer loyalty for home grown or domestically produced products.

Deep Pockets Advantage Analysis

To be able to exploit the advantage of an entrenched position, a firm must have substantial financial and managerial resources to outlast competitors in terms of discriminatory pricing, capital, infrastructure investment and expansion. Currently, Panda lacks the financial resources and technical expertise to compete aggressively against local as well as established foreign rivals entering the domestic market. It does not have any significant deep pocket competitive advantage over its competitors. With the local competitors (Chang Hong and Kang Jia) each holding 15% (as compared to Panda's current 18% market share) combined with a growing interest by foreign competitors, the company is in danger of losing market leadership. Furthermore, with exports of less than 5% annually, Panda is in need of political and financial muscle to compete locally and internationally.

(i) ***Panda's Current Deep Pocket Strategy:*** To give it the required technological leverage and to build up its financial resources, Panda has been actively seeking joint ventures or cooperative business arrangements with foreign firms. So far, it has transacted technology transfer arrangements with established Japanese electronics giants, such as National and Panasonic, and other European companies such as Ericsson and Philips. In April 1995, it entered into a joint venture arrangement with Motorola Inc. for the production of pagers, cellular phones and telecommunications equipment for the Chinese market. The two companies plan to sell 500,000 Motorola numeric pagers in the Chinese market under the name "Panda by Motorola" in 1995, and to set up a joint venture factory in Nanjing in 1996.

    In October 1995, it entered into yet another joint venture agreement with Motorola Inc. to produce computers. Sales growth is expected to reach at least 50% per annum over the next five years. In a 40:60 equity split with Motorola, the firm, known as Nanjing Power Computer Limited, will develop, produce and sell computer systems for the growing domestic Chinese market with a vision of supplying U.S. markets in the future.

    According to the Chairman of the Board of the Panda Group, Mr. Chen Xiang Xing, these joint ventures "have been formed to capitalise on the domestic growth potential and in contribution to China's national development policy for the country's computer industry". The growing confidence of MNCs, such as Motorola and other Japanese electronics giants, in Panda is indicative of management's commitment to business cooperation. The experience of these significant others with Panda will become an important learning reference for all types of potential business partners.

(ii) ***Financial Sourcing Through Public Listings:*** The successful alliances with foreign companies have renewed Panda's confidence in the international market. Going beyond joint venture partnerships, Panda is trying to establish a deep pocket advantage by preparing for its debut listing on the Hong Kong Stock Exchange by the end of 1996. Through this initial public offering, Panda hopes to raise about US$250 to US$500 million to fund its ambitious business expansion programme. For Panda, this debut listing is significant because it will help to establish potential investors' confidence in the company and its management.

(iii) ***Drawing on Alliances with Larger Firms:*** As a newcomer to competitive consumer marketing, and as one in need of financial and managerial resources, Panda definitely needs to consider aligning itself with larger established firms that have an international reputation and business aspirations to tap the lucrative consumer electronics market in China. Through an equity or co-operative joint venture arrangement, foreign partners can provide the required manufacturing technology, raise funds and offer management, marketing expertise and training skills while Panda can provide the factory facilities, production equipment and the necessary labour. Clearly, Panda has already embarked on some experimentation in this regard but much more still remains to be done.

BUSINESS PARTNERSHIPS: POTENTIAL ISSUES AND CONSIDERATIONS

As discussed above, Panda possesses attractive business opportunities for serious potential business partners who wish to penetrate the growing consumer market in China and the region. Panda has specific business plans to build up and sustain its competitive advantage *vis-à-vis* competitors in the short and long run. Its needs are clear; access proprietary technology in CRT production and in advanced TV manufacturing and design technology; acquire modern management and marketing techniques; and search out capital resources to fund its expansion and growth programmes. But before deciding on a business arrangement with Panda, potential investors need to consider several factors and these are discussed in the following sections.

Shared Goals and Business Aspirations

The experience with previous joint ventures has convinced Panda that there must be a congruence of goals. While potential business goals may not necessarily be the same, they certainly should not be in conflict, which would destroy hopes of mutual cooperation. According to company sources, Panda's joint venture with an established Japanese firm did not materialise because the foreign partner could not agree on Panda's brand name being on the product. It is important that potential business partners review their business goals and understand the indigenous factors for business partnership with Panda.

Similar advice has been sounded by others. For example Murray (1994, p.158) cites the Chinese experience with the now defunct American Motor Company (AMC) where there was a rift in the joint venture management due to differing business goals in the jeep market. The American company had hoped to exploit the relatively low labour costs to produce low end jeeps in China while the Chinese joint venture partners were more interested in acquiring new manufacturing technologies to launch into other regional markets. However, for cautious investors, the Ericsson and Motorola equity joint ventures with Panda can be useful benchmarks for evaluating the latter.

International Reputation of the Business Partner

Panda believes that business cooperation requires mutual affinity and business compatibility between the partners. The past and current joint venture arrangements with Ericsson and Motorola are reflective of its corporate stance. Panda is therefore anxious to joint venture with established companies that have an interest in launching into the lucrative domestic market, and new markets in Latin America, parts of the Middle East and Asia.

Commitment to Panda Brand Name

For Panda, it is important that all potential partners share or respect Panda's commitment to its brand name. As disclosed by Mr. Kong, Vice-Director of the Panda Electronics Group, some joint ventures with foreign companies have not been successful because both parties could not agree on Panda's continued use of its brand name on the products. Panda's brand name is highly treasured and eagerly protected by management due to the well-established quality image. As such, Panda is not keen to manufacture products for original equipment manufacturers (OEMs), even though it is aware that many developing countries, such as Taiwan and Korea, have successfully adopted the OEM strategy to gain market share, acceptance, recognition and the experience of manufacturing to high standards.

Foreign Exchange, Inflation and Continued Political Stability

China has been pursuing a policy of stepped devaluation of its currency. The devaluation in 1993 was a high point when the currency dropped from RMB 5.76 to RMB 8.33 to the U.S. dollar. Since 1993, the RMB/US$ exchange rate has remained in the range of RMB 8.0 to RMB 8.5. It is not envisaged that floating the RMB as a freely convertible currency will become a reality within the Ninth Five-Year-Plan from 1996 through to the year 2000. According to UNIDO sources, foreign exchange reserves are expected to increase from US$21.2 billion in 1993 to US$80 billion by 1997, which should give some confidence to businesses in China. There is no doubt that the central government in Beijing will carry out its commitment to the many infrastructure development projects in Jiangsu province, and other SEZs, to facilitate industrial growth and economic reforms (Yang *et al.*, 1995).

In addition, potential investors need to monitor government efforts at managing the inflation rate in China. It peaked at 22% in 1994 but it fell below 17% in 1995. The government has affirmed its commitment to keep inflation at 10% until the end of the decade. The central government is taking the necessary fiscal and monetary precautions to control the overheated economy. However, inflation is still a major consideration for foreign companies doing business in China. In particular, the continued funding of SOEs, including Panda, may be constrained. Last, but certainly not least, it is in the interests of potential investors to monitor China's political and economic relationships with its neighbours and other key political players on the international scene.

CONCLUSION

To serious minded business interests, Panda offers attractive reasons for considering a joint business partnership. The belief is that it possesses the prerequisites for market leadership in the consumer electronics industry. Despite a lack of advanced technological knowledge and financial resources, it has substantial intangible assets in the form of a current reputation for quality products, an established distribution network and a pro-business management that can complement the business needs of potential partners and global suppliers. However, in reviewing Panda as a potential business partner, it is necessary to track China's monetary policies in managing an overheated economy and fluctuating foreign exchange rates, and its political disposition and economic relationships with regional and international trading partners.

In addition, potential investors most certainly have to evaluate the impact of China's imminent membership of the WTO as well as its MFN status with the U.S. The latter threat may be dampened because of the enormous potential waiting in the "wings" from the European Community and Japan. Then too, it is comforting for potential investors to know that Beijing will not adopt policies that in any way endanger the going concern of huge successful SOEs such as Panda.

REFERENCES

A Brief Introduction to the Policies and Regulations on Investment in Nanjing, China (publication distributed by Mr. Chen De Ming, Vice-General Secretary of the People's Government of Jiangsu Province), Nanjing, 1995.

"China Plans to Cut Tariffs to 13% by Year 2000", *The Business Times*, 20 December 1995, p. 1.

"China Spells Out Ways to Breathe Life into State Firms", *The Straits Times*, 28 December 1995, p. 12.

D'Aveni R.A., *Hypercompetition: Managing the Dynamics of Strategic Manoeuvring*, Maxwell Macmillan Inc., New York, 1994.

Editorial, *Asian Wall Street Journal*, 31 October 1995.

Forestier K. and Z. Abdoocarin, "China Investors Play a New Game", *Asian Business*, September 1994, pp. 20–4.

Hamel G and C.K. Prahalad, *Competing for the Future,* Harvard Business School Press, Boston, Massachusetts, 1994.

Interviews with Mr. Kong Junxiang, Vice-Director of the Panda Group, Mr. Shi Qui Sheng, Economist to the Panda Electronics Group; and Mr. Loo Sao Foong from the Nanjing local government, December 1995.

MacMurray T and J. Woetzel, "The Challenge Facing China's State-Owned Enterprises", *The McKinsey Quarterly*, No. 2, pp. 61–74.

Murray Geoffrey, *Doing Business in China: The Last Great Market*", St. Martin's Press, New York, 1994.

UNIDO Industrial Development Review Series, *China: Towards Sus-*

tainable Industrial Growth, Blackwell Publishers, Oxford, 1992.

Yang Mu, John J. Williams and Cao Yong, "Resurrecting Shanghai for the 21st Century: The Shift in China's Regional Economic Strategies", *China Business Review*, December 1995, pp. 11–29.

Young Susan, *Private Business and Economic Reform in China,* M.E. Sharpe, Armonk, New York, 1991.

Chapter 14

Shanghai Jahwa Corporation*

BY
LIM San San
Patrick CHONG
Orlando TAN
YEUNG Hung-Kung

INTRODUCTION

THIS CHAPTER PRESENTS a case study on a Shanghainese company, Shanghai Jahwa Corporation. Information about the company was acquired through interviews during site visits to Shanghai Jahwa Corporation. Shanghai Jahwa Corporation's core businesses are in skincare, cosmetic and household cleaning products. The focus of this chapter is on the marketing of its products using the classic "Four Ps" framework. The marketing strategy of Shanghai Jahwa Corporation regarding product, price, promotion and place are discussed. Whenever relevant, the positioning of Shanghai Jahwa Corporation relative to its competitors, both local and global (such as Proctor & Gamble (PG), and Unilever), is analysed.

This case study is based on interviews that were conducted with representatives of the company. Due to the status of Shanghai Jahwa, a state-owned enterprise, detailed financial information is confidential and cannot be released for circulation.

---

* Special thanks are extended to Dr. Choo Teck Min for his guidance during this project; thanks also to Mr. Li Tao and Mr. Ye Tao from Shanghai Jahwa Corporation for their kind cooperation in providing valuable information.

Potential of China's Consumer Market

Since 1985, China has boasted double-digit GDP growth, bringing along with it high inflation rates of over 20% per annum. As China continues to expand and grow, the threat of the economy being overheated becomes more imminent and inevitable. To counter this threat, the Chinese government has implemented a series of austerity programmes which have led to a slowdown in economic growth. Despite this, figures show that China's private consumption growth has continued to increase. Sales of consumer goods in the second quarter of 1995 rose 11.6% in real terms, as compared to the same period in 1994. This figure is also higher than the 9.6% growth in the first quarter of 1995 as well as the 7.8% growth for all of 1994. This trend shows that there is still strong potential in the Chinese consumer market despite a slowdown in economic growth (Citibank, 1995).

China's consumer market represents an enormous sales and marketing opportunity for consumer goods manufacturers and distributors. With an average growth rate of 1.3% per annum, China's population is expected to reach 1.3 billion by the year 2000. Around 40% of China's population live in coastal provinces where retail sales account for 53% of the country's total. While the interior provinces have been developing at a slower pace than the coastal regions, their market potential is also enormous, especially in the densely populated provinces like Sichuan and Hubei. Although 1993 GDP per capita was RMB 2,626, residents in the coastal cities possess a much higher purchasing power than the national average (Hong Kong Trade Development Council Research Department, 1994). This explains why retail sales for consumer goods have been stronger in the coastal regions. Moreover, in cities such as Shanghai, where income levels are among the highest in the country, the demand for brand name products is growing fast (Montagu-Pollock, 1994).

Purchasing Behaviour of Consumers

The opening of the Chinese economy means that cultural interaction between the East and West is inevitable. The style of living and the consumer behaviour of the West has become a source of influence on Chinese consumers whose preferences are changing in various ways: demand is now more focused on products of high quality which have modern, diversified designs. Branded products, especially world famous names in fashion and accessories, will no doubt remain popular among the young and the newly rich entrepreneurs (Hong Kong Trade Development Council Research Department, 1994).

COMPANY BACKGROUND

Shanghai Jahwa Corporation was established in 1898. It was known originally as Guang Sheng Hang Pte. Ltd. With almost a century of history, it is the oldest enterprise in China selling traditional Chinese cosmetics.

History

Because of China's reform movement in 1978, Shanghai Jahwa has undergone a major internal restructuring. The present organisation structure is shown in Figure 14–1. Shanghai Jahwa has successfully cooperated with renowned foreign-based cosmetic companies such as Johnson and Johnson, Kanebo and Lion. It has adopted high-technology production techniques, quality control and marketing expertise from foreign partners. Equipped with these skills, Jahwa has emerged as the country's biggest domestic cosmetics and skincare enterprise in the past few years.

In 1992, Shanghai Jahwa adopted its present name Shanghai Jahwa Corporation because their previous name, Shanghai Toiletries Company, no longer represented their diversified range of business activities. Although the company's core business is still in skincare, cosmetic and household products, it has recently ventured into other businesses such as investment in real estate, imports and exports, food outlets and optical shops (see Figure 14–1).

Performance

In 1990, the company's sales in the domestic market reached RMB 450 million with a profit of RMB 105 million. Not only was Shanghai Jahwa the leading domestic producer of cosmetic and skincare products, it was also earmarked as one of the top 500 enterprises in China for its distribution model and profitability.

Shanghai Jahwa's products are concentrated in three main areas: personal skincare (85%), cosmetics (10%) and household cleaning products (5%). These products are manufactured in seven high-tech factories located on the outskirts of Shanghai. The company is the largest producer of cosmetics and household products in China. Shanghai Jahwa has projected an annual growth rate of 40% over the next five years as compared to an industry average of 27%. In 1995, sales were RMB 700 million, or 6% of the total market share of cosmetic, skincare and household products.

FIGURE 14–1
Organisation chart

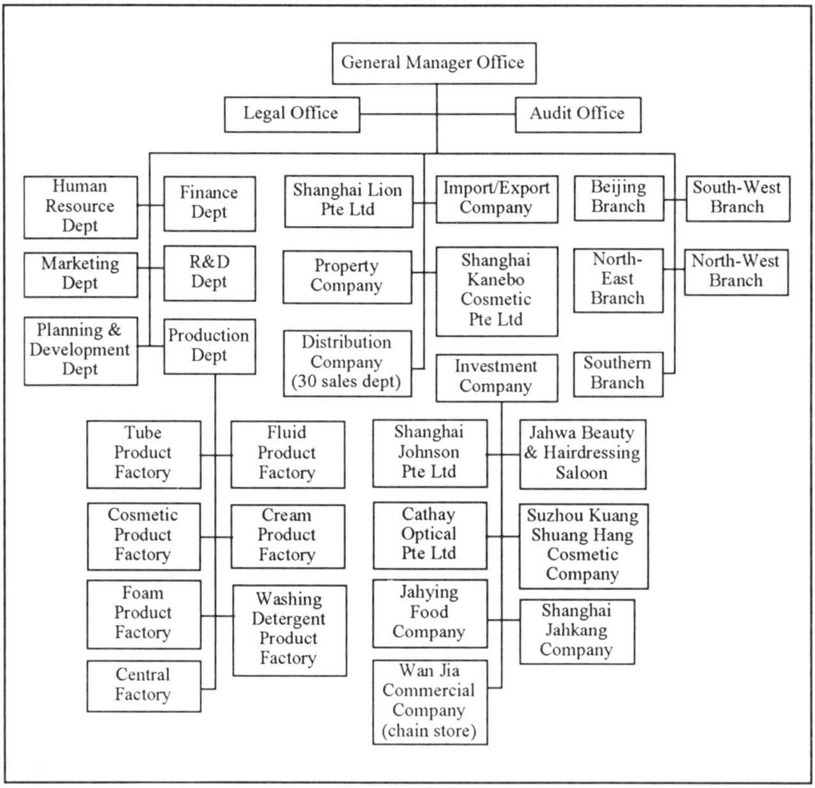

Management Philosophy

For the 1990s, Shanghai Jahwa has adopted a philosophy of brand name management as its core objective; market research is its foundation, and service, advertising and public relations its key marketing tools. It has also adopted advanced technology in product innovation and quality control, and implemented some of the latest techniques in market research and surveys.

Human Resources

At the management level, more than 50% of the staff have tertiary education and there are 30 members of the staff with MBA and PhD qualifications. In addition to a strong top management team, Shanghai Jahwa also has in place a strong sales and marketing department which maintains excellent relations with its customers.

Impression of the Company

Shanghai Jahwa is conveniently located in its own seven storey building in the heart of Shanghai at 527 Bao Ding Road, which is about a ten-minute drive from the famous Bund. The entire exterior and interior of the building were renovated in 1994 at a cost of RMB 7 million in order to project a new revitalised and modern image of the company to the public.

Shanghai Jahwa's staff are all housed in the building except for the production personnel. The interior of the building has been redesigned to reflect the firm's image. There are brass figurines of famous historical personalities, such as Mozart and the Mona Lisa, lining the passageway of the fifth floor convention and meeting area. These figurines are intended to convey an impression of class and sophistication. The conference rooms bear special names which identify visitors with their home countries: the Paris Room is used to entertain French visitors and the Tokyo Room to host Japanese visitors. Shanghai Jahwa's main joint venture partners are from Japan and France.

The training rooms bear the names of the company's product ranges, and they have colour schemes which match them. As an illustration, the Chinf Chinf room's black and red colour scheme matches the packaging on the Chinf Chinf range of cosmetics products. On other floors, several banners bearing various quality, service and productivity related slogans hang on the walls to remind staff of the company's corporate mission. Overall, the impression created is just the opposite of the stereotyped "backward" image that is traditionally associated with state-owned enterprises in China.

Description of Interviewees

Interviews were conducted first with Mr. Li Tao, the Vice-Director of Marketing, and a second session with Mr. Ye Tao, Manager of Marketing Research, who reports to Mr. Li Tao.

Mr. Li Tao has more than ten years of experience in the toiletries consumer goods industry. His responsibilities involve coordinating the various marketing functions of pricing, promotion, new product development, marketing research, marketing strategy and budget formulations.

Mr. Ye Tao has been involved in market research for over ten years as well. His responsibilities involve research on consumer profiles and their evolving tastes and preferences. He is also concerned with competitors' products and strategies, and he is forever devising strategies counter to the competition.

MARKETING STRATEGY

The marketing strategy of Shanghai Jahwa has been analysed using the classic "four Ps" marketing framework: product, price, promotion and place (Kotler, 1994).

Product

Shanghai Jahwa offers three main types of products, namely personal skin care, cosmetics and home cleaning products. The unique selling points of the company's products are elaborated on below.

(i) ***Unique Seasonal Products:*** Shanghai Jahwa has successfully differentiated itself from other competitors in one of their personal skin care product ranges, known as Liushen, by adding local flavour and herbal content. The Liushen eau de toilette, called Florida Water, is said to contain six rare herbal medicines as key ingredients. It is made by a process that combines advanced imported cologne processing technology with the traditional method of processing. It is considered to be a new generation of Florida Water with the special capabilities of suppressing prickly heat, relieving itchiness, refreshing the mind and preventing bites from mosquitoes and other insects. The Liushen shower gel, which contains rare natural Chinese medicinal herbs and pearl hydrolysate, is known to be especially effective for disinfecting and treating inflammation.

The popularity of these two products shows that Shanghai Jahwa understands the local needs and consumption patterns of Chinese consumers and has incorporated them into their products. As a result, Shanghai Jahwa has overtaken its main competitors, PG and Unilever, in terms of sales for 1995. Even though sales for its range of products is very seasonal, sales are high during the summer and this has helped Shanghai Jahwa to become the market leader for this range of personal skin care products.

(ii) ***Familiar and Reliable Brand:*** The other two ranges of personal skin care products, Maxam and Yashuang, are also doing considerably well because they both have a very long brand history of more than 50 years in China. This gives Chinese consumers brand confidence, which has resulted in very stable sales over the years.

(iii) ***Extensive Coverage of Target Markets:*** In the case of cosmetics, Shanghai Jahwa is still a relatively young company and it has to compete fiercely with many well-known imported brands from Japan and France. However, these imported brands tend to carry very high prices and they usually cater to the rich or tourists in China. Therefore, it gives Shanghai Jahwa the opportunity to capture a niche in the lower to mid-end market segment for cosmetics.

Shanghai Jahwa has further sub-divided this target segment into three sub-segments to better cater to the needs of its customers. The K series brand, the result of a joint effort with the Japanese company Kanebo for the past five years, is targeted at the higher-end Chinese consumers. This joint effort has been so successful that Kanebo finally concluded a joint venture contract with Shanghai Jahwa in 1995. The salient feature of the K series is that it is being viewed more as a "Japanese" product, thus attracting consumers who prefer Japanese or imported products.

The mid-price cosmetic products offered by Shanghai Jahwa are known as Chinf and Chinf. For example, the Chinf de Chinf eau de parfum incorporates both an ancient and modern image and has a classical and romantic character blend. It is a perfume that combines both Eastern and Western cultures to appeal to the needs of Chinese consumers. It is compounded with natural fragrances and alcohol from modern French perfumes and kept in a uniquely-shaped bottle which has very oriental features. Its colour combination of red and black reminds consumers of the ancient Chinese official or scholar and the cap on the bottle is specially designed to resemble the hat of the ancient officials.

This unique composition and packaging is targeted at the middle income group of more adventurous, younger female consumers. This strategy works in the Shanghai market because Shanghainese are known to be fun-seeking and they are very receptive to change.

The lower-end Ruby series is targeted at contemporary working professionals who are more conservative in their purchasing behaviour, for example, nurses and teachers.

(iv) ***Imported Raw Materials:*** The raw materials used in the products are imported, mainly to ensure consistent quality which, in turn, brings confidence to Shanghai Jahwa's customers. As a result, production costs are higher but Shanghai Jahwa overcomes this problem through mass volume production which reduces the overall production cost. But material cost is still higher than the competitors' because international companies have even higher production volumes due to worldwide sales. However, this disadvantage has not changed Shanghai Jahwa's strategy of selling higher volume at a lower price when competing against rival companies.

(v) ***Product Strategies:*** Shanghai Jahwa is not an international company like PG and Unilever and, therefore, it still does not enjoy such strong name recognition. As a result, the company is unable to compete directly. Even though Shanghai Jahwa has succeeded in "summer" products, such as Liushen, it is contemplating developing products for other seasons to capture other Chinese market segments. As for cosmetics, Shanghai Jahwa's strategy of using several product ranges to target a wide range of customers in the hope of increasing market share, may not work. The difficulty is that the company may eventually lose focus. Moreover, this strategy may drain its resources by covering such a large range of target customers.

Pricing

This section introduces Shanghai Jahwa's key competitors, PG and Unilever, and the pricing strategies which they used during their initial entry into the Chinese market. This analysis serves to contrast Shanghai Jahwa's pricing strategies.

PG is an American multinational which carries a wide range of toiletries, skincare products and detergents. Labels carried by the company include "Head and Shoulders" (shampoo), "Tide" (detergent) and "Crest" (toothpaste). Unilever is a British multinational which also carries similar product ranges. Their products include "Organics" (shampoo), "Ponds and Lux" (skincare) and "Breeze" (detergent), to name just a few.

(i) ***PG and Unilever's Pricing Strategies:*** When PG and Unilever entered China in the 1990s, the consumer market was still very young. However, these two companies adopted a long-term, forward looking strategy of selling in the country. Although driven by margin considerations, the pricing strategy of each relied on the desire of Chinese consumers to demand higher quality in the future.

For example, they positioned their brand names at the upper-end of the market in a bid to differentiate their products from the local ones. They retailed their products at prices that were three times higher than local brands. They also advertised heavily to create product awareness and desirability when other firms did not advertise. Their initial strategy resulted in a smaller market share and net losses from premium pricing because they had to compete with lower quality, but much cheaper, local brands produced by state-owned enterprises.

According to many market researchers, this competitive approach should not have worked in China. Yet after just three years of losses, PG and Unilever made profits in 1995. More importantly, they have created a niche market for themselves in the upper-end market where their position as a market leader is unshakeable at the moment. Their combined market share is 30% of the total market for skincare products.

Their success is attributable to a number of factors. First, both companies carry brand names which are renowned all over the world. Second, they have the financial resources to sustain losses as well as the heavy cost of advertising. Third, they have adopted a premium pricing strategy in line with the long-term plan for economic progress carved out by the Chinese government which is the economic development of the coastal areas followed by the inner provinces (Yang *et al.*, 1995). The combination of these factors has proven to be successful because changes in consumer patterns have paralleled the economic progress of the country.

(ii) ***Shanghai Jahwa's Pricing Strategies:*** Traditionally, products produced by state-owned enterprises are controlled by the government through a regulating body. As a state-owned enterprise, Shanghai Jahwa's products were priced at affordable rates to the public during the early 1950s. Although prices are no longer government controlled, the company's pricing strategy has not been changed in terms of affordability. Of course, there has been an improvement in the quality of the products due to new techniques transferred by various joint ventures with foreign based companies.

With prices deliberately set at 50% below imported products of comparable quality, Shanghai Jahwa's products have captured a large segment of the domestic market. In fact, one skincare product, Liushen, had the largest market share in 1995, displacing the Unilever product from its number one position. Hence, Shanghai Jahwa prices its products below the competition but above other local brands. However, Shanghai Jahwa's products offer quality comparable to the foreign competition, but much superior to other local products.

Skincare products such as Maxam, Liushen and Yashuang which are produced by Shanghai Jahwa have been accepted by consumers for some time. Therefore, their prices have been comfortably maintained at a traditionally affordable level. These products bring in the most profits since they target a large base of customers. On the other hand, for cosmetic products such as Chinf and Chinf, the K series and Ruby, the prices tend to be at the higher-end but they are 50% lower than imported products. The main strategy for the former products is not based on price but, rather, on creating an elitist image for the products while staying within an affordable price range. The unit selling price is highest for these products; yet the net margin is lower than for the skincare products due to the high promotional expenses incurred in promoting the high-end cosmetic products.

One of the pricing strategies that Shanghai Jahwa has intelligently exploited is the "pyramid effect" as shown in Figure 14–2. The pyramid effect is a phrase used to describe a typical consumer market. Consumer markets can be viewed as a pyramid consisting of three groups based on income levels: high, middle and low. Low income consumers make up the base of the pyramid. This group of customers is the largest and, also, it is the most price sensitive. At the apex of the pyramid is the high income customer group. This group is the smallest but it is the least price sensitive.

FIGURE 14–2
Pyramid effect

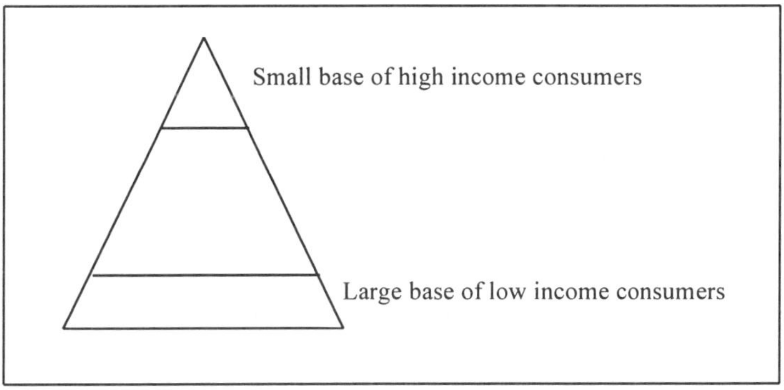

The competition's products and other imported products have already established themselves at the upper-end of the market. Shanghai Jahwa does not price its products in this range because of financial constraints. At the same time, there is no intention of cheapening its products by competing at the lower-end of the market with the other local manufacturers. Since the company has a long brand name history and good quality products, it has priced in the mid-range very successfully.

An interesting phenomenon regarding pricing systems in China is that different regions have different prices. For example, prices in the coastal and southern regions are lower than in the hinterland regions due to transportation costs incurred in bringing these goods to the hinterland. This is ironic because the purchasing power in these rural areas is generally much lower. To overcome this non-uniform pricing system, Shanghai Jahwa will be one of the first companies to implement standardisation in the price of one of their skincare products, Liushen, throughout the country in 1996. If this scheme is successful, then it would certainly enhance the company's name and would encourage it to introduce this scheme to other products.

One major problem faced by Shanghai Jahwa is counterfeit products. It is well known that when products sell very well in China there will be counterfeit products appearing in the market within a year. These counterfeit products are identical to the real ones, differing only in price and quality. The government is trying to stamp out counterfeit products but, due to regional protectionism, the local authorities may not put in much effort to resolve this issue. In fact, the bigger the counterfeit syndicate, the greater is the likelihood that more protection is given to them. This occurs because these syndicates bring in huge benefits for the local community. This problem continues to pose a threat to Shanghai Jahwa's pricing strategy and it will continue to be an obstacle to any company which sells products in China.

Promotion

A company's advertising budget and the type of product it promotes are important considerations when choosing a medium for product promotion. Shanghai Jahwa spends 10 to 15% of its total sales revenues on promotion annually, of which television (TV) advertising takes up more than 50% of the total budget.

According to Mr. Li, Vice-Director of the Marketing Department, television is by far the most effective method of promotion in the country because it helps to familiarise viewers with a company's name and reputation. However, it is also the most costly method. Mr. Li feels that Shanghai Jahwa is disadvantaged because it has a limited advertising budget as compared to international companies such as PG and Unilever. Hence, the company cannot create as much impact through this method of advertising as it would like to *vis-à-vis* its two key competitors.

For instance, China Central Television (CCTV), the country's national channel, charges RMB 60,000 for a 30-second slot during the peak hours from 7:00 p.m. to 9:00 p.m. (Greaves and Baldwin, 1994). Due to the high rates and a limited budget for advertising, TV advertising is only used for certain products and it concentrates on regions with higher purchasing power such as Shanghai, Guangzhou and Beijing. TV advertising is used extensively for introducing new products as well as for market penetration; less TV advertising is used for products in mature markets or where the company is already a market leader. Further, TV advertising is mainly used for products that are targeted at the mass market, such as the personal skincare range of products.

For the range of cosmetics, promotion is carried out through sales counters in major departmental stores as well as through advertisements in women's magazines because these sources are deemed to be the most feasible methods for the cosmetics range. The target customer group for cosmetics products is much smaller and it does not justify TV advertising. Shanghai Jahwa also has two beauty saloons under its umbrella selling the Ruby and Chinf and Chinf range of products, as well as a beauty training centre to train its own sales and beauty saloon staff on the company's range of products. Each training session lasts for a period of ten to 15 days after which time the sales staff, in turn, can educate customers on the proper use of the company's products.

As part of their promotion strategy, Shanghai Jahwa also participates regularly in mini trade fairs. In October 1995 alone, the company spent RMB 70 million at a mini trade fair in Beijing using lucky draws to entice customers to visit the company headquarters in Shanghai, with airfares and accommodation provided. The objective of the company's participation in trade fairs and the organisation of lucky draws is to promote brand awareness and, consequently, enhance the corporate image in the public's eye.

Throughout Shanghai, Suzhou and Nanjing, there are several billboards bearing the Maxam range of products. However, the ads are not sufficiently eye-catching to capture one's attention. Moreover, the sales staff at the beauty counters in several departmental stores that were visited uniformly recommended imported cosmetics as well as fragrances. The reason cited by them was that imported products are generally regarded to be better quality then local products. This clearly reinforces the earlier statement that brand awareness is catching on fast among Chinese consumers.

It is not easy for Shanghai Jahwa to break through this newly erected psychological barrier. The company is aware of the shift in brand consciousness and, as a start, they have obtained ISO 9000 certification to increase public awareness of the quality of its products. Corporate image and brand awareness are very important considerations in promoting consumer goods in the Chinese market. Forming a joint venture among foreign international companies and local companies is one of the best ways for local companies to enhance their corporate image. At the same time, it provides an opportunity for local firms to bring in foreign products for distribution in China as well as to obtain foreign technology.

Place (Distribution)

In this section, Jahwa's strategy on "place" is discussed. Place refers to the distribution system that is used. In other words, it is the way in which products are distributed from the production centres to the sales outlets and the way these sales outlets are used to sell products.

(i) ***Distributors and Warehouses:*** Jahwa's main production centres are concentrated in the outskirts of Shanghai (with branches in other parts of China). This location gives Jahwa a competitive advantage because Shanghai is strategically located in the centre of the main markets of China where distribution can be most efficiently started. The main markets are along the coastal area with Beijing and Tianjin in the north, Shenzhen and Guangzhou in the south and Shanghai in the middle (Murray, 1994). Products are distributed using distributors. In the past, any distributor could carry Jahwa products. However, since the restructuring of the company, distributors are now selected by Jahwa and the number of distributors is limited. This change in policy has given Jahwa better control and an overview of what is happening with their products.

Currently, Jahwa has warehousing facilities in each of its 25 distribution centres. There are 23 distribution centres which cover the eastern half of China, and two distribution centres which cover the western half of China. The former has a better coverage of distribution centres because it is better developed and the market is concentrated in this part. The warehouses have about a two months' supply of inventory. Contrary to modern concepts of inventory such as just-in-time (JIT), where stocks are kept to a minimum (Atkinson *et al.*, 1995), Jahwa keeps a large volume of stock. This results in additional costs for storage and the insurance of goods.

However, it makes sense to stock up on goods since the transportation infrastructure in China is still not well developed, efficient or reliable. To be able to maintain small amounts of stocks, or virtually none, JIT, buyers must rely on suppliers for the frequent and consistent delivery of goods. This is not easy to achieve given the current status of China's transportation infrastructure.

(ii) ***China's Transportation Infrastructure:*** As industrial output has been growing at 20% in recent years, China's transportation system has not been able to keep pace with this growth (Murray, 1994). The road and rail networks are already operating at full capacity. The railways carry about 70% of domestic freight, but only 60% arrives on schedule (Murray, 1994). Rail freight costs also have increased substantially in the past few years because of the increased fees to finance rail development.

(iii) ***Sales Outlets:*** Stores that sell Jahwa products are supplied through warehouses and distributors. Most of Jahwa's sales are concentrated in Shanghai where it has about 4,000 outlets. These 4,000 stores make up 85% of thc total number of department stores, retail shops and supermarkets in Shanghai. Furthermore, there are 100 beauty counters in department stores on a contractual basis promoting Shanghai Jahwa's products.

To stay in touch with customers' perceptions and purchasing patterns of its products, Jahwa has implemented a feedback mechanism. The sales of products at Jahwa beauty counters are registered at the end of each working day. At the end of each week, sales are consolidated at Jahwa and used for monitoring and review. Furthermore, Jahwa employs people to monitor stocks of Jahwa products at sales outlets. This measure is to prevent sales outlets from running out of inventory.

(iv) ***Credit Terms:*** The credit terms that Jahwa uses are different from PG, Unilever and local competitors. PG and Unilever are able to demand payment within seven days of delivery because they have well-established brand names and a greater market share. The credit terms for Jahwa are 60 days and for local competitors it can be more than 100 days. A problem that originates from extended credit terms is the existence of immoderate bad debts which causes Jahwa cash flow problems although the volume of sales is large.

The credit terms also could be an indication of the bargaining power of Jahwa relative to the distributors. Based on this criterion, PG and Unilever have the highest bargaining power, followed by Jahwa and the local competitors. The fact that Jahwa's distributors also carry products for the competitors could be a disadvantage for Jahwa. Since PG and Unilever have more bargaining power, they may receive preferential treatment by the distributors.

(v) ***Regional Blockades:*** Even companies with solid distribution networks might encounter problems with selling their products in a certain region. Thus, is important to understand the structure of the Chinese economy. As Lester Thurow, Dean of MIT's Sloan School of Management advises, "One way to think of the Chinese economy is as a series of economies run by economic warlords on a provincial level – and they are very non-cooperative sometimes" (Batson, 1994). Each "economic warlord" is trying to build his own small empire. The result is that provinces are not always very cooperative towards each other. Moreover, many provinces have started building trading blockades to protect their tax base as the Chinese economy becomes more and more decentralised. This means that companies are given incentives to buy from local suppliers within the province. For Jahwa's future expansion strategy, this could be an incentive to set up subsidiaries with production facilities in different provinces so as to by-pass these trading blockades.

STRENGTHS AND WEAKNESSES

This section focuses on the strengths and weaknesses of the company. It is important for Shanghai Jahwa to capitalise on its strengths and devise strategies to overcome its weaknesses so that it can successfully exploit whatever opportunities that are available in the external business environment.

Strengths

(i) ***Long History of Brand Name:*** Shanghai Jahwa has enjoyed a long history of well-established brand names. The company has been around for almost one hundred years and it is known for quality products at affordable prices. Although intense competition has forced many local companies to either raise prices, or use lower quality raw materials for production, Jahwa has been able to maintain consistently high standards for its products without resorting to drastic price increases. This intangible asset gives the company an extra edge over local competitors, especially in the event of new product introductions or new market penetration.

(ii) ***Human Resources:*** With the entry of foreign multinational companies such as PG and Unilever into China over the last few years, Shanghai Jahwa has experienced strong competition with regard to human resources. Although wages are comparable to foreign companies, this Chinese company offers better staff benefits and accommodation (most wholly-owned foreign companies or foreign joint ventures do not provide accommodation). As a local firm, cultural conflicts within Jahwa are at a minimum which leads to less staff problems. Foreign firms do not enjoy this same benefit and, thus, staff problems can be more significant for them.

Weaknesses

(i) ***Limited Financial Resources:*** Jahwa's financial resources are limited to those from retained earnings and bank loans. As a result, the company cannot compete head on with the foreign competition and has had to carve out different target markets. It also has to settle for less advertising and using cheaper advertising, and this reduces the impact of the kind of elite corporate image that it hopes to achieve.

(ii) ***Reliance on Imported Raw Materials:*** Currently, more than 70% of Shanghai Jahwa's raw materials are imported. This puts the company in a vulnerable position because production volume and cost depend largely on the availability and prices of these imports which are beyond its control. Shanghai Jahwa should thus explore the feasibility of sourcing for quality raw materials locally so as to reduce the dependence on imports.

(iii) ***Overdependence on Foreign Technology:*** Although Shanghai Jahwa enjoys the latest technology, especially in production and quality control, this is the result of technology transfer arising from joint venture efforts with foreign companies. This dependence hampers the company's efforts to create a better corporate image for itself. The public still perceives it as a local company with limited technological capabilities and regard it as inferior to foreign companies. Shanghai Jahwa, therefore, needs to consider investing more research funds and manpower in the areas of technology so as to enhance its corporate image and break free from this public psychological barrier.

CONCLUSION

In order to have extensive coverage of the Chinese market, Shanghai Jahwa has regionalised by setting up four branches with full production facilities outside Shanghai. These branches are located in the south-west, the north-east, southern China and Beijing. Another production site is coming up soon in the north-western part of China and should be ready by 1997.

There are several advantages to regionalisation. First, it provides better service to the regions supported by the branches. This includes being able to respond faster to changes in situations, purchasing behaviour and the tastes of consumers in each region. The company is also able to monitor more closely the sales of each product and react accordingly. Secondly, regionalisation is part of an expansion plan adopted by Shanghai Jahwa to capture a bigger market in China. Thirdly, shifting the production sites out of Shanghai will curb the problem of rising production costs in Shanghai. However, such a move may result in the company not being able to enjoy economies of scale. Lastly, having production facilities within the provinces means that Shanghai Jahwa can effectively by-pass trading blockades imposed by the provinces.

The Chinese market is very different from other overseas markets because it is not only huge, but it is non-uniform throughout China. Due to different levels of economic reforms throughout the country, the purchasing power of consumers in different regions can be quite varied. Consumers within cities, especially Shanghai, Guangzhou and Beijing, have a very high level of purchasing power compared to those in the hinterland. However, Shanghai Jahwa's product pricing strategy at present is such that prices are higher in the hinterland due to transportation costs. Thus, foreign businesses of any kind need to consider the merits of a fixed pricing strategy for their products and focus on having a higher sales volume in order to absorb the transportation costs into the hinterland.

Consumers in China are generally very brand conscious. Due to the efficient mass media and good communication systems, consumers are now more aware of the products available in the market and, hence, have higher expectations of product quality. Due to rapid economic reforms, consumers' purchasing power is increasing exponentially and pricing is becoming less of a concern to them as compared to brand name. Generally speaking, consumers are starting to prefer branded imported products even though they may cost a lot more than local products.

REFERENCES

Atkinson A.A., R.D. Banker, R.S. Kaplan and S.M. Young, *Management accounting*, Prentice Hall, London, 1995.

Batson Bryan, "Chinese Fortunes", *Sales and Marketing Management*, March 1994, pp. 93–8.

Citibank, *Monthly China Review,* Economic Research Department, Hong Kong and China, 1995.

Greaves Jane and Peter Baldwin, *Distribution in China: Getting Down to the Nuts and Bolts*, The Economist Intelligence Unit, November 1994.

China's Consumer Market, Hong Kong Trade Development Council Research Department, 1994.

Kotler Philip, *Marketing Management: Analysis, Planning, Implementation and Control,* Prentice Hall, London, 1994.

Montagu-Pollock Matthew, "The Drawcard for the World's Multinationals", *Asiamoney*, September 1994, pp. 51–3.

Murray Geoffrey, *Doing Business in China: The Last Great Market,* St. Martin's Press, 1994.

Yang Mu, John J. Williams and Cao Yong, "Resurrecting Shanghai for the 21st Century: The Shift in China's Regional Economic Strategies", *China Business Review*, December 1995, pp. 11–29.